HANDBOOK
OF
INDUSTRIAL
RELATIONS

Handbook of Industrial Relations

Editor: Derek P Torrington

First published in Britain by Gower Press Limited
Epping, Essex
1972

Set in 11 on 13 point Times and printed in Britain by
Tonbridge Printers Ltd
Peach Hall Works, Tonbridge, Kent

Contents

Notes on the contributors   xiii

Preface   xix

PART ONE: THE NATIONAL FRAMEWORK

1 Management and Industrial Relations   3
D P Torrington
The Industrial Relations Act   4
Trade unions   6
The organisation   7
Future developments   8

2 Collective Bargaining   11
E G A Armstrong
Definition   11
Underlying principles   12
The extent of collective bargaining   13
Methods of operation: industry-wide bargaining arrangements   15
The importance of collective bargaining   19
Substantive and procedural rules   22
Examples of rules from collective agreements   23
References   27

3 The Industrial Relations Act 1971   29
J L Cookson
The rights of workers   30
Collective bargaining   36
Registration and conduct of organisations   40
The new system of industrial relations justice   43
Guiding principles for the conduct of organisations   47
Requirements of an organisation's rules   48

4 Personnel Management and the Code of Practice   49
D P Torrington
Responsibilities   50
Employment policies   53
Communication and consultation   57
Collective bargaining   59
Employee representation at the place of work   60
Grievance and dispute procedures   62
Disciplinary procedures   62

5 Central Government Services in Industrial Relations   65
R Naylor
Government intervention in employment questions   68
Assistance offered by government   68
Subject areas in which outside advice may be valuable   71
Types of assistance offered and example   71
Locations of departmental advisory services   79

6 Employers' Associations and Trade Unions   81
R Naylor
Employers' associations   82
Trade unions   85
Agreements   90
References   95

7 Sources of Information   97
D P Torrington
Types of information   97
Information from governmental, professional and similar bodies   99
Information from employers' associations and trade unions   101
Information from other employers   103
Information from the academic world   104
The use of publications   104
Earnings surveys   106

PART TWO: THE COMPANY FRAMEWORK

8 Management Responsibility   109
L F Neal
Balance of bargaining power   109
Responsibility for industrial relations   111
Allocation of responsibility for industrial relations   114
Line or staff   116
References   120

9 Plant Agreements   121
D P Torrington
Agreement strategy   123
Procedural content   131
Substantive content   137
Other contents   138

10 Communications Structure   141
R H Jeffrey and C Howarth
Why communicate?   142
Formal and informal organisation structures   144
Effects of organisation structure   145
Communications structures   147
Factors essential to communication   156

11 Methods of Payment   159
D H Langton
Payment of manual employees—selecting a system   160
Payment systems   166
Payment of staff employees   173

12 Shiftwork   179
R Sergean
Practical problems for management   180
Social implications   188
Organisational implications   191

13 Racial Integration in Employment   193
T J Connelly
Employment and integration   194
Immigrant disadvantage   196

Immigrant needs 199
Racial discrimination and the Race Relations Act 200
Dangers in assumptions 205

14 Women and Equality 207
R Naylor
The campaign for equal pay—some important dates 208
Impact of equal pay 209
The Equal Pay Act 1970—requirements and implication 212
The phasing of equal pay 216
Equal opportunity 218
Trade union membership 219
Future developments after the Act 219
References 220

15 Training in Industrial Relations 221
C V Kettle
Approach to training in industrial relations 222
Categories of training 225
Current sources of training and course content 231
Comparison of training courses 233

16 The Conduct of Negotiations—A Viewpoint 239
R Naylor
Getting the feel of the subject 239
Preparation for negotiations 241
The negotiation/confrontation situation 246
Outcome 250
References 252

PART THREE: THE UNION VIEWPOINT

17 Working with the Union 255
R Lyons
Individuality of unions 256
Contact 257
Procedural agreements 258
Negotiations 259
Effective co-operation 260
Establishing sound industrial relations 265

18 **The Role of the Shop Steward in Industry**   269
    J Murray
    Conception of shop stewards   269
    Birth of shop stewards   271
    Shop stewards and works committee agreement   271
    Central Conference   275
    Duties of shop stewards   277
    Shop stewards' relationships   278
    Politics and shop stewards   281

PART FOUR: THE SOCIAL FRAMEWORK

19 **Lessons from the Behavioural Sciences**   285
    A W Gottschalk
    People in organisations   286
    Groups in organisations   291
    The organisation   297
    References   301

20 **The Social Implications of Industrial Relations**   303
    E R Wickham
    The search for reform   303
    The Code   304
    Requirements for good industrial relations   306
    Extrinsic factors in industrial relations   307
    Social goals—attainment   308
    Intrinsic factors in industrial relations   309
    Model of industrial organisation   310

    Bibliography   313

    Index   319

Illustrations

5 : 1   Government intervention in employment questions   66

5 : 2   Principal causes of unofficial strikes   69

5 : 3   Services available from Department of Employment   70

6 : 1   Employers' views on advantages of federation   84

6 : 2   Dispute procedure agreements   92

9 : 1   Plant agreement programme   126

10 : 1   Benefits of good communication through joint
         consultative machinery   143

10 : 2   Results of an opinion survey   145

10 : 3   Comparison of centralised and decentralised
         networks   146

10 : 4   Organisation structure showing separation of staff
         and line functions   148

10 : 5   Composition of typical works council   150

11 : 1   Main categories of work occurring in industrial
         activity   160

11 : 2   Main categories into which payment systems fall   161

11 : 3   Manning arrangements   162

11 : 4   Wage structure based on six job-evaluated grades and proportional standard performance incentive bonus   163

11 : 5   Earnings under various payment by result systems   168

11 : 6   Comparative earnings; bonus varying proportionally less than output   170

11 : 7   Staff report   175

11 : 8   Staff salary structure   176

14 : 1   Numbers and percentage of women employed in thirteen selected industries—April 1969   210

Notes on the Contributors

Derek P Torrington, the editor of this book, is Senior Lecturer in Industrial Relations at Manchester Polytechnic, where he runs a full-time post-graduate one-year course in personnel management. He is also an industrial consultant and a member of the Institute of Personnel Management Examinations Committee. Ex- Manchester Grammar School and Manchester University, he gained much of his industrial relations experience as Manager of the Personnel and Training Division at Oldham International Limited. His extensive lecturing activities included a five-year run of seminars for the British Institute of Management on *Successful Personnel Management*. He has published various articles in management journals, and two books: *Successful Personnel Management* (Staples, 1969), and *Face to Face* (Gower Press, 1971).

E G A Armstrong, BA, MCom, PhD, is Senior Lecturer in Industrial Relations at the Manchester Business School and prior to that, was a lecturer in Industrial Relations and Industrial Law at the University of Aston. Soon after leaving the University of Birmingham where he obtained his degrees, he became a manager with Cadbury Brothers Limited where he had special responsibility for industrial relations and factory legislation. He has written various articles in academic and management journals and is the author of *Industrial Relations—An Introduction* (Harrap, 1969).

Tom Connelly is the Chief Conciliation Officer at the Race Relations Board and was, until 1968, a member of the Greater London Conciliation Committee on Race Relations. He was educated at Oxford and afterwards studied Industrial Relations in the United States for one year. In 1955, he became Research Officer of the Amalgamated Society of Woodworkers, where he remained for eight years, until his appointment as Head of the Research Department of the General and Municipal Workers' Union. Prior to his current position, he was an industrial relations adviser to the Prices and Incomes Board.

J L Cookson is lecturer in Industrial Law, and tutor in Industrial Relations at Manchester Polytechnic. He was educated at a northern grammar school and read law at Cambridge, after which he emigrated to Canada for three years. Here, he was employed in different aspects of corporate planning, first with Gulf Oil (Canada) and later with the Algama Steel Corporation. He has held his present post since 1969, when he returned to this country.

Andrew Gottschalk is a staff tutor in Social Psychology in the Department of Adult Education at the University of Nottingham, where he teaches Industrial Relations and Social Psychology to a variety of groups from both sides of industry. He has observed the negotiation and implementation of several productivity agreements and is co-editor and contributor to *Bargaining for Change*, *Productivity Bargains* and *British Industrial Relations* (Allen and Unwin, 1972).

Christine Howarth is a research officer at North, Paul and Associates Limited and was, for three years, employed by The Thomson Organisation in advertising and marketing and as a business economist. She is a graduate of the University of Sheffield, where she obtained a BA(Econ) Honours degree in Sociology in 1967.

R G Jeffrey is a management consultant with North, Paul and Associates Limited. He was formerly a consultant with AIC, where he worked on one of the first productivity deals with dockers at Teesside

Port Authority. During the eight years previous to this, he was involved in work study for ICI Limited and Richardsons Westgarth Limited. He is a graduate of New College, Oxford, where he read an Honours degree in French.

E V Kettle, Group Personnel Manager of Lankro Chemicals Limited, has nineteen years of personnel experience. Working up from the shop floor as an electrician, his first personnel position was with Esso Petroleum Company, Fawley. He spent some time with Brotherton and Company and Associated Chemical Companies before taking up his present post. He is Chairman of the Northern Region of the Institute of Personnel Management as well as being a member of the National Executive and Council of the IPM.

Denis H Langton is the Manufacturing Manager at Oldham and Son Limited. He was awarded his MA in Chemistry at Balliol College, later following this up with a post-graduate diploma in Management Studies. The next ten years were spent in production management working for The Distillers Company and BP. His work in productivity bargaining assumed greater importance in his two years of management consultancy at AIC. He has continued this interest in drawing up the recent Oldham and Son productivity agreement.

Roger Lyons is National Officer of the Association of Scientific, Technical and Managerial Staffs, and is based at the head office in London. He gained his experience from a training period with ASSET (which later merged with the AScW to form ASTMS) where he was appointed the Merseyside official in 1969. Mr Lyons is a graduate of University College, London, where he was awarded an Honours degree in Economics.

Jim Murray is Chairman and Works Convenor of Vickers' Shop Stewards, Newcastle upon Tyne, where he is responsible for negotiations on behalf of twelve unions. After leaving school at the age of fourteen, he served an engineering apprenticeship at Clarke Chapman

Marine Engineers, Gateshead, until joining the Merchant Navy as an engineer. He was the Labour Party Parliamentary Candidate for Louth in the 1970 General Election.

Rachel Naylor, MA (Oxon) is lecturer in the Department of Management Sciences at the University of Manchester Institute of Science and Technology, where her special interests are Industrial Relations and Manpower Administration, which she teaches to post-graduate level. Miss Naylor also holds a social Sciences Diploma from Liverpool University and is a Fellow of the Institute of Personnel Management. She has held general management and personnel management posts in large and small firms and was, for a time, Personnel Management Adviser in both the Midlands and North West regions of the Department of Employment.

L F Neal, MA(Cantab), MInstT, MIPM, was appointed Chairman of the new Statutory Commission on Industrial Relations on 1st November 1971. In 1955 he joined Esso Petroleum Limited and later, as Employee Relations Manager at the Fawley Refinery was closely associated with the Fawley productivity agreements. Later he was appointed Deputy Employee Relations Adviser and until December 1966, was Labour Relations Adviser to Esso Europe (Inc). He then became a member of the British Railways Board with responsibility for all staffing functions. He was appointed Professor (Part Time) of Industrial Relations at the University of Manchester and Fellow (Visiting) of the University of Lancaster. He is joint author with Andrew Robertson of *The Manager's Guide to Industrial Relations*.

Robert Sergean is an industrial psychologist, at present attached as an independent research worker to Sheffield University's School of Librarianship and Information Science. His degree at Edinburgh University was in Psychology and Social Anthropology, and for fifteen years he was a member of the Medical Research Council scientific staff. A regular contributor to many management and scientific journals, his book, *Managing Shiftwork* was published in 1971 by Gower Press.

The Rt. Revd. E R Wickham (BD) has been Bishop of Middleton for the Diocese of Manchester since his consecration in 1959. Previous strong involvement in industry led him to found the Sheffield Industrial Mission, of which he was Director 1944–1959. For the five years ending in 1970, he was Chairman of the World Council of Churches Department for Urban and Industrial Mission. His publications include: *Church and People in an Industrial City* (Lutterworth Press, 1959); *Encounter with Modern Society* (Lutterworth Press, 1965); and *Task of the Church in Relation to Industry* (Church of England, 1959).

Preface

This book is an attempt to help managers in their handling of industrial relations within the organisations they run. The contributions are from a wide variety of people. There can be few books for managers with chapters by trade union officials and even fewer that close with a chapter by a bishop! The common factor of all the contributors is expertise in the field of industrial relations, even though the standpoint of the writers varies considerably. All have widespread experience in handling industrial relations issues, and all have some specialist wisdom to offer.

I hope that the book will be both read and used, rather than merely read. The coverage includes material that is intended to inform and to stimulate thinking, as well as material that is intended to be of practical value immediately in handling the details of day-to-day affairs.

The material in this book was written just as the Industrial Relations Act was coming on to the statute book, but before anyone really knew what the effects of the legislation would be in practice. It is hoped that what is said may help some managers cope with the new, post-legislation situation.

I would like to acknowledge the ready co-operation of the other contributors in providing material which I have found of absorbing interest and real value. I trust that the variety and quality of their contributions make this a readable and useful book.

February 1972   *Derek Torrington*
                                                                              Editor

Part One

THE NATIONAL FRAMEWORK

1

Management and Industrial Relations

D P Torrington

Senior Lecturer in Industrial Relations, Manchester Polytechnic

Industrial relations is a subject of interest to all sections of the community, either as participants or observers. For a time during 1970 it rivalled sex and sport in the acreage of newsprint devoted to it and, through television, it has become an armchair spectator sport in which we, the viewers, are involved; savouring the stimulation of conflict.

Unlike some spectator sports, there is an unusual spice of excitement through the feeling of personal danger, similar to sitting close to the track during a grand prix motor race. At any time the spectator is likely to be involved in the backwash of the conflict. At the motor race he may be hit by a flying wheel or sprayed with petrol from a ruptured tank. The industrial relations spectator is exposed to a different type of hazard. While relishing the television account of the latest stoppage, he will have the tantalising uncertainty of not knowing whether his commuter train will be running the following morning, or whether his new car will be completed, his post delivered, his dustbin emptied, his children taught in school or whatever; according to the current spectacular being played.

3

Politicians and economists observe the industrial relations scene for different reasons, but both see the incidence of industrial disruption as having a major influence on the economic health of the country and the prospects for prosperity. Others may see it as an aspect of our way of life where social revolution is both overdue and likely to be achieved. The growing interest being taken in industrial relations by the outside observer is in most cases a source of discomfort to those directly involved. The actual participants are those who employ and are employed, and their representatives.

The subject of this book can be defined as the regulation of the working relationships between employers and groups of employees through the intermediary of managers and employee representatives. Here the attention of the outside world is often unwelcome, as the observers do not seem to understand the rules by which the game is played and they introduce a note of melodrama and hysteria that makes solutions harder rather than easier to reach. Personnel managers and trade union officials feel misrepresented, while employers and employees alike feel that they are vilified as being responsible for socially undesirable behaviour. Nevertheless, industrial relations is no longer a private matter between employer and employees, if it ever was. The whole community is now concerned about the way in which working relationships are regulated, so that managers and employee representatives are being required to conduct their arrangements in a way which can be seen and understood by those outside.

The Industrial Relations Act

Since 1965, when the Donovan Commission was set up, the scene for public accountability by the industrial relations specialists has been developing, reaching its climax in the Industrial Relations Act of 1971. Even before the Donovan Report was published there were already signs of both employers and unions taking a long, hard look at their industrial relations policies and behaviour in order to re-assess their attitudes and practices. This gathered momentum slowly after publication of the report and its attendant, invaluable research papers.

During the late sixties both major political parties were committed to some sort of intervention in industrial matters and these were set out in two policy documents: *Fair Deal at Work* stating the case of the Conservative party, and *In Place of Strife* setting out the proposed legislation of the Labour government. Following the Conservative election victory of 1970, the Industrial Relations Act and the associated Code of Industrial Relations Practice were introduced. Government has set down the rules within which it requires industrial relations practitioners to work in regulating the working relationships between employers and groups of employees. State intervention has come as the result of managers and trade union officials appearing to the observers as being incapable of conducting their affairs in a way which provided reasonable safeguards for those outside the tight little world of the experts.

Some readers of this book, and some contributors to it, will loathe the Industrial Relations Act, others will welcome it. Some may think it will help and others may think it will hinder industrial relations. What seems inevitable is that there will be change. At least it will change the form even if it does not change the substance of industrial relations. The Act sets up a new legal framework within which managers, trade union officials, shop stewards, individual employees and government servants all have to find new ways of working together to avoid breaking the law. There is no chance of managers and shop stewards getting together and agreeing tacitly to ignore the law. At so many points the provisions for individual workers' rights prevent the possibility of such collusion. It needs only one person to challenge an existing closed shop agreement, or to be unfairly dismissed and the machinery of the new legal system to deal with industrial relations comes into operation, whether the full-time officials and personnel managers want it to or not.

This book is not concerned principally with the political or philosophical debate about the new legislation. This book is concerned with the practice of industrial relations; it is intended for managers in the industrial relations business and for students of management. The objective of the book is to set down in one volume the main matters which the manager needs to know in order to be able to manage the industrial relations affairs of his organisation. In the end if there is to be an improvement in industrial relations in this country, or in any individual organisation, this improvement will be made at the initiative of those who are principally concerned: shop stewards and managers. Throughout their report the members of the Donovan Commission emphasised the importance of getting managers to bring about the

improvement that is needed. Here is a brief extract from the introduction to the report (paragraph 18):

'With a continuing growth in the size of industrial units
and the amalgamation of companies there has developed
a managerial society in which ownership has become
divorced from control. The running of large businesses
is in the hands of professional managers. They are responsible to Boards of Directors who can be regarded
broadly as trustees for the general body of shareholders.
While in the long term shareholders, employees and
customers all stand to benefit if a concern flourishes, the
immediate interests of these groups often conflict.
Directors and managers have to balance these conflicting
interests and in practice they generally seek to strike
whatever balance will best promote the welfare of the
enterprise as such.'

The report further emphasises the importance of Boards of Directors
recognising their own responsibility for industrial relations activity.
There has been a strange tendency amongst directors of companies to
avoid this particular area of responsibility and leave it to specialists.
Presumably this may be because of the inevitable conflict and overt
ill-humour that goes along with industrial relations negotiations. Perhaps
it is also because it lacks the glamour and characteristic attractions of,
for instance, marketing, advertising, public relations and financial
matters.

The first Code of Practice — opened with: 'Management has the
primary responsibility for good industrial relations and should take
the initiative in creating and maintaining them.' However, industrial
relations is as central to the running of a business as it ever was, and
there is a serious danger that the handling of industrial relations may
remain a fragmented professionalism, rather than being the principal
pre-occupation of those who mainly control the business.

Trade Unions

Industrial relations and trade union membership are both tending to
increase rather than contract. In the beginning, trade unionism was

restricted to those having manual skills. By the latter part of the nineteenth century general workers too were also organised in trade unions. Later came the clerical and technical workers and in the last ten to twelve years there has been a considerable increase in the number of supervisory and managerial personnel who are not only joining trade unions, but also becoming militant and determined in their trade union membership.

Trade union membership is by no means restricted to manufacturing industry. There is extensive union membership and representation in the public services. There is an efficient and determined union for airline pilots. There are others for nurses, teachers, doctors, and members of other professions. Total membership of the TUC now exceeds 10 000 000.

The developing unionisation of the professions is, perhaps, due to increased government intervention in industrial relations affairs. Professional employees may feel happier about joining a representative body which is both publicly accountable and bureaucratised in a way that the professional understands. In this context two factors of the late sixties, which contributed to the present situation, should not be overlooked. The research that was instituted by Donovan provided the first hard information on many industrial relations matters, getting through some of the long-standing mystery and mystique. Secondly, the National Board for Prices and Incomes produced some pioneering investigations and reports on aspects of industrial relations. They were commendable not only for their readability and realism, but also for the way in which they replaced dogmatic assertion with systematic enquiry as a means of basing understanding on data rather than prejudice.

The Organisation

As industrial relations is being subjected to public scrutiny, so is management as a whole having to reconsider its place in society and its objectives in relation to employees: What is industry for? What is the place of work in the life of the individual and the life of the community?

Personnel managers for a long time saw their function as being to stand between the rapacity of the employer and the helplessness of the employees, or as the agent of a paternalistic employer distributing benefits to the deserving employees while protecting the helpless employer from the rapacity of the trade unions. Later, came the pre-occupation with efficiency. Competition became tougher and profitability more difficult. Survival was seen to be the main objective of employer and employee alike, so that the personnel manager became the executive who made sure that the people (who are now known as human resources) in the undertaking were deployed in the most efficient and therefore the most profitable way.

It is now, perhaps, realised that even a combination of efficiency and justice is not enough. Debate is emerging about the social role of the organisation and the ways in which employees can achieve personal fulfilment in their work. This may need quite radical changes in practice and attitude, such as reducing competition, running a factory as a miniature democratic state, and making the work suit the people rather than deploying the human resources to fit the work.

It is not the aim of this book to propose answers to this type of question, but it is accepted that answers to more mundane questions, such as how people should be paid, need to be considered against this type of background and the book takes into account the social and philosophical setting.

Future developments

Some of the gradually changing attitudes that have developed in recent years are the following:

1   The traditional system of command of authority from the manager and obedience by the employee is not the only way to run a business.

2   The manager and the employee have different frames of reference and different interests in their approach to work. The Institute of Personnel Management has defined personnel management as an attempt to achieve both efficiency and justice, neither of which can be achieved without the other. The manager's main objective is to achieve efficiency. Perhaps the main objective of the trade unionist or other employee representative is to see that justice is done.

3   The different set of interests which are represented by the manager on the one hand and the employee representative on the other, have traditionally been seen as a regrettable waste of energy and as a dichotomy which is harmful to the best interests of the organisation.

This conflict of interests can be used constructively for both sides if the conflicting nature of the interests is recognised and attempts to reconcile conflicting views are based on an understanding of the reality of the situation.

4   It seems strange that it should be a Conservative government which introduces wide-ranging legislation designed to strengthen and establish the position of trade unions in society, but trade unions find the type of establishment which is envisaged for them as being largely repugnant. For a long time employers appeared to regard trade unions as being both unnecessary and undesirable. Now, the majority of employers and the majority of managers regard trade unions as being not only desirable but essential, although perhaps most managers still would like trade unions to behave in a way in which trade unions would not accept as being reasonable.

There is a steadily increasing proportion of those at work who are what are loosely classified as white-collar employees; they comprise some 14 per cent of the working population. Industry is increasing the number of technicians but is not increasing the number of craftsmen who are employed. There are no fewer than 25,000 new management posts created every year. In the next decade the number of people employed in basic industries, such as coal-mining and farming, is likely to decline with the introduction of further mechanisation. The number in manufacturing is not expected to increase although there will be a larger section of the working population who are engaged in public service and in other types of service work. There is likely to be a further substantial increase in the number of married women in the working population. What will be the industrial relations effect of these various developments?

At the moment there is an unusual phenonomen; a relatively high level of unemployment associated with steady overtime by those who are in employment but, on the basis of both efficiency and justice, this seems an inconsistent situation. Is the number of hours spent at work going to come down, after having remained almost unchanged for the last 25 years, despite the steady reduction in the number of hours in the nominal week? Are we coming in the 1970s to the levelling off in the boom of demand for consumer durables that have become commonplace during the post-war period? Is the dwindling of raw materials and the increasing anxiety about the manifold effects of pollution likely to curtail the output of manufactured goods? What will be the effect of these possible developments on industrial relations?

Is there a possibility of achieving a greater degree of industrial democracy and workers' participation in management? In the next few years, is it likely that there will be control of industry by the workers? If this happens, what will be the effect on industrial relations and the management of industrial relations within the enterprise?

The Donovan Report, the Labour Party Bill and the 1971 Industrial Relations Act have all been considered necessary because of a need by society for industrial relations to improve and to become less destructive. In recent years we have had our fill of moral exhortation as those outside the field of industrial relations say what ought to be done and how terrible everything is. Exhortation of this type will not succeed in putting things right; neither will legal frameworks nor revised trade union rules, although all these may help.

It is the structure and intent of work-place relationships that will bring good industrial relations. Here the manager has the prime responsibility and controls the right to livelihood and to self respect. The people who work in the factory may be members of a trade union; the trades union controls the right to challenge the manager's authority.

2

Collective Bargaining

E G A Armstrong

Senior Lecturer in Industrial Relations, Manchester Business School

A useful way of looking at the sum of activities which constitute industrial relations, is to see the product of those activities as rules which regulate and influence life at work. Some of these employment rules are laid down by Act of Parliament such as the safety, health and welfare requirements of the Factories Act. Other rules develop informally by convention, by *custom and practice*. Probably the most important sets of rules are those established by collective bargaining. If this were not true, governments would hardly take the trouble they do to change the behaviour of the bargainers with prices and incomes policies and industrial relations legislation. This chapter is therefore concerned with defining collective bargaining, assessing its extent, method of operation, importance and achievements.Elements of specific collective agreements will be examined.

Definition

Although the Industrial Relations Act 1971 contains a lawyer's definition of 'collective bargaining' (Section 167), the following description from the Ministry of Labour's *Industrial Relations Handbook*[1] is more suitable for everyday use:

'The term "collective bargaining" is applied to those arrangements under which wages and conditions of employment are settled by a bargain, in the form of an agreement made between employers or associations of employers and workers' organisations'

(In the above quotation, to wages should be added salaries.) Essentially, collective bargaining is a representative process in that some men bargain on behalf of others, be they managers representing the interests of the firm, or of many firms in an industry; shop stewards representing the interests of one or a group of union members, or full-time trade union officers bargaining in national negotiations for hundreds of thousands of *their members*, or for a few hundred in a particular category. Similarly, although there can be workers' organisations which are not trade unions, any employment rule bargaining they do as organisations is on behalf of their membership.

In short, collective bargaining is concerned with the employment rule bargaining which is carried out by organised groups with varying degrees of power.

Underlying principles

For years, there has been a strong system of voluntary collective bargaining and the trade unions still place great value on the voluntary principle. In broad terms, voluntary meant minimal legal regulation of power group bargaining. Specifically, *voluntary* could be applied to the following elements that compose collective bargaining.

The British people have long enjoyed a wide measure of freedom of *association*. Almost daily the mass media bring this fact home to us as groups of demonstrators associate to wave their banners and shout their slogans. Workers have been free, in this sense, for 100 years to protest in a more permanent form by creating trade unions. Once formed, it is in the nature of a trade union (or employers' organisation) to try and recruit members. The recruitment pressures invoked have been of a moral (occasionally perhaps immoral) social, economic character. They have not emanated from the law courts. For example, a union has not been able to go to court and say: 'compel this man to join our union'. The law intervened only marginally in the operation of the closed shop. Similarly, it was long lawful for an employer to make it a condition of employment that an employee should not join a union. The law had little to do with voluntary *organisation*.

Mutual recognition by the bargainers is a pre-condition of collective bargaining. Although public policy, as expressed through nationalisation acts and government practices, has encouraged employers to concede, under conditions, trade union claims for recognition, there has been no general law on *recognition*. Similar remarks apply to the *bargaining* which should follow recognition. The purpose of bargaining is to reach agreement, but collective *agreements* have been binding in honour only, sustained by voluntary support. They have had no contractual and, therefore, no legal force. In a free society, the bargainers are bound to fall out from time to time. In the event of *disagreements* the law has sometimes suggested but not imposed solutions. Acceptance by the parties of a Court of Inquiry's findings, for example, is voluntary not compulsory.

So in relation to association, organisation, recognition, bargaining, agreement, disagreement, the key word has been voluntary not compulsory. With the Industrial Relations Act, the law is or can be, dependent on the circumstances, introduced into all the above elements of collective bargaining. Whether the Act is thus a straitjacket to restrict voluntary collective bargaining, or a framework in which it can operate more effectively, depends on one's own viewpoint. Both viewpoints may well need to be modified in the light of events.

The extent of collective bargaining

While only slightly more than 40 per cent of the national work force are members of trade unions, it is probable that upwards of 80 per cent have their pay and conditions directly or indirectly affected by collective bargaining. Where a firm is party to, or observes a particular collective agreement, the union rate will be paid to union and non-union members alike among the grades of workers affected. As the result of a collective agreement reached on behalf of the manual workers in a firm, the salaries of the unorganised, non-manual workers and even managers, may well be revised. A commercial laundry with no union members on its payroll may well increase its wage levels when it is discovered that some of its workers have left for better paying jobs in the local hospital laundry where, as the result of a recent national agreement in the National Health Service, hospital laundry pay has been increased.

B

(There may well be relatively few actual trade union members among the hospital laundry staff.) Many *non-federated* firms pay close attention to the agreements reached in their industries by the appropriate employers' associations with trade unions.

In a variety of ways, therefore, the number of people affected by collective bargaining can become very much greater than the numbers in membership of the respective *collectives*.

'According to the Ministry of Labour's evidence, there are about 500 separate industry-wide negotiating arrangements in Britain for manual workers alone . . .' (Donovan Report, 1968)[2]

In their evidence to Donovan,[3] the Ministry of Labour (now the Department of Employment) listed those 'Negotiating and Statutory Wage Fixing Bodies Covering 100 000 Workers or More.' Leaving aside, for the moment, the white collar sectors, nineteen industry groups constitute the big league, namely: agriculture, coal-mining, food manufacture, engineering, shipbuilding and ship-repairing, cotton spinning and weaving, woollen and worsted, clothing, general printing, building and contracting, civil engineering, electricity supply, British Rail, road passenger transport, road haulage, the Post Office, National Health Service (Ancillary Staffs Council—Manual Workers), motor garages, local government service (manual workers).

This list includes private and public employment, most of our oldest industries and some of the important services. Other services are to be found in the white collar group of retail distribution, education, catering and national government.

As a further dimension of size, at one end of the scale among the 'five hundred' industries is engineering with some 3½ million employees and at the other, the tiny industry of pin, hook and eye consisting of some twenty firms whose small labour force is affected by a statutory Wages Council for the trade. Additionally, (this point will be amplified later) industry-wide collective bargaining has developed unevenly within particular industries. Catering is a large industry but actual trade union membership among catering workers is thought to be less than 10 per cent of the potential and the various collective agreements established for different sectors of the industry such as pubs and clubs are of meagre quality. Conversely, newspaper printing is a relatively small industry, in terms of manpower employed, but it is highly unionised with its work force usually at, or near, the top of the manual workers' earnings table.

Methods of operation: industry-wide bargaining arrangements

A broad division may be made between *voluntary* and *statutory* industry-wide bargaining arrangements. By voluntary is meant those institutions formed essentially by the voluntary exertions of the joint bargainers themselves. A stimulus to organisation has sometimes been provided by the State in the form of exhortation and example. The acceptance and application by Governments of *Whitleyism* following the Whitley Report of 1917, the requirement in the nationalised industries that the management work with the unions to fashion joint negotiating machinery—illustrate the point. By 'statutory' is meant those arrangements which derive directly from Acts of Parliament. Such legislation has created our Wages Councils system.

The Whitley Committee was set up by the Government during the First World War and given the task of making recommendations about how best to secure 'a permanent improvement in the relations between employers and workmen.' A major Whitley recommendation was the encouragement of the extension and strengthening of industry-wide collective bargaining. In industries where trade unions and employers' associations were sufficiently well organised, the bargainers should jointly form Joint Industrial Councils. The Government agreed and *Whitleyism* became public policy. Whitley Councils were formed for civil service pay negotiations and later for the National Health Service. JICs or their equivalent were established in the nationalised industries. Not until the Donovan Report of 1968 were misgivings about the operation of industry-wide bargaining publicly and authoritatively expressed. These misgivings will be briefly examined later in this chapter.

The archetypal institution for conducting industry-wide collective bargaining has been the Joint Industrial Council. (The first Appendix of the Ministry of Labour's *Industrial Relations Handbook* comprises a 'Model Constitution and Functions of a Joint Industrial Council.') *Joint* obviously implies two parties—the employers' grouping, in one or more employers' associations and the employees' grouping in one or more, usually more, unions. *Industrial* may constitute a complete industry as with building, or furniture, or a sector such as biscuit manufacture within the multisectoral food manufacturing industry. In its evidence to Donovan, the Ministry of Labour estimated that something like 200 JICs currently operated. *Council* implies a constitution, committees, procedures—the terms of the treaty for the conduct of orderly negotiations founded on the concept of *self-government* within an industry. Hopefully, this should promote better understanding, better conditions of employment and improved productivity.

In some of our older industries, and here engineering is the pre-eminent example, JICs have not been formed. Industry-wide collective bargaining has nonetheless been practised for many years. Such arrangements, particularly in engineering and shipbuilding are commonly labelled *ad hoc*. The reasons for the absence of JICs in these industries are complex and lie outside the scope of this chapter. It would be misleading to suggest the existence of a direct relationship between the absence of a JIC and the presence of a high degree of industrial strife, but it may be that the lack of JIC 'ideology and tradition' in engineering and shipbuilding is one important cause of conflict. (It is notable that Donovan, the CIR and, to some extent, the Code of Industrial Relations Practice advocate the formation of *mini-JICs* within the plant. The Industrial Relations Act's provisions for the bargaining agent/unit are also consistent with this approach.)

Wages Councils are the 'poor man's JIC'. More than fifty of these Councils are currently in operation and the results of their negotiations apply, at least on the technical and legal level, to some 3 000 000 work people. With a Wages Council the State provides the bargaining machinery which the unions and employers in a 'poorly organised trade' (in the collective bargaining sense) have been unable to fashion for themselves. Thus, Wages Councils are to be found where unions traditionally have been weak and wages poor, in retail distribution, catering, sectors of the clothing trade and small manufacturing industries where high proportions of women have been employed.

Wages Councils are tri-partite in structure. On either side of the bargaining table sit the representatives of the employers and trade unions but the chair is taken by an Independent, supported by two other Independents, all three being appointed by the Secretary of State for Employment. The function of the Independents is to help along not control, the bargaining process which remains the responsibility of employers and unions. However, if an *impasse* arises, then by use of their voting powers, the Independents can tip the scales for or against a particular wage claim. Agreements reached by a Council are submitted for ratification to the Secretary of State for Employment who has no powers of veto but may delay the implementation of the settlement. Such delays have occurred at times of government wage restraint policies.

Once the modification to the industry-wide collective agreement has been ratified by means of a Wages Regulation Order, every employer in the trade in question, whether he has union employees or not, is under a statutory duty to pay wages and observe conditions not less favourable than those set out in the relevant Orders. Wages Inspectors are continually checking samples of wages records and arrears of pay are regularly recovered for workers found to be underpaid. On the whole, however, the legal minimum standards are not difficult, in economic terms, for an employer to meet. It is thought that most infractions arise from administrative failures.

It has long been the intention of public policy that the statutory Wages Councils should disappear as the bargainers became better organised, to be replaced by voluntary JICs. Progress in this direction has been slow and the Industrial Relations Act contains features designed to speed up this process.

In some sectors of employment, voluntary and statutory bargaining arrangements overlap. For example, the pay of every shop assistant employed by a grocer is protected by the Wages Regulation Orders of the Retail Food Wages Council. Some of these assistants are, however, entitled to higher pay as the result of a voluntary agreement reached by the Union of Shop Distributive and Allied Workers with the Multiple Grocers grouping. Two-tier arrangements of this kind are to be found in a number of industries. Our total bargaining structure at industry level is, therefore, complex. Since the end of World War II, the structure has become even more intricate with the growth of work-place bargaining, the second of the 'two systems' of industrial relations.

The two systems

'Britain has two systems of industrial relations'—in the judgement of Donovan—the formal and the informal. By *formal* is meant the system so far outlined in this chapter of industry-wide collective bargaining arrangements and agreements. The *informal* system is centred on the work place. Plant and work-place bargaining are considered in detail later in this book, but the relationship between the two systems needs to be indicated here, because the two systems are not separate and distinct—they interact. The Donovan Report summarised the situation thus:

> 'The informal system is often at odds with the formal system. Actual earnings have moved far apart from the rates laid down in industry-wide agreements; the three major elements in the "gap" are piecework or incentive earnings, company or factory additions to basic rates, and overtime earnings. These are all governed by decisions within the factory (or other establishment such as a construction site or an office, the word "factory" not being used in the report in a restricted literal sense). At the same time, disputes procedures laid down in industry-wide agreements have been subjected to strain by the transfer of authority to the factory and workshop.
>
> The bargaining which takes place within factories is largely outside the control of employers' associations and trade unions. It usually takes place piece-meal and results in competitive sectional wage adjustments and chaotic pay structures. Unwritten understandings and "custom and practice" predominate.
>
> These developments help to explain why resort to unofficial and unconstitutional strikes and other forms of workshop pressure has been increasing.
>
> This decentralisation of collective bargaining has taken place under the pressure of full employment . . .'

Other pressures have also contributed to the process of decentralisation. The widespread application of payment by results entails the measurement of work where the work is done—that is, in the work place. Measurement entails the setting of standards—a potential challenge to and commonly constant haggling about those standards—at work-place level. Productivity bargaining with its concern for the more efficient use of labour enhances work-place bargaining. From surveys carried out for Donovan it is clear that many managers prefer to bargain with shop stewards rather than the full-time officers of unions. This preference clearly indicates the importance of the union bargainer—in the work place. Some unions, notably Britain's two biggest, the TGWU and the AUEW have latterly developed policies designed to foster work-place bargaining in the interests of democracy. As part of a widespread social phenomenon, people seek increasing influence over their immediate environment, over the decisions that affect them. To this end, in the employment situation, the main focus of attention must be the work place.

This is not to argue that industry-wide collective bargaining will or should disappear. Some employment rules can best be fashioned at industry level and others within the company or plant. Donovan recognised this and so does the Code of Industrial Relations Practice. Different industries will have different mixes of the two systems—and the mixes will alter over time. The burden of the Donovan message, and this now seems accepted public policy, was that the prime responsibility for good industrial relations rests with management and specifically with the boards of companies. Workpeople are not managed by JICs or Wages Councils. They *are* managed by supervisors, production superintendents, works managers, office managers, shift managers— whose own behaviour may well reflect the adequacy or inadequacy of *the board's* industrial relations policy. There is now no shortage of guidance on what constitutes a *good* industrial relations policy. The Donovan Report, reports of the PIB, the CIR, the Code of Industrial Relations Practice, are replete with advice. What is needed is movement and the Industrial Relations Act and the Code may generate pressures, particularly on management, to move in the desired directions.

The importance of collective bargaining

Viewed from a variety of perspectives, collective bargaining is an important process. Hints have already been given about its economic importance, as seen by governments anxious to operate incomes policies of whatever subtlety or crudity. It would be pointless to discuss here whether rising wages, salaries and earnings are the cause or consequence of inflation but as wages and prices both rise faster than productivity, to harmonise the three growth rates inevitably means some form of intervention into our basically free-wheeling collective bargaining practices.

The various forms of intervention and the extent of their success/

failure are discussed in a recent book by Professor Clegg.[4] Having analysed the mistakes of past incomes policies, Professor Clegg suggests a variety of ways in which fresh interventions into collective bargaining might be made. A recurrent theme of this interesting work is 'the injustice of our existing income distribution.' Some people are paid too much and some too little as the result of the *untidy* operation of collective bargaining. Intervention must, therefore, be made not only into industry-wide bargaining but work-place bargaining, otherwise 'there is a danger that the policy will control rates while earnings control the economy.'

Whatever the present government decides to do, or not do, about collective bargaining as an economic process, it is clear that this government is firmly determined to intervene in collective bargaining as a political and social process. The Industrial Relations Act and the Code of Industrial Relations Practice bear witness to this determination. The Act significantly modifies, or has the potential for so doing, some of the important procedural rules of collective bargaining and the rules which are to apply to the bargainers, notably in relation to trade union registration. Many of these changes are designed to serve political rather than economic ends, although the changes may have economic consequences.

By political is meant concern with the use of power, with defining anew the boundary lines between the rights of the individual, the group, the trade union, the employer(s), the community. The rules of the game of collective bargaining are being changed, so as to strengthen, in the government's view, the rights of the individual *vis-à-vis* his employer and *vis-à-vis* his trade union (if he is a member), and to strengthen the rights, by making legal remedies available, of those hurt by the unfair industrial practices (defined in the Act) which sometimes arise during collective bargaining. In practical terms, an example would be the putting at legal risk of the leaders of an unofficial strike.

Quite apart from the law's redistribution-of-power type of intervention into collective bargaining, collective bargaining is in its own right a vitally important political and social process. In our kind of society, collective bargaining, to quote Professor Dubin:[5]

'Is the great social invention that has institutionalised industrial conflict. In much the same way that the electoral process and majority rule have institutionalised political

conflict in a democracy, collective bargaining has created
a stable means for resolving industrial conflict'

British collective bargaining in recent years may not have been resolving
industrial conflict particularly well but this deficiency may be due more
to the inadequate operation of outdated institutions than the inherent
nature of collective bargaining itself. It was with the reform of institutions and procedures that Donovan was much concerned. Supporters
of the Industrial Relations Act contend that this legislation also seeks
to change institutions so that conflict can be handled more sensibly and
with less damage to the community.

As mentioned above, collective bargaining is political because it is
concerned with the operation of power—be it power at the industry-
wide bargaining, company, plant, work place or work group level. The
Industrial Relations Act itself is concerned to check the abuse of power,
as seen by the authors of this law, the abuses being described as unfair
industrial practices. Collective bargaining is an important political and
social process in that many people engage in it. An unknown but
substantial number of managers and employers' association officials are
bargainers. Whatever the number, it is certain to increase under the
pressures generated by the Industrial Relations Act and the Code of
Practice. Some 3000 full-time trade union officers and an estimated
200 000 shop stewards are engaged in bargaining and many lay members
are caught up in the process, as part of the bargaining teams. Their
numbers too are likely to increase as workpeople become more involved
in the decision-making processes at their place of employment. In
broad terms, this is a healthy development as it tends to check the
exercise of arbitrary power from whatever direction this may come.
Collective bargaining, and this has been particularly true of genuine
productivity bargaining, can promote better understanding of the
complex nature of how an enterprise—be it factory, oil refinery,
government department—operates. In short, it can be an educational
exercise in democratic industrial citizenship.

Collective bargaining, therefore, is more than bargaining about
money. It enables unions to agree with management the type of shift
systems that are acceptable to the workforce rather than the employees
being told what they are to be. Manning ratios, the criteria by which
workers shall be selected for redundancy or for promotion, can be
subject to jointly agreed rules rather than management imposed rules.

The same applies to grievance and disciplinary procedures, to the operation of work study, job evaluation techniques—to what Professor Allan Flanders has called *job regulation*. Flanders in fact, has gone so far as to say:

> 'That the value of a trade union to its members lies less in its economic achievements than in its capacity to protect their dignity.'[6]

Collective bargaining, whatever its imperfections and there are many, gives people a chance to count for something. In its absence, they would be faced with the alternatives of State control of incomes or individual bargaining with their much greater imperfections.

Substantive and procedural rules

Collective bargaining is multi-faceted in character and this is illustrated by the fact that the employment rules established by collective bargaining are conventionally separated into substantive rules and procedural rules. The Code of Practice itself follows this convenient distinction. To oversimplify, the substantive rules are those with largely an economic content such as wage rates, incentive standards, hours of work, overtime and shift premiums but the procedural rules are designed to regulate the relationships between the parties. Such rules would commonly embrace grievance and disciplinary procedures, union security (for example the operation or otherwise of the check-off), shop steward facilities and other rules relating to rights, privileges and duties. (The Industrial Relations Act is much concerned with new procedural rules.)

Dependent on the kind of industry and firm in which he is employed, an individual manager may find the exercise of his managerial prerogative hedged about by a complex of national, local and work-place substantive and procedural rules. In many cases, the procedural rules are likely to be less well codified than the substantive. There is usually a better chance of an employee knowing what he is to be paid for what he has to do than there is of his knowing the circumstances that warrant his suspension with or without pay for misconduct. The remainder of this chapter will, therefore, be concerned with examples of collective bargaining procedural rules which are important to workpeople and which have special significance for management. In essence, the following examples (by no means exhaustive) of some procedural rules are grouped around—the scope of the agreement; the degree of local autonomy; the deployment of labour; the handling of conflict.

Examples of rules from collective agreements

Scope of the agreement

To whom does the agreement apply? This question is easily posed but less readily answered. An engineering agreement is presumably applied to engineering workers but do canteen assistants employed in an engineering factory canteen count as engineering workers? (The answer will not be found here as the question is purely illustrative.) In an industry that is much more homogeneous than engineering, rubber, it is found that the 1968 NJIC Agreement for the Rubber Manufacturing Industry devotes its first page to 'scope' of the agreement. The rubber manufacturing industry is defined as an 'establishment, branch or department' and the agreement applies to 'all work incidental to the operations specified.' The agreement also specifies some of the jobs considered to be 'incidental' viz:

> ' "Work incidental" includes the work of general factory
> labourers and storemen'

Rubber is not all it seems, for the agreement applies to people working with gutta percha, balata and various compounds, 'if such substitutes are processed on machinery of the kind normally used for processing rubber.' Further,

> 'Unless otherwise mutually agreed at local level this
> Agreement will not apply to canteen workers, clerks and
> bookers, commissionaires, engineers (including workers
> employed as stokers and boiler firemen in raising steam
> heat for vulcanisers) and maintenance workers'

From the above, it is reasonable to suppose that from time to time problems have arisen about whether a particular group of workers should be covered by the Agreement or not. The pay and conditions of general factory labourers and storemen is to be regulated by the JIC

Agreement but, in relation to other groups of workers, boiler firemen for example, the national Agreement will not apply—unless management and the unions in the local situation agree to the contrary. This national agreement thus permits local flexibility and autonomy as the following excerpt further demonstrates:

Local autonomy

'The minimum basic weekly wages payable to all workers to whom this Agreement applies shall be . . .' there then follows a table of 'Minimum Weekly Wages'. These are open to improvements by local bargaining as this clause makes clear:

> 'Subject to (hours, shift and overtime conditions attached to "Minimum Weekly Wages") the wage rates and systems of payment for all workers, including earnings for skill, responsibility and productivity shall relate to increases in productivity or efficiency or to changes in job evaluation or similar assessments'

Relating pay increases to productivity increases often entails changes in the deployment of labour, and many productivity agreements have featured *flexibility of labour* provisions.

Deployment of labour

Two major areas of deployment are briefly considered here.

The first concerns the movement of craft or process workers across the hitherto rigid boundary lines marking off the job preserve of another group of craft workers. Genuine productivity agreements provide numerous examples of this kind of flexibility serving the purpose of the more efficient use of labour.

Here is an illustration of the erosion of demarcation and of traditional working practices taken from an oil refinery productivity agreement.

> Inter-Craft Flexibilities
> 'Boilermakers and Fitters will carry out tack welding for structural work . . .'
> Craft/Non-Craft Flexibilities
> 'Suitably trained members of the TGWU will carry out

bolting and unbolting (for example manhole covers, heat
exchangers . . . etc) when craftsmen are unavailable'

The next example is taken from an early productivity agreement in a
major service industry:

'. . . the following general principles shall apply where
such arrangements would assist in the proper progress of
the job.
(*a*) Craftsmen on related work should be interchangeable
as far as is practicable . . .'

The next example shows 'greater flexibility,' it is one of many:

'Glazing and associated work: to be done by
Plumbers
Joiners
Painters'

The second area of deployment concerns mobility, the movement of
workers between a variety of jobs entitled to the same or different rates
of pay under a job evaluation or similar scheme. A collective agreement
applying to manual workers in a particular food processing plant
devotes three pages to 'Conditions Relating to Transfers Between Graded
Work'. Upgrading entails qualifying periods at the existing grade rate.
When qualified, the worker is paid the higher grade rate. (Clearly,
there will be bargaining about qualifying periods.) Dependent on the
circumstances of a worker's transfer to a lower grade—the higher level
of pay will be made for a stipulated period or the lower rate may be
applied immediately. Downward transfers, because of poor quality
work or for disciplinary reasons, would mean payment at a lower rate
immediately.

Usually, there can be more than one point of view about poor quality
work and punishment for disciplinary offences, particularly if a reduction in income is involved. In short, out of the operation and administration of the many facets of collective agreements arise grievances.
Collective bargaining and collective agreements are therefore much
concerned with conflict-handling procedures, avoidance of dispute, or
more popularly grievance procedures.

Grievance procedures

Such procedures will be examined more thoroughly in a later chapter and it is possible to mention only one or two points concerning their purpose and operation here.

The central purpose of a grievance procedure can be easily stated; it is to ensure continued production while the grievance is processed through one or more stages of joint management/union discussions/ negotiations. In many industries and many more firms this purpose is achieved reasonably well. In a few well-known cases, and this applies particularly to engineering, strikes in breach of procedure are all too common. The reasons why some procedures work well and others far less so, are complex and not completely established. The engineering grievance procedure comes under particular strain because it is used so extensively for wage improvement bargaining purposes; that is for bargaining about *substantive* issues, rather than strictly *procedurally* for the interpretation and application of substantive agreements. If, so the argument runs, substantive bargaining at engineering work-place level were enriched and this might be done by creating Works Committees and formalising their activities along the lines of JICs, then a grievance procedure could do what it is supposed to do; effectively handle procedural issues. This explanation naturally does far less than justice to engineering's problems but the basic proposition is of general concern, that is whether within any particular collective agreement there is an adequate balance between the substantive and procedural rules of employment. The role of arbitration in relation to either or both sets of rules also merits conscientious examination.

Finally, and the whole trend of British industrial development over many years confirms this, it is expected that the substantive rules of employment will become more generous in content and the procedural rules will improve in quality. Collective bargaining is likely to become more, rather than less, complex but, at the same time, more rather than less orderly.

References

1 *Industrial Relations Handbook*, Ministry of Labour, HMSO, 1961
2 *Royal Commission on Trade Unions and Employers' Associations* 1965–1968, report, HMSO, 1968
3 *Royal Commission on Trade Unions and Employers' Associations*, written evidence of the Ministry of Labour, HMSO, 1965
4 *How to run an Incomes Policy—and why we made such a mess of the last one* by H CLEGG, Heinemann, 1971
5 'Constructive Aspects of Conflict' by R DUBIN, *Collective Bargaining* edited by A FLANDERS, Penguin Modern Management Readings, Penguin, 1969
6 'Collective Bargaining: a theoretical analysis' by A FLANDERS, *British Journal of Industrial Relations*, March 1968

3

The Industrial Relations Act 1971

J L Cookson

Lecturer in Industrial Law, Manchester Polytechnic

In a sense, the voluntary system of industrial relations in Britain is finished. When the Industrial Relations Act received the Royal Assent, the policy, traditionally followed by our Governments for the last 150 years, of generally keeping out of industrial relations came to an end. The occasion marked the fulfilment of the Conservatives' promise to introduce legislation 'to establish a framework of law within which improved industrial relations can develop,' but the framework is imposed, not voluntarily created by the two sides of industry.

The Government's reason for departing from tradition is simple. It believes that the voluntary system no longer works effectively; that the deterioration in the relations between management and workers testifies to this fact; and that, therefore, the Government is justified in (and has a responsibility for) intervening with legislation designed to set standards of conduct to which parties should conform and, thereby, to persuade both sides to behave in a more orderly and responsible manner towards each other.

The purpose of the Act is made expressly clear by Section 1. It is to promote good industrial relations in accordance with four general principles; these are:

1   That collective bargaining be conducted freely and responsibly and with due regard to the general interests of the community

2   That orderly procedures be developed and maintained for the peaceful settlement of disputes—by negotiation, conciliation or arbitration—with due regard to the general interests of the community

3   That workers and employers should enjoy free association in independent trade unions and employers' associations, such unions and associations to be representative, responsible and effective bodies for regulating the relationship between employees and employers

4   That workers be free and secure, protected by adequate safeguards against unfair practices by employers and others

This chapter will examine those sections of the Act which seem most likely to have an impact on the practice of industrial relations. For the sake of clarity and easier appreciation, the following points are made at the outset:

1   Three institutions play key roles in the operation of the Act
  — the National Industrial Relations Court ('the Court')
  — industrial tribunals
  — the Commission on Industrial Relations ('the Commission')

2   The Trade Disputes Acts of 1906 and 1965 (upon which the immunity from actions in tort enjoyed by trade unions was largely based) are repealed. In their place, the Act introduces a new legal concept, that of 'unfair industrial practices.' These will be examined in due course but the reader might be helped by his appreciating that such unfair practices, whether committed by employers, employers' associations, trade unions, organisations of workers or individuals, enable the party injured by the unfair practice to sue the offending party for damages

3   Reference in this chapter to 'registered' trade unions is to those unions which have registered themselves with the new Registrar of Trade Unions and Employers' Associations.

The rights of workers

Prior to the Act, certain fundamental rights for workers were conspicuously missing from the statute book. They had no right to belong to a union that they could protect through legal redress via the courts.

Pre-entry closed shops were lawful—here, a worker was compelled to join a union (like it or not) in order to get a job. Nor did the law recognise the concept of unfair dismissal—a worker could be fired for any reason whatsoever and he looked in vain to the law for protection. It is to these situations that Part II of the Act is largely directed.

Trade union membership (sections 5–10)

The Act confers a statutory right on an employee to belong to a registered union and to take an unfettered part in its activities. It is an unfair practice for an employer to infringe this right (or to attempt to do so) in any way either by refusing to employ a person or by discriminating against him or by dismissing him because he is a union member. Similarly, it is an unfair practice for a union or anyone to try to persuade an employer to infringe this right.

Equally, the Act confers on an employee the right *not* to belong to a union. This makes pre-entry closed shop agreements void. It is an unfair practice for employers and unions to operate closed shops or for anyone to try to persuade an employer to do so. However, employers may 'encourage' an employee to join a union which he recognises for bargaining purposes but such encouragement must stop short of offering material inducements.

Agency shop agreements (sections 11–16)

Whatever may have been the Government's motives in outlawing pre-entry closed shops, the Act impliedly recognises that they were useful devices so far as industrial relations practice is concerned, particularly since they enabled employers to fix the terms of employment of all closed shop members in a single negotiation. Since pre-entry closed shops are now unlawful, the Act attempts to preserve their practical usefulness by making it possible for employers and registered unions to operate agency shops (a device common in North America).

Where an agency shop exists, it will be a condition of employment for workers covered by it that they should be or become members of the union(s), or, alternatively, pay an appropriate contribution to it in lieu of membership. However, should a worker have conscientious objections to exercising either option, he may pay an equivalent amount to a charity (agreed between himself and the union)—disputes concerning the amount of the contribution or to which charity it should be payable will, ultimately, be determined by a tribunal.

Where a worker refuses to exercise any of the three options, it will be lawful for the employer to dismiss him.

Agency shops can be established in two ways. Firstly, by simple agreement between management and registered union(s). Secondly, if management rejects a request for an agency shop, procedures exist whereby the union(s) can create an agency shop by order of the Court following a ballot of the workers supervised by the Commission. Such an order will be made if, on the ballot, *either* the majority of workers eligible to vote *or* two-thirds of those who actually vote are in favour of the union(s) having an agency shop. On the other hand, if a majority is not obtained the Court will order the employer not to establish an agency shop for two years. Similarly, the Act has provisions whereby workers can challenge an agency shop already in existence though, here, one-fifth of the workers must endorse the initial application to the Court.

It is an unfair practice for anyone to prevent workers exercising their rights in relation to obtaining an agency shop, and for unions or workers to induce (or attempt to induce) employers to establish an agency shop during the two years for which the Court has ordered no agreement to be made or whilst an application for an agency shop is before the Court.

Approved closed shop agreements (sections 17–18)

The Government's original intention was to outlaw closed shops totally. During the Bill's passage through Parliament, however, it promised to reconsider the special circumstances of certain unions whose existence depends on the fact that a worker must hold a union card to get a job in industries where employment is usually short term.

Accordingly, the Act allows an employer and a registered union to enter into an approved closed shop agreement by order of the Court. The procedure requires both parties to submit a draft agreement to the Court for reference to the Commission, which must consider whether a closed shop is desirable for certain purposes. These include maintaining reasonable terms of employment, reasonable prospects for continual employment and stable machinery for collective bargaining, and these purposes must be considered incapable of being satisfied by an agency shop. If the Commission's report is favourable to the establishment of a closed shop, the Court may order one or may order a ballot to ascertain whether the majority of the workers concerned favour a closed shop.

As in the case of an agency shop, a worker may opt to pay to a charity, and an employer may lawfully dismiss (or refuse to engage) a worker who refuses both to join the union and to pay to the charity.

Contracts of employment (sections 19–21)

The Contracts of Employment Act 1963, provides that, subject to certain excepted employment, (including workers ordinarily employed for less than twenty-one hours a week), employees shall be entitled to minimum periods of notice based on their length of continuous service. As amended by the Industrial Relations Act, this minimum notice is as follows:

> after 13 weeks' continuous service—1 week's notice
> after 2 years' continuous service—2 weeks' notice
> after 5 years' continuous service—4 weeks' notice
> after 10 years' continuous service—6 weeks' notice
> after 15 years' continuous service—8 weeks' notice

The 1963 Act placed employers under an obligation also to provide employees with 'written particulars' of their terms of employment. These particulars are now extended to include the following:

1 A statement of the employee's right to join or not join a union and details of any agency shop or approved closed shop if these concern him
2 An explanation of the grievance procedure available to him, a description of a person to whom he should apply to invoke this procedure and the manner of making this application
3 Information concerning his holiday and holiday-pay entitlement (in sufficient detail to enable him to calculate precisely such entitlement, including his entitlement to accrued holiday pay on termination of his employment).

An employer continues to satisfy his obligations by referring workers to a document containing the statutory information and by making such document reasonably available to them.

Unfair dismissal (sections 22–32)

A worker now enjoys the right not to be dismissed unfairly. It is an unfair practice for an employer to dismiss without reasonable cause or for anyone to induce him to do so. Workers who feel that they have been dismissed unfairly can complain to a tribunal. If the tribunal finds the allegation justified, it has the power to recommend the employer to re-engage him in his former position (or in a reasonably suitable one) or to award him compensation against his employer. Such compensation is based on his loss of earnings, subject to a maximum period of 104 weeks and to maximum earnings of £40.00 per week. Fair grounds for dismissal include the following:

1 Incompetence
2 Misrepresentation of skills or qualifications
3 Redundancy
4 Misconduct
5 Striking—but if other strikers are not dismissed and if the reason for selective dismissal is that the worker belonged to or participated in a union *before* the strike, his dismissal will *not* be fair
6 Lock-out—if the worker is not offered re-engagement when work resumes

These provisions do not apply to employment which is, ordinarily, for less than twenty-one hours a week. Nor do they apply to workers who have reached normal retirement age or who have been continuously employed for less than 104 weeks *unless* the reason for dismissal is the worker's membership of, or activity in, a trade union (or his non-membership).

Further, the parties to a procedure agreement can apply, jointly, to the Court for an exclusion order whereby these provisions shall not apply to workers covered by such procedure. The Court will make an exclusion order if it is satisfied that his union is independent; that the procedure agreement enables him to contest the grounds for his dismissal and provides him with remedies generally as beneficial to him as are the remedies via a tribunal; and that the procedure agreement provides for independent arbitration on the matter of his dismissal.

The introduction of a statutory right to join a trade union is to be welcomed mainly because it brings British law in line with the legal systems of the West. But it is a right to join only a registered union so that workers belonging to unions which decide not to register continue to have no protection in law. It is clear that workers whose rights to join, or not join, a union are infringed will usually be hard-pressed to substantiate unfair practice before a tribunal because discrimination and coercion can be discreet or subtle (though this is a problem which legislation cannot erase).

The abolition of pre-entry closed shops is a radical move. Potentially, it threatens both a union's negotiating strength and its ability to control its members although agency shops (whereby workers must *pay* to exercise their right not to join a union) may help to offset these difficulties. Certainly it can be expected that agency shops will be established not merely to replace previously-existing closed shops—the Act's provision on recognition and sole bargaining agents (see below) suggest that agency shops—might become a common feature of our system.

Where agency shops exist employers must be careful to extend the *same* terms and conditions of employment to union members and non-members alike (or nearly the same) because failure to do so might lead to their being hauled before a tribunal to answer allegations that they have, thereby, discriminated against their workers' rights to join or not join the union.

So many employers fail to fulfil their obligation under the Contracts of Employment Act that it is easy to exaggerate the significance of extending minimum periods of notice and written particulars. However, the extended statutory notice (which workers are usually more concerned to see implemented) represents a benefit to longer-serving employees. Those employers who are anxious not to break the law will have to give careful consideration to their grievance procedures, particularly 'staff' procedures which are often non-existent or, at best, ill-defined (that is, if they want such procedures to be successful in enabling grievances to be dealt with effectively and not merely something hastily conceived and put on paper to satisfy the law).

The right to belong to a union and the new legal right not to be dismissed unfairly are both long overdue. However, it is difficult to see how the provision relating to unfair dismissal reinforces the Act's opening principle that workers be 'secure, protected by adequate safeguards.' True, the onus of proving reasonable cause rests with the employer but the odds are heavily in his favour (for which the Act is *not* responsible). A worker must finance a complaint himself since legal aid is not available in tribunal cases, though he may receive assistance—cash and/or lawyer—from his union. If he loses his case he may find himself having to contribute to the employer's costs. If he wins, he is compensated only for loss of earnings (which he must take immediate steps to mitigate)—the personal indignity he has suffered is discounted. Nor does the Act protect him against 'constructive' dismissal—where he voluntarily resigns because his employer unfairly makes life intolerable for him. Further, the right not to be dismissed unfairly is not given to part-time workers nor to those with less than two years' service.From the worker's point of view, and as the law stands, it is to be hoped that employers will implement those recommended disciplinary procedures contained in the Code of Practice.

Collective bargaining

It is a pre-condition of collective bargaining that employers recognise unions for negotiating purposes. Historically, recognition has been difficult to win, the more so because the unions' only weapon has been industrial action—unlike the United States, Britain has had no legal procedures by which employers could be compelled to negotiate.

Perhaps the most obvious result of ineffective negotiation has been that collective agreements, substantive and procedural, have been too frequently broken. Such agreements were not legally enforceable unless they contained an express intention to be so (which they rarely did) and because of this some argued that they were hardly worth the paper they were written on. Procedure agreements have been so generally unsatisfactory (or non-existent) that the inability of both sides to settle their disputes in an orderly fashion is not surprising.

Substantive agreements have been broken also, it seems, because what seemed a good bargain at the time subsequently 'turned sour;' a development which (the unions argue) resulted from unions having to negotiate 'in the dark' because of the refusal of employers to disclose material information during negotiation.

Part III of the Act is the result of the Government's awareness of these difficulties.

Collective agreements (sections 34–36)

Written, collective agreements entered into after the Industrial Relations Act are presumed to have been intended to be legally binding (and are, therefore, enforceable) unless the contrary is stated in relation to all or part of the agreement. This presumption applies to substantive and procedural agreements *and* to awards or decisions of voluntary joint negotiating bodies.

It is an unfair practice for either party to break an enforceable agreement, or to fail to take all reasonably practicable steps to prevent its agents or members from doing so.

Procedure agreements (sections 37–43)

Where, in relation to a unit of employment in a business, there is no procedure agreement *or* where one exists which is unsatisfactory for settling disputes promptly and fairly *or* where the agreement is broken, the Secretary of State or the employer or the registered union which is party to the agreement (or which has negotiating rights in respect of that unit of employment) may apply to the Court for the matter to be referred to the Commission for investigation. Such applications by employer or union must be preceded by notice to the Secretary of State to enable him to advise and assist the parties with a view to promoting agreement on the matter.

If the Court believes that the reference is necessary, to prevent good industrial relations from being impeded, the Commission is authorised to examine the procedures (or the lack of them) and to propose new or improved ones. If the parties accept such proposals, the matter ends. If not, the Commission reports its recommendations to the Court and either party may, within six months, ask the Court to make the procedure legally enforceable by order.

It is relevant to mention here that sections 58–59 of the Act enable the Secretary of State to make regulations whereby employers are compelled to inform him of their procedure agreements within six months of their being made. Fines are imposed for failure to do so and for giving him false information.

Recognition of sole bargaining agents (sections 44–55)

The Secretary of State or employers or registered trade unions may ask the Court to refer to the Commission a claim by a registered union (or joint negotiating panel representing registered unions) for exclusive negotiating rights, as sole bargaining agent, for all the employees in a bargaining unit. Again, such an application by an employer or union must be preceded by notice to the Secretary of State to allow him opportunity to assist the parties, and the Court will refer the claim to the Commission only if it is satisfied that the parties have tried sincerely to settle their dispute *and* that a reference is necessary to get a satisfactory settlement.

The Commission's tasks are to recommend, firstly, what bargaining units it defines (that is, which employees can appropriately have their terms and conditions of employment settled in negotiation between the employer and a union or joint negotiating panel) and, secondly, which registered union or negotiating panel should have exclusive bargaining rights in respect of each bargaining unit thus defined.

In considering these matters, the Commission will take into account the extent to which employees have 'interests in common' (for example the nature of their work, their training, experience and qualifications); which union has 'the support of a substantial proportion of the employees' in the bargaining unit; and whether it has the resources and organisational competence to represent those employees effectively as sole agent. The Commission will *not* recommend as sole agent a union or panel unless it is 'independent' and unless its recognition is in accordance with the general wishes of the employees concerned.

Within six months of the Commission's recommendation, the employer or the union (or panel) can ask the Court to make it enforceable. The Court will do so if the employees endorse the recommendation by secret ballot. Equally, the Court can *end* recognition of a union if a majority of the employees in the unit favour the same by ballot—such a ballot is possible, however, only if one-fifth of the employees endorse the initial application to the Court (or two-fifths if the union is recognised by order of the Court and two years have elapsed since the order was made).

It is an unfair practice for an employer to fail to negotiate with a sole bargaining agent or to negotiate with another organisation in respect of the employees in a bargaining unit; and for anyone to threaten or induce industrial action either to challenge the position of a sole agent determined by order of the Court or while a recognition

issue is before the Court and for six months after the Commission
has made its recommendations.

Disclosure of information (sections 56–57)

Employers have a duty to disclose to representatives of registered
unions information relating to the business without which they would
be materially impeded in conducting negotiations *and* which it would
be good industrial relations practice to disclose (to be determined
partly by considering the Code of Practice on disclosure). Thus, management must try to meet reasonable requests on matters relevant to
the negotiations and should make conveniently available the substance
of that information which it gives to shareholders or which it publishes
in annual reports. Employers will *not* (per s. 158) be required to disclose information if to do so is contrary to the interests of national
security; which is seriously prejudicial to their interests other than in
its effects on collective bargaining; which is given to them in confidence; or which concerns an individual (unless he agrees).

Further, employers of more than 350 persons are required to give
those persons, every year and within six months of the end of the
financial year, information to be specified in regulations which will be
approved by Parliament. This requirement does not apply to persons
with less than thirteen weeks' service or who, ordinarily, work for less
than twenty-one hours a week.

Enforceability of collective agreements

The Government's decision to make written, collective agreements
enforceable unless they contain an express provision to the contrary is
based on their belief that lack of enforceability has been a major cause
of their being broken so consistently, that enforceability will help to
prevent their being broken in the future and that both sides will be
prepared to go to the Court for damages if they are broken. This
thinking is utterly contrary to the report of the Donovan Commission.
It remains to be seen whether the Government or Donovan is proved
right *and* whether enforceable agreements materialise. The outcome is
hard to predict. Most (though not all) unions will probably oppose
enforceability and will try to insist upon an appropriate 'exemption'
clause being written into their agreements. Either, negotiations could

get completely bogged down on this issue or management might decide that it is better to have a non-binding agreement than no agreement at all and concede the point.

The Secretary of State appears to have anticipated *this* consequence by arguing that the *creation* of binding agreements is less important than the fact that the *presumption* of enforceability introduces a new consideration to the bargaining situation 'tending towards greater care and precision in the thinking, drafting, making and keeping of the agreement.' On the other hand, a new negotiation strategy could emerge whereby management makes *two* offers, one in return for a binding agreement and one (less favourable) for a non-binding one. This is not quite so naïve as it sounds, and if it happens, life for union negotiators will become more difficult than ever because their members want the best deal they can get and cannot be expected to show too much concern for legal niceties.

The fact that unions must now take 'all reasonably practicable steps' to prevent their representatives and members from breaking enforceable agreements may become a powerful instrument of pressure if binding agreements do materialise. No longer will they be able to give tacit encouragement, or sit passively, while their members engage in lightning strikes but will have to 'stand up and be counted.' As it is reasonably practicable to expel or discipline a shop steward, for example, this duty could make the steward's position even more difficult than it is at present—his members will want results: his executive will expect to get his co-operation to prevent binding agreements being broken and may have to discipline him if it is not forthcoming. The provisions on recognition and exclusive bargaining rights will certainly be a 'shot-in-the-arm' for those unions which have been vainly struggling for recognition by employers and which are willing to register in order to get it. On the other hand, they may be disruptive in so far as they seem likely to produce rivalry between registered unions for exclusive negotiating rights. There is reason to believe, however, that they will lead ultimately to more rational (and, therefore, more effective) negotiation.

Registration and conduct of organisations

The Government feels that the rights which the Act confers on organisations of both workers and employers should be available only to those which, by registering, accept statutory standards in relation to their rules and their behaviour. The objective is clearly to subject such organisations to closer and more rigorous public control than hitherto.

A Chief Registrar of Trade Unions and Employers' Associations has been appointed. His first task has been to establish a provisional register covering organisations previously registered under the Trade Union Acts 1871–1964 and, subsequently, he will transfer such organisations to a permanent register if, in his opinion, they are eligible for registration and satisfy certain conditions. He *must*, however, cancel registration if requested to do so by an organisation.

To be eligible for registration an organisation must be independent (this relates to workers' organisations); must have power to alter its rules and control the application of its property and funds; and must submit to the Registrar a copy of its rules, a list of its officers and the names and addresses of its branches. A federation of workers' organisations cannot register unless all its affiliated organisations are also registered. If these conditions are satisfied, the organisation will receive a certificate of registration on payment of a fee. After issuing a certificate, the Registrar must examine the rules of the organisation with a view to ensuring that they are consistent with certain 'guiding principles' (see page 47) and comply with the requirements of Schedule 4 (see page 48).

It is an unfair practice for an organisation, its officials or agents to take or threaten any action in contravention of the 'guiding principles.' Complaints may be presented direct to a tribunal, or through the Registrar (after he has tried to promote agreement between the parties) to a tribunal or the Court, both of which have the power to make a declaration as to the parties' rights or to award compensation. If the Registrar is not satisfied that the rules conform to the Act's requirements, he will inform the organisation what changes are necessary and fix a reasonable time in which the changes can be made. If the defects remain uncorrected, he can apply to the Court for the registration to be cancelled (though the Court can allow further time for the organisation to do what has to be done). Additional procedures are available to enable the Registrar to present a complaint to the Court if he suspects that a registered organisation is persistently contravening any of the 'guiding principles,' and to present a winding-up petition to the High Court if he believes the organisation is insolvent. Conversely, an organisation may appeal to the Court against the Registrar's refusal to register it.

A registered organisation must comply also with administrative requirements. It must maintain proper accounting records and establish a satisfactory system of control over its cash-holdings. It must submit to the Registrar an annual return (containing revenue accounts and year-end balance sheet) and a copy of the auditor's report. It must publish a yearly report on its activities containing the annual return, and must make this report available to all its members. It must, finally, inform the Registrar of any changes made to its rules, in its officers or to its principal address. Failure to comply with any of these requirements is punishable by fine.

The provisions concerning registration are self-explanatory. The crucial issue is whether trade unions *will* register and accept statutory standards of conduct instead of their own. This is a bitter pill for them to swallow and many of them have expressed an intention to 'contract out' in protest against the legislation. Time will tell whether their opposition to registration is maintained. Certainly the advantages from registration are compelling. They include retention of tax concessions (worth by some estimates, over £1 000 000 a year to the bigger unions); the freedom to induce or threaten a breach of contract in furtherance of an industrial dispute; the benefit of compensation 'ceilings' for committing an unfair practice; the rights to enter into agency shop and approved closed shop agreements, to win exclusive bargaining rights and to receive information relevant to negotiations. These advantages seem desirable if a union is to further the interests of its members. Moreover, if some unions fail to register they will face the possibility of losing members to rival organisations 'waiting in the wings' which *are* prepared to register. Others may find themselves in the odd position of having to register because their rules require them to do so (their rules could of course be changed but sometimes only by delegate conference decision) and the Registrar could, on this ground, refuse an application to be taken off the register

Emergency procedures (sections 138–145)

Where an industrial dispute has begun (or is likely to begin) and where its likely effects will be to gravely injure the economy or imperil national security or create serious risk of public disorder or endanger life and limb *and* where a deferment or discontinuance of industrial action would be conducive to a settlement of the dispute, the Secretary of State may apply to the Court for a restraining order.

This order will restrain named organisations and/or named individuals from calling, organising, procuring or financing a strike, irregular industrial action or a lock-out in relation to a specified area of employment. It may also require those organisations and individuals to take specified steps to secure the deferment of such action. Similarly, where a dispute has begun (or is threatened) which will likely produce any of those effects or possibly threaten the livelihood of a substantial numbers of workers in the industry concerned *and* where doubt exists that a majority of the employees support the dispute, the Secretary of State may apply to the Court for a secret ballot order. The order will specify what issues are to be voted upon; who is eligible to vote; how the ballot will be conducted; and will suspend industrial action until the result of the ballot is reported to the Court and made known to the parties concerned.

The object of a restraining order (which can be effective for up to sixty days) is to provide both sides with 'breathing space' in which tempers can cool, negotiation continue, conciliation be attempted or the dispute be referred to arbitration. The order cannot directly compel workers either not to strike or to return to work but indirectly it is capable of having these effects by compelling organisations or individuals to secure deferment or discontinuance of a stoppage. American experience suggests that, far from having a cooling effect, such orders signal more heated disagreement and a hardening of attitudes (which it has been suggested, secret ballots produce) round the bargaining table. Its usefulness in Britain, as a device for enabling agreement to be reached, remains to be seen and it is to be hoped that it does not provide the excuse for complacency or irresponsibility in the early stages of negotiation. The emergency procedures do not prevent strike action following a secret ballot whatever the ballot's result but in practice, if the ballot reveals opposition to a strike this effectively cuts the ground from beneath the strike's organisers.

The new system of industrial relations justice

The Act intends that legal proceedings arising from industrial disputes should normally be brought before the National Industrial Relations

Court or an industrial tribunal. Its introduction of unfair practices largely extinguishes traditional remedies in the civil courts. For example, only the Industrial Court may entertain proceedings based on the breach of an enforceable collective agreement and no proceedings in tort may be entertained by a civil court where the cause of action occurred in the context of an industrial dispute.

Two unfair practices, not previously examined, deserve special mention here:

1   It is unfair practice for anyone other than a registered union, *or a person acting on its behalf*, to induce or threaten a breach of a contract of employment in contemplation or furtherance of an industrial dispute (s. 96).

This is designed to reduce the number of unofficial strikes; but s. 147 makes a strike *not* a breach of a contract of employment if it is preceded by 'due notice'. Thus, the *only* unofficial strikes which amount to unfair practices are 'lightning' strikes and strikes in breach of a 'no-strike' agreement.

2   It is unfair practice to induce or threaten a breach of a commercial contract where the inducement or threat is directed at someone who is neither a party to the original dispute nor supporting it (s. 98).

A sympathy strike is not in itself unfair, but it will be unfair to induce a third party to break a commercial contract which he has entered into with one of the parties to the dispute (for example, to supply goods). It is clear that the third party will not be 'supporting the dispute' merely by fulfilling a commercial contract entered into *before* the dispute began. The Act repeals those provisions by which criminal penalties could be imposed on workers in electricity, gas and water undertakings who deliberately break their contracts and so deprive the community of supplies. It reduces the scope of peaceful picketing by excluding the right to picket a person's home. It does, however, maintain protection for organisations of workers (registered or not) from criminal prosecution based on their being in unlawful restraint of trade.

National Industrial Relations Court

The Court consists of presiding judges from the higher judiciary (appointed by the Lord Chancellor) and lay members having special knowledge or experience of industrial relations (appointed by the Lord Chancellor and Secretary of State jointly). Its central office is in London but it will sit in Divisions anywhere and at any time. Its proceedings will be informal—parties may represent themselves, or be represented by a lawyer or a representative of a trade union or employers' association or by others, and usually proceedings will not be governed by formal rules of evidence. The Court will hear evidence publicly but it has the right to sit in private. Legal Aid is available on the usual terms.

The Court's jurisdiction is generally exercised over issues of a collective nature (though 'individual' complaints to industrial tribunals may be transferred to the Court if they involve matters of special significance). Thus, it hears and adjudicates upon complaints of unfair practices (except those involving the right to membership of a union or unfair dismissal); allegations of breach of duty by an employer (for example failing to enter into an agency shop agreement or to disclose information to a trade union); applications from the Registrar to cancel an organisation's registration; and appeals from organisations against the Registrar's refusal to grant registration. Such proceedings must normally be instituted within six months of the cause of action arising. The Court's powers are threefold: to make orders compelling someone to do/not to do something; to declare the rights of the parties; and to award compensation. Appeals from decisions of the Court, on a point of law only, lie to the Court of Appeal.

Industrial tribunals

A tribunal consists of a legally-qualified chairman and two lay members with relevant industrial experience. Like the Court, it normally sits in public (but has the right to hear proceedings privately) and proceedings are informal. However, Legal Aid is *not* available.

Its jurisdiction extends to disputes based on the Contracts of Employment Act, redundancy, industrial training and equal pay. So far as the Industrial Relations Act is concerned, its function is to hear complaints by individuals of unfair industrial practices, specifically those involving the right to membership or non-membership of a trade union, not to be dismissed unfairly, contravention by a union of one of the 'guiding principles' (though the individual can alternatively complain to the Registrar) and failure by his employer to disclose information. Such complaints must normally be initiated

C

within four weeks of the cause of action arising. Its powers are to make orders determining the rights of the parties, to recommend re-engagement of an employee who has been dismissed unfairly and to award compensation. Appeals from its decisions, on points of law only, lie to the Industrial Court.

Commission on Industrial Relations

The Commission now has a statutory permanence. It consists of a full-time chairman and between six and fifteen members (part-time or full-time), appointed by the Secretary of State.

Its functions are to consider (and to make recommendations in respect of) matters of specific or general concern including how employers and workers are organised, or ought to be organised; procedure agreements or the need for them; recognition and bargaining rights; disclosure of information; and facilities for training in industrial relations. To discharge these functions it is empowered to hold inquiries, compel documents to be produced for inspection and witnesses to attend for examination.

It arranges ballots relating to agency shops, approved closed shops, recognition and emergency procedures. It has replaced *ad hoc* commissions under the Wages Councils Act 1959. It must present an annual report to Parliament on the general condition of collective bargaining in Britain, drawing attention to specific problems.

Industrial Arbitration Board

This is the former Industrial Court re-named. It consists of an independent chairman and equal numbers of employers' and employees' representatives. Its functions are to arbitrate in disputes and (if authorised by the Court) to entertain claims from registered unions for new terms and conditions.

The Industrial Relations Act has, inevitably, provoked great argument. The opinions of employers, trade unions, academics and individuals are divided upon whether this legislation will succeed in its purpose or, on the contrary, make the problems of industrial relations more difficult than ever to solve. No one believes that the Act will automatically put right all that is wrong. It is merely a first step (the Government believes in the right direction) towards achieving certain objectives dear to both sides. Current judgement as to the Act's wisdom is based almost entirely on speculation as to its *likely* consequences, and it remains to be seen whether it provides merely a framework surrounding industrial relations activity or becomes its focus. If the law is invoked only when voluntary efforts fail to produce satisfactory results (on which premise the proposed extended functions of the Department of Employment's conciliation service is based) some aspects of the traditional system may endure. To improve the quality of industrial relations, permanently, requires intensive and constructive effort by both sides. Final judgement depends upon whether the Act, supported by the Code of Practice, promotes or prevents such effort.

Guiding principles for the conduct of organisations (sections 65 and 69)
The principles are:

That anyone appropriately qualified for membership be not excluded arbitrarily or unreasonably
2 That members have the right to terminate their membership subject to giving reasonable notice and complying with reasonable conditions
3 That members be not arbitrarily or unreasonably excluded from holding office, from nominating candidates, from voting in elections and ballots, and from attending and participating in meetings
4 That ballots be kept secret
5 That workers be free to vote without interference or constraint
6 That members be not subjected to disciplinary action for failing to take any action constituting an unfair industrial practice, or for failing to take part in a strike or lock-out otherwise than in contemplation or furtherance of an industrial dispute
7 That no disciplinary action be taken against a member unless he has received a written notice of the charge brought against him; is given a reasonable time to prepare a defence; is afforded a full and fair hearing; receives a written statement of the findings; and has exercised any right of appeal available to him under the rules (these principles do *not* apply to disciplinary action for non-payment of contributions)
8 That a person's membership be not terminated by the organisation unless reasonable notice is given
9 That members be not restricted from instituting proceedings before a court or tribunal, or from giving evidence in such proceedings

Requirements of an organisation's rules (schedule 4)

The rules must specify:

1 The name of the organisation, the address of its principal office and its objects

2 The names of its branches and its power to control them

3 How its governing body is to be elected, re-elected at reasonable intervals, and how members of its governing body are to be removed

4 How its officers and officials (including work-place representatives) are to be elected or appointed and removed

5 The powers of the governing body, officers and officials

6 How meetings are to be convened and conducted

7 How rules are to be made, altered or revoked

8 By whose authority and in what circumstances industrial action can be taken

9 How elections are to be held or ballots taken; who is eligible to vote; the procedures preparatory to such elections or ballots, for counting votes or ballot papers, and for declaring results

10 The circumstances in which the organisation has power to conclude agreements on behalf of constituent or affiliated members

11 Eligibility for membership, the procedure for dealing with applications and provision for appeals against decisions made in relation to such applications

12 The contributions payable by members and the procedure and penalties in case of default

13 The conduct for which specified disciplinary action can be taken, the procedure to be followed in taking such action and provision for appeals

14 The procedure for investigating members' complaints

15 The manner in which, and the purposes for which, its property and funds may be applied.

4

Personnel Management and the Code of Practice

D P Torrington

Senior Lecturer in Industrial Relations, Manchester Polytechnic

The Code of Industrial Relations Practice was first published in June 1971 by the Department of Employment, it was later revised and approved by Parliament after consultation on the original draft. The Code is complementary to the Industrial Relations Act, and the degree to which the legal remedies contained in the Act *are* sought, will largely depend on the extent to which the practices in the Code are *not* followed. The Code sets down what one has to do to stay out of trouble.

The then Secretary of State for Employment, Mr Robert Carr, introduced the first draft of the Code with the following sentence:

'An essential part of the government's policy for industrial relations is to produce a code of practice, the purpose of which is to set standards and give practical guidance on the conduct of industrial relations and the development of policies to improve human relations in all types of employment'

One of the important aspects of the Code is the need for practice to seem fair to those outside the close circle of industrial relations practitioners.

The practice of industrial relations is full of language and methods which make sense to those who live with them in industry, but which are, probably, incomprehensible to the outsider. The terms and methods will in future need to be able to withstand the scrutiny of lawyers and others outside industry, so that practice will not only have to be fair, but be seen and understood to be fair. The Code attempts to summarise some of the main points that outsiders may look for in coming to a judgement.

The Code is not legally enforceable but there will be strong pressure to conform to it. This will come from the agencies of central government, such as the Department of Employment, from the vigorous union official seeking improvements in the conditions of employment of his members and, most of all, the pressure will come from the very existence of the Industrial Relations Act. The Code may be used in the determination of an appropriate remedy, and individual company practices may be quoted as evidence of whether the behaviour of the employer has been reasonable or unreasonable in a particular situation that may have become the cause of a dispute.

There can be no substitute for reading the Code itself, and it has the merit, unlike the Act, of being in straightforward English that is readable and lucid. This chapter examines the seven sections of the Code and considers some of the major implications for personnel management within the undertaking; the ways in which both policy and practice are likely to be affected.

The Code includes comment on how trade unions and individuals should conduct themselves, but this chapter will be limited to comment on the suggestions for management behaviour, as this is a book for managers.

Responsibilities

Management responsibilities under the Code

The section of the Code on the responsibilities of management, starts with two significant sentences:

'One of management's major objectives should . . . be to

develop effective industrial relations policies which command the confidence of employees. Managers at the highest level should give, and show that they give, just as much attention to industrial relations as to such functions as finance, marketing, production or administration.

These two statements may involve a radical change of attitude by many employers. The fact that the management of the undertaking has this primary responsibility was one of the cornerstones of the Donovan Report. The members of the Royal Commission were seriously disturbed by the degree to which many managements did not accept this premiss; these managements believed that industrial relations was a disease introduced by trade unions and that the way to cure the disease was to stamp out the trade unions. The approach of many managements has been to delegate this responsibility too readily. Either they have joined an employers' federation solely to avoid having to come into close contact with trade unions or they have appointed a personnel officer to deal with it. In each case the management as a whole gives the impression that it is a distasteful task that they want to be rid of; it is rather like contracting a firm of outside caterers to run the staff/works canteen.

The attitude presumably stems from the belief that employees ought to do what they are told to do without argument as the employee rents his services to the employer for him to do with it whatever he thinks fit. Furthermore, industrial relations tend to be activities of a fairly earthy nature in which spades are called spades and the social niceties are often absent; it is frequently difficult and damned hard work.

The Code endorses the Donovan proposal that management should accept responsibility at the highest level for industrial relations. This means that the Company board should have one of its members with overall responsibility for personnel and industrial relations matters and that this should be a full-time responsibility in all medium and large organisations. The board needs also to commit itself to a personnel policy within which industrial relations can be conducted. All other members of management should receive appropriate training in how to discharge this aspect of their managerial responsibility with the support of personnel specialists who have professional skill and training in industrial relations practice.

Collective bargaining

Management are required to take certain initiatives in setting up collective bargaining in the plant if trade unions are recognised. Apparently there is no initiative—Only consultation and grievance procedures are expected if unions are not recognised or if employee representation comes from an organisation of workers that is not a trade union. Otherwise, the management has the responsibility for taking the initiative in setting up, jointly with the trade union, the procedures for negotiation, consultation, communication and the settlement of grievances and disputes.

This requirement changes the traditional emphasis. Previously, most employers have taken a defensive attitude towards trade unions, grudgingly conceding recognition and reluctantly following nationally agreed procedure. Now the management is required to seek such arrangements.

Some managers may find a bitter pill in the advice that they should encourage employees to join a recognised trade union and to play an active part in its work. Those who have previously actively discouraged employees from union membership, sometimes to the point of not employing union members, will find this a difficult practice to follow.

Organisation of work

Among the duties of management in personnel practice is the informing of employees and groups of employees what they have to do, and what progress they are making towards their objectives and giving them opportunities for job satisfaction.

These duties recognise the fact that work will be more efficiently done if it is well organised in a way that gives the individual an emotional stake in it. It requires the management to have a comprehensive organisation chart and statement of responsibility for individual members of management so that they know what they are supposed to be doing, to whom they report and who reports to them. It also requires production figures to be supplied to work groups and for work to be set up in a way which is not only efficient from a mechanical point of view but which is also likely to be done well by the employee because it gives him some satisfaction.

Supervisors

The position of the foreman has become uncertain with the growth of shop steward influence and plant-level negotiation, both of which make it inevitable that the first-line supervisor is often by-passed. This has caused him to lose face in the eyes of the people in his work group and in his own eyes. The Code gives little help with this dilemma. It simply says that he should be appropriately trained and in charge of a group that is small enough for him to control so that he can act as an effective communicating link between management and employees with particular reference to management policy.

In view of what the Code says later about communication we may see the foreman finding a new role for himself as the key man in the interchange of information between management and men. As immediate practical steps in line with the Code, managements may check that the training they provide for foremen is appropriate for their needs (Mr Kettle's chapter in Part II (Chapter 15) may help here), and then consider the number of people he controls. The precise number that a supervisor can handle depends on the nature of the process and the amount of direct supervision that the individual employee requires but it would seem unlikely that any first-line supervisor can cope adequately with more than twenty or thirty people without introducing section supervisors under him. If managements also re-consider their procedures for the dissemination of information to ensure that the foreman knows of innovations before they happen, they will support his authority and help to develop his function as a two-way link in the communication process.

Employment policies

Planning and use of manpower

Manpower planning is a technique for avoiding the twin dangers of having too many people for the work to be done or being short of the number of people needed. If there are too few people the undertaking does not make the progress it should. If there are too many, there is frustration among individual employees who have no scope, expense for the employer in unnecessary wage and salary payments and eventually there may be the acute personal hardship of redundancy.

If manpower planning is to be undertaken it requires a very detailed study, which is beyond the relatively sketchy comments that can be made in this chapter. At the same time there is no need for any but the largest organisations to plan manpower requirements on an elaborate scale. A straightforward, practical guide to what can be done is published by the Department of Employment; it is entitled *Company Manpower Planning* and sets out how the job may be done. There is also a useful bibliography. As a preliminary to manpower planning managements could make sure that their personnel records are up-to-date.

The Code also suggests that absenteeism and labour turnover could be reduced by identifying causes through appropriate records being kept and that a system should be set up to arrange transfers within the undertaking for employees who seek them, so that employees move inside the firm rather than leave it. For absenteeism and labour turnover records there is a useful publication *Design of Personnel Systems and Records*, compiled by the Industrial Society and published by Gower Press in 1969. The question of arranging a system of transfers can help reduce turnover as long as it does not establish certain departments in the organisation as threshold areas where people take jobs to get a foothold in the organisation before moving on to better jobs as they become vacant. The most useful safeguard is to have a time limit, so that applications for transfer out of a department will not be considered until after a set term of weeks or months has elapsed. Even if the transfer is still sought at the end of the time the employee will settle more readily in his first department than he might if he was hoping to move out at any minute.

Recruitment and selection

In considering management action about what the Code says on recruitment and selection, one needs to take this in conjunction with parts of the Industrial Relations Act; particularly those on the rights of individual workers to join or not to join a trade union. The executive responsible for the selection of employees has to know the rights which people have in relation to union membership so that he does not reject an applicant on that ground. Equally, however, the executive has to be aware of the situation within the plant so that if there has traditionally been a closed shop situation, and if there is 100 per cent trade union membership, he will consider the likely repercussions of engaging someone who does not hold the appropriate union membership card. He has the responsibility for keeping within the law at the same time as maintaining a viable employer/employee relationship in the department. If an agency shop is established the executive needs to explain to the new recruit the three alternatives open to him; union membership, union services, or contribution to charity in lieu of agency fee.

The Code requires selection to be based on job analysis without arbitrary conditions and a selection decision based on adequate evidence about the candidate after the possibilities of internal transfer have been considered. The selector should explain terms and conditions of employment to applicants and check, periodically, on the results of the selection process being used.

Managements not operating systematic selection already could benefit from having an executive trained by the National Institute for Industrial Psychology, or by attendance at one of the admirable short courses run by the British Institute of Management or the Institute of Personnel Management. Alternatively there are a number of books on this subject which has been extensively researched and documented.

Training

Emphasis in training is needed for induction and job training as well as broadly based schemes for young persons coming into industry and for re-training in new skills, adults with obsolescent skills. This ground has been well-trodden by the industrial training boards and any employer needing help will doubtless get in touch with the board appropriate to his industry.

Payment systems

The Code says that the lack of soundly based pay policies and systems is a frequent cause of disputes and comments on effective systems in a mere dozen lines. Donovan pointed out that wage problems were the cause of half of all strikes. For guidance on setting up satisfactory payment systems, readers are referred to Mr Langton's chapter in Part II (Chapter 11) of this book.

Status and security of employees

After explaining the desirability of stability and security in employment the Code makes a number of specific suggestions.

Managements should, 'where practicable' provide pension and sick pay schemes to supplement statutory arrangements. A substantial minority of British employees are without one or both of these fringe benefits; the cost of establishing them could be prohibitive. Furthermore, anyone who has negotiated productivity agreements knows that trade union negotiators at plant level do not place great importance on pension arrangements although there may be more concern about levels of sick pay. Now employers are being told they should provide these benefits, despite the fact that in some situations both employer and employees might prefer to see the money spent on additions to earnings. This is one reason why some critics have described the Code as paternalistic.

For help with sick pay schemes readers could usefully consult *Sick Pay* by E G Rutter and K Otway, published by the Industrial Society. A useful review of pension schemes is *The Complete Guide to Pensions and Superannuation* by G D Gilling-Smith, published by Penguin Books.

Another far-reaching suggestion is that differences in status and conditions of employment between manual and white collar employees should be progressively removed unless they are related to the responsibilities of the job. There are many problems here and personnel managers in organisations which have differential standards will probably blench at the prospect of levelling up however much they may applaud the principle. The main problems are likely to be the cost and the white-collar reaction. The cost comes about through, for instance, improving the provisions for payment to employees who are off sick. The idealist will argue that the greater sense of security will induce a greater sense of responsibility and that the employee will be off sick less with improved sick pay conditions. The hard, unpalatable fact is that sickness absence rises if the conditions of sickness payment improve. More obviously, an increase in the number of days holiday that are allowed will reduce the number of days worked for a fixed annual level of earnings. This makes it a costly operation to reduce differentials. The other main problem is that there is a long-established practice of 'staff' employees regarding themselves as being socially superior to manual employees. For many years this sense of superiority was buttressed by the fact that they were paid more money and had more job security. The financial differential has largely disappeared or been reversed and job security has vanished. All that is left is the trivia of two days more holiday and starting work half an hour later in the morning. The development of white-collar unionism is seen by some observers as a symptom of disenchantment among staff employees consequent upon this loss of differentials. There are relatively few examples of undertakings that have removed all artificial status differentials between manual and white-collar employees. Most of those that have succeeded are in fairly new organisations and in undertakings which have a predominance of white-collar employees.

The problems associated with redundancy, perhaps, need little elaboration. It could, however, be useful to read some of the ways in which productivity bargainers have approached this question. One of the best examples is in *Productivity Agreements and Wages Systems* by D T B North and G L Buckingham, published by Gower Press. Collective subscribers to the BIM could obtain their Information Summary 137 *Company Redundancy Policies*, which summarises the practice in thirty-three different companies.

Working conditions

The advisability of introducing standards of physical working conditions above those laid down by law is a sound suggestion. The Code sees the need for this to be done, at least partly, on a basis of consultation with employee representatives. Companies that do not already have a safety committee should consider the advantage of setting one up to consult on matters of safety and to demonstrate that safety at work is not simply a question of providing a safe environment; it is also a question of developing and maintaining safe working practices and the sense of personal responsibility that those involve. Whatever general form of joint consultation there may be within the plant, it could be used as a vehicle for extending the scope of co-operation on good housekeeping and improving the environment.

Communication and consultation

The Code sets down the fact that efficiency in industrial operations is improved if people know what is happening and can offer their views on matters that affect them. It is one of the responsibilities of management to ensure that this happens.

Communication

The interesting aspect of this section is that prime importance is placed on word-of-mouth communication between managers and employees, with more formal methods being used only where it is necessary to supplement this. There are many bureaucratic organisations with good-looking formal communications channels in which communication does not happen. Elaborate, centralised procedures are no substitute for face-to-face encounter.

Employees should be given information in two categories. These are, information about their own job and their personal conditions of employment, and information on how the organisation is getting on, what is happening in consultation and what changes are made in the organisation.

The first category can best be dealt with through an employees' handbook and the second through the effective use of notice-boards, but these are not hard-and-fast distinctions between the two categories as the specific means are not mentioned in the Code. There is a useful publication on handbooks *Producing an Employee Handbook* by Liz McLeod, published by the Industrial Society.

The blasé personnel manager who says that the Code of Practice simply suggests what has happened for years in his company should look at this section of the Code carefully. The main question is, how many employers give *all* employees information about agreements with trade unions, statements of individual responsibility, circumstances which can lead to suspension or dismissal, the name of someone to approach for advice, and the training needed to achieve promotion?

Consultation machinery

For this item there is a specific statement about which organisation is big enough to be responsible. 'Establishment with more than 250 employees should have systematic arrangements for management and employee representatives to meet regularly.' So all medium-sized and large companies should have such a committee and it is up to the management to take the initiative in setting one up. Furthermore, they are required to do this even if there are not recognised trade unions covering all categories of employee.

Managers needing to set up consultative machinery may find some help in the chapter of this book on plant agreements. Alternatively they could refer to *Some Examples of Effective Consultative Committees* by Joan Henderson, published by the Industrial Society.

This section of the Code concludes by distinguishing between consultation and negotiation.

Collective bargaining

Dr Armstrong, in Chapter 2 discusses collective bargaining and demonstrates the difference between industry-wide and plant-level bargaining. The Code gives some guidance on the aspects of collective bargaining below industry level but this section of the Code has to be considered with the Industrial Relations Act in mind.

Bargaining units

The Act specifies that negotiations should be carried on by a bargaining agent acting on behalf of a group of employees who form a bargaining unit. The Code now sets down some of the factors to be considered in establishing what is an appropriate bargaining unit. It suggests that it should be based on the consistency of the work and conditions of the employees: duties, training, qualifications, place, hours, payment, etc. It also makes allowance for fitting the bargaining unit into the structure of both management and union and contains with a reference to the wishes of the employees concerned. The drafters of the Code also specify that the units should cover 'as wide a group of employees as practicable,' and then suggest various ways in which disagreement between management and prospective bargaining agent may be resolved before finally making an application to NIRC if all else fails.

If both the management and the unions, representing employees in an undertaking, are satisfied with the existing situation, it does not seem that either side need do anything, and they can proceed in the conduct of their affairs in their customary fashion without invoking the new legal framework. It is only if one side is not satisfied that there may be a change; this could arise where an employer feels that he is recognising too many unions and conducting too many negotiations independent of each other.

Recognition of trade unions

Suggestions are made about what the management should consider in receiving a claim for recognition from trade unions and it is stated that the management is entitled to know the number of employees who are members of the union making the recognition application. Furthermore, this can be taken to a secret ballot if the degree of support is in doubt. This is a new aspect of trade union recognition.

At least one aspect of this section of the Code may worry some managers. The first is the advice to receive representations from union officials on behalf of groups of employees or on behalf of individuals even if the union is not recognised. This is, in effect, Government endorsement of representation being valid with or without the union being strong enough to be recognised.

Also, there is the simple piece of advice that so many ignore: 'Contacts (with trade union officials) should not be left until trouble arises.' In this statement the Code demonstrates the need for negotiation, consultation and communication to become a normal part of the manager/employee relationship through the intermediary of the representatives with managers taking the initiative in seeking and developing such contacts. It is contrary to the widespread management practice of using contact with trade union officials reluctantly and as a means of last resort to avoid serious trouble. Where this is the way industrial relations are conducted, it is not surprising that trouble recurs.

Collective agreements

The remainder of the section of the Code dealing with collective bargaining is referred to in the chapter of this book dealing with plant agreements, so little need be said here, except that the Code attempts to distinguish between what is appropriately negotiated at national level and what is best done on a plant basis.

Employee representation at the place of work

The section on shop stewards makes a number of requirements on trade unions and managements. There is a much fuller treatment of the question of shop stewards in the report of the CIR that was published in the spring of 1971.

Appointment and qualifications

Trade unions and management should agree on the basic qualifications required of an employee who is to be a steward, as well as the number to be elected and the areas they will represent. It is also suggested that management should offer facilities for the election of stewards, including the internal management publicity machine to make sure that the process is as widely known and understood as possible. Not all unions will welcome such assistance, and it is to be offered, not imposed.

Status

Trade unions are advised to seek agreement with management on issuing not only trade union credentials but credentials signed by management and union which set out the rights and obligations of both steward and management. This is a rare practice and its extension could be beneficial.

Facilities

A further development, of the principle that management accepts trade unionism, is the requirement for stewards to be given facilities by the management to carry out their duties. The specified minimum is that they should be allowed reasonable leave from work and have their earnings maintained while carrying out their functions. There is further reference to office equipment, accommodation and access to a telephone, lists of new employees—'appropriate to the circumstances.'

Training

Relatively few employers provide training for their stewards, either because they think that this is putting weapons into the hands of the enemy, or because the union is suspicious of their motives in providing the training. The Code requires managements and trade unions to agree on arrangements about what training is needed and how facilities for it should be arranged. It is also suggested that there are areas in which the training should be jointly undertaken. There is no mention that the training should be arranged for joint groups of stewards and managers even though much of the training will be concerned with the understanding of the same material. The TUC education service sponsors a number of courses for stewards that are run by universities, polytechnics and technical colleges.

Grievance and disputes procedures

The Code emphasises one point that needs attention here; *all* employees should have the right to seek redress for their grievances. This means that there has to be a procedure that any individual can follow, whether he is a trade union member or not, and whether his trade union is recognised by the management, or not.

Disciplinary procedures

One of the biggest potential changes in industrial relations practice that the Industrial Relations Act could bring about is in the question of dismissal. Hitherto this has often been on an arbitrary basis. The introduction of the concept of unfair dismissal with the opportunity for cases to be heard by an industrial tribunal, makes sure that dismissal of employees with more than two years' service will only be on fair grounds.

Managements need to reconsider their procedure for dismissal and discipline to make sure that it conforms with the standards laid down in the Code and that it is operated scrupulously; it should then be possible to keep out of the tribunals. It is worth quoting in full the first major statement in the Code on disciplinary procedures:

> 'Management should ensure that fair and effective arrangements exist for dealing with disciplinary matters. These should be agreed with employee representatives or trade unions concerned and should provide for full and speedy consideration by management of all the relevant facts'

Although the Act does not recognise unfair dismissal, if it occurs in the first 104 weeks of employment, there is no such time limit mentioned in the Code, before which presumably all men are regarded as being equal no matter what their length of service.

Another point of interest is that supervisors should not have the power to suspend or dismiss without reference to more senior management. There is an outline hierarchy of penalties:

1   Informal (not recorded) warning by immediate superior
2   Formal (written) warning with note of further action that could take place if the offence is repeated, and a copy going to the employee
3   Final warning, suspension without pay, dismissal
4   Right of appeal

Any wise manager or supervisor will welcome the restraint of not being able to dismiss or suspend from duties single-handed, although some other managers may feel that their authority is undermined. The authority to dismiss is an awesome one to be on the shoulders of one person, particularly when he is so close to the situation that he can not see it clearly and when there may be the suspicion of prejudice or victimisation. The supervisor who sees an employee dismissed as a result of his initiative, but with the concurrence and declared support for this action from a senior manager, is in a much more secure position through sharing that particular responsibility.

To avoid claims for unfair dismissal the management must follow the detail of the Code and must be scrupulously fair and consistent. This involves careful records being kept of disciplinary actions that are taken and a centralisation of disciplinary actions in the control of the personnel manager. Only if the personnel manager is involved is there a view of what is happening in all parts of the organisation; and disciplinary practice has to be consistent throughout, not only in the factory or with the members of one bargaining unit. If the managing director wishes to dismiss an employee he should ask the personnel manager to vet the details first and he should welcome the opportunity for the wisdom of his action to be confirmed by someone else. The line manager or supervisor takes the action with the employee; the personnel manager merely agrees to the action taken. The personnel manager will need to satisfy himself that the action proposed is consistent with the company's disciplinary procedure as written down and consistent with the company's disciplinary procedure as practised.

Despite some disparaging comment in the press, the Code of Practice is well worth close and thoughtful reading by all managers, however good they think their present practices are and however little they wish to be involved in industrial relations. It will be developed in the future and we all need to keep up with these developments.

5

Central Government Services in Industrial Relations

Rachel Naylor

Lecturer, Department of Management Sciences, UMIST

Even with the passing of the Industrial Relations Act in 1971, the Government's view remains that 'management has the primary responsibility for good industrial relations and should take the initiative for creating and maintaining them.' (Code of Industrial Relations Practice Consultative Document) Nevertheless successive governments have built up a range of services to support and assist. This chapter deals with:

1 The growth of government interest and intervention in employment questions
2 The assistance offered; the current statutory bodies
3 The subject areas where assistance may be useful
4 The type of assistance given—immediate and longer term
5 The location of the Manpower Advisory Services

The legal powers of the Secretary of State to intervene are dealt with in the chapter on the legal framework and are only touched upon here.

A. ABUSES AND REMEDIES

Poor working conditions	Factories Act 1961 Offices, Shops and Railway Premises Act 1963
Excessive or unsuitable hours worked by women and youngsters	Employment of Women and Young Persons Act 1922
Sudden redundancy without compensation	Redundancy Payments Act 1965
Sudden termination of employment; unspecified terms and conditions	Contracts of Employment Act 1963
Inadequate training opportunities. Insufficient contribution to training costs	Industrial Training Act 1964
Severe drop in earnings due to sickness or unemployment	Earnings-Related Benefit Legislation
Low income in retirement	National Insurance Acts 1965-71 consolidated earlier legislation from 1908 onwards
Wage discrimination against women employees	Equal Pay Act 1970
Discrimination in employment based on race, colour, creed	Race Relations Act 1968

B. LEGISLATION RELATING TO INDUSTRIAL RELATIONS

Conciliation Act 1896	Provides assistance in bringing together the parties to a dispute or, on the application of both parties, for the appointment of an arbitrator(s) Committees of Investigation may be set up by the minister responsible

Figure 5:1   Government intervention in employment
questions

The Industrial Court Act 1919	Provides for voluntary arbitration by the Industrial Court, now the Industrial Arbitration Board; or by a single arbitrator or an arbitration panel. Expenses borne by Exchequer for state arbitration
Terms and Conditions of Employment Act 1959	Provides for unilateral application by employers' or workers' organisations to the Industrial Court in cases where it is claimed that terms and conditions established for *the industry* are not being observed
The Fair Wages Resolution 1946	Ensures fair remuneration and conditions for employees on government contracts
Wages Councils Act 1959 (a continuation of the Trade Boards Act 1909) *N.B.* Wages Councils under review 1972 by CIR	Consolidates Wages Councils where employers and/or employees are poorly organised. Ensures minimum standards of wages, hours, holidays, etc., in trades such as catering. Government encouraged development to Joint Industrial Council as organisation improved
The Industrial Relations Act 1971	Establishes National Industrial Relations Court, Commission on Industrial Relations, Industrial Arbitration Board to replace Industrial Court; widens scope of industrial tribunals to include appeals against dismissals, against unfair practices either by employer or by a union against a member; establishes Chief Registrar of trade unions. Empl. Assoc. extends power of Sec. of State

Figure 5:1 *continued*

Government intervention in employment questions

As H A Clegg says in his book *Industrial Relations in Great Britain* (1970), the great bulk of industrial relations has been until very recently outside the scope of the various statutes governing the work situation. The remedy of 'abuses' so considered has of course always been government policy and examples of such action are given in Figure 5:1. Part B of Figure 5:1 shows the increase in legislation specifically concerned with industrial relations. The table shows the change in government outlook from little intervention to considerable intervention. Except for legislation on social security benefits and race relations, the Department of Employment now administers most of the Acts listed. Great social and economic changes have taken place during the period and latterly industrial relations have been troubled in some, but not all, areas. In 1970, days lost through strikes totalled 10 980 000; in 1971, 13 558 000[1].

Assistance offered by government

Given that the quality of working relationships is made or marred in the daily interchanges at all levels of the organisation—and the silent interchanges may be the most significant of all!—and given that the Government's view of management's responsibility is as stated above, internal resources may yet be considered insufficient for the situation. There are many private sector forms of assistance: employers' associations, professional bodies such as the British Institute of Management or the Institute of Personnel Management, their literature, courses and conferences. A stream of books, to which one adds with some trepidation, pours off the presses and there are many consultants in general or specialist fields.

The Government's advisory services in the industrial relations field are also well known. These are free and offered through the Conciliation and Advisory Service of the Department of Employment at the addresses given at the end of this chapter. They are public services offered to employers and trade unions alike. This is part of their strength since advisers are thus well known on both sides of industry and in fairly close touch. Since no payment is made, there can be no accusations of leaning to either party—particularly by the trade unions. The Department Adviser has no commercial worries and is free to say whatever he feels necessary to any party involved. He can spend as much or as

PRINCIPAL CAUSE	NO. OF STRIKES IN ALL INDUSTRIES
1 Wages	1052
2 Working arrangements, rules and discipline	646
3 Redundancy, dismissal, suspension, etc.	326
4 Demarcation	57
5 Hours of Work	30
6 Closed Shop	29
7 { Trade Union recognition { Sympathetic Strikes	18 18
8 Alleged victimisation for trade union membership, and other disputes about trade union status	16

Source: Royal Commission on Trade Unions & Employers, Associations 1968, Report Cmnd 3623

Figure 5:2 Principal causes of unofficial strikes

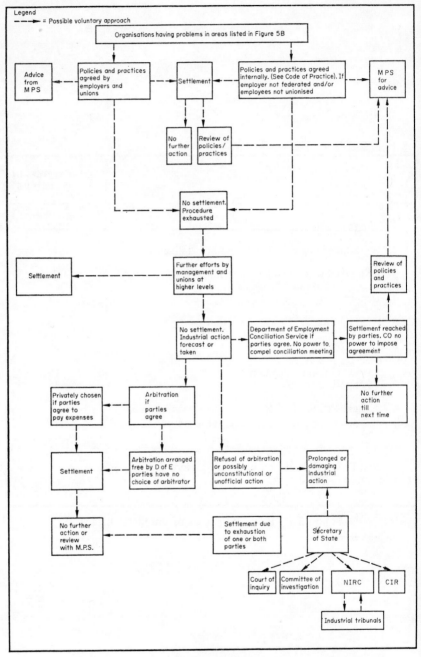

Figure 5:3 Services available from Department of Employment

little time on the case, either intermittently or consecutively, as appears appropriate or as his time-table allows. A disadvantage may be that advice which is free is not valued; but even expensive and excellent advice may not lead to action. At the time of writing at least the advantage in access, in known impartiality and in freedom of action seems to lie with the free service.

Subject areas in which outside advice may be valuable

These may be taken as similar to those used in the Donovan Report to analyse the causes and extent of unofficial strikes, since these accounted for 95 per cent of all strikes in the period reviewed (1964–1966). Figure 5:2 gives the principal causes in order of importance for number of strikes caused in all industries.

Types of assistance offered and example

Figure 5:3 shows in simplified form the course a contentious issue might take and the various points at which services may be offered and the equal opportunity to accept or reject these until the point is reached at which the Secretary of State intervenes, though even this intervention is hardly authoritarian in character. These questions are discussed further below. The direction lines in the chart are dotted rather than solid to indicate the voluntary nature of the arrangements. The arrows leading to both post- and pre-industrial trouble reviews by the advisers indicate the importance the Department of Employment now gives to this advisory part of its work.

Assistance with an immediate problem, such as a strike, a strike threat, or other cause of industrial discontent

Conciliation Service The difference between the conciliator's and the adviser's role is not a hard and fast line and in each the element of 'non-directional counselling' is strong. The aim is that the parties shall think through their problems and arrive at their own—non-imposed—solutions. The conciliation service is normally available for immediate assistance, subject to the demands on staff time, with any of the problems listed in Figure 5:2 where either there is a problem to discuss or where the agreed procedure has been used and has not produced a settlement. Either unions or managements may request conciliation. The possible outcome might be:

1   That a meeting is by agreement held. The conciliation officer may, if the parties wish, chair the meeting. He is certainly likely to be looking for possible ways to break any deadlock. For this he will draw on a wide experience. Normally conciliation staff remain in post for a fair length of time, know the area well and acquire considerable professional expertise in their job. There may be a settlement resulting from the meeting or meetings

2   The parties may refuse to meet. The conciliation officer cannot compel them to do so. He may take suggestions from the unions meeting in a pub to the managers closeted in their office and vice versa. Thus some link is maintained. If all communication were severed, a resumption of work or negotiations would be unlikely. There may be many ultimately useful 'talks about talks.' If these are refused the conciliation officer has no powers in the matter

3   No acceptable settlement may emerge, and industrial action starts or fails to cease. This is still entirely the responsibility of the parties to the dispute

4   Current attempts at an incomes policy may limit the conciliator's freedom to offer conciliation services in wage claim disputes[2]

5   Any settlement obtained must be jointly agreed. Otherwise, of course, it would have little chance of lasting

6   The parties may voluntarily agree to go to arbitration

Arbitration (Conciliation Act 1896 and Industrial Courts Act 1919)   These Acts encouraged industries to set up their own arrangements either through Joint Industrial Council machinery referring unsettled disputes to the Industrial Court (now the Industrial Arbitration Board), or by Arbitrators appointed by the Department of Employment, sitting singly or as a panel, who would make an award. These awards are binding in honour only, except in so far as they may become part of a contract of employment to which the Terms and Conditions of Employment Act, 1959 may apply and on which the unions may make a unilateral claim for arbitration. In all other cases, the Government prudently insists that both parties must agree to arbitration. Otherwise the award would risk rejection by one or the other of them. Interestingly, the rejection of an arbitration award is rare. Compulsory arbitration has been unacceptable to both management and unions in this country except in time of war. But it is possible that both sides are re-thinking their positions. Examples of disagreements in all the categories in Figure 5:1 have been dealt with by arbitration. Possibly there have been more cases recently concerned with redundancy, dismissals and non-recognition union issues such as shop steward facilities, 'check-off' arrangements, etc.

Industrial action—the cooling-off period—unofficial action   In spite of the agreed machinery for dispute settlement strikes still occur. They are unlikely ever to disappear from the scene in a free society. If a strike is widespread, damaging to the economy or otherwise the focus of public attention, it may be dealt with by headquarter's staff of the Department of Employment. In this, as in all other cases, the role of the Department is to try to find a basis for the resumption of negotiations. A new development under the Industrial Relations Act 1971 is the power given to the Secretary of State at the Department to apply to NIRC for a 'cooling-off' period of up to sixty days *if the industrial action begun or planned is sufficiently widespread or injurious to the national economy, national security, etc.* (see Industrial Relations Act 1971, Emergency Procedures, Part VIII). Under this section also an order may be made requiring a ballot to determine support for the strike. In the light of present knowledge, it appears unlikely that either of these provisions will be used other than most sparingly. The increasing number of unofficial strikes noted in Chapter VII of the Donovan Report produces as many difficulties for the Department of Employment services as for anyone else. The rigid stance on the concept that there can be no contact with unofficial strikers is no longer completely adhered to by the Department—if it ever was—any more than managements in fact rather than in theory always refused any contact before a return to work or at least to the agreed procedure had been achieved. Such a return is however always the aim of the Department. Increasing stress is now being put by the Department on its advisory role designed to deal with the problems of industrial relations policy and personnel practices which produce industrial strife within undertakings. Hence the employment of specialist Departmental Advisers whose role in the improvement of industrial relations is discussed in the second part of this section which deals with long-term assistance.

Disclosure of information to trade unions for purposes of collective bargaining   Trade Unions believing that the employer is not fulfilling his duty to do this as laid down in section 56 of the Industrial Relations Act may complain to the National Industrial Relations Court which may determine the rights of the employer and the registered trade union.

This obligation is further spelled out in the Code of Practice and the Department of Employment's advisory staff will no doubt assist firms in complying with it.[3]

Industrial tribunals   These statutory bodies comprising management, trade union and independent members dealt originally with queries under the Industrial Training Act and the Redundancy Payments Act. They established a reputation for speedy and fair resolution of difficulties, the published reasons for their decisions forming a code of practice on the issues with which they dealt. Since the reaction of the unions to the passage of the Industrial Relations Act was to instruct members to withdraw from these tribunals, it seems at the time of going to press that they will be much hampered in fulfilling their additional duties under the Act of dealing with 'unfair practices' such as curtailment of the worker's right to belong to a trade union or not to belong to one (section 5), unfair dismissal (section 22), disputes relating to charity contributions by workers objecting to payment of contributions to trade unions (section 10), and appeals against a trade union by a member or former member (section 107). The last section refers to employers' associations also. Again, the Code of Practice makes specific recommendations on these points, and Departmental Officers are available to advise.

The National Industrial Relations Court and the Commission on Industrial Relations   Agreement on appropriate bargaining units is normally reached on a voluntary basis as the Code of Industrial Relations Practice indicates. Where there are, for example, contending unions and where the agreed voluntary machinery including conciliation and arbitration has produced no settlement, the matter may be referred by *either* or *both* parties to the Secretary of State for Employment for examination by the Commission of Industrial Relations—with no *imposed* settlement in view. If this fails to produce a resolution of the problem, an application may be made to the National Industrial Relations Court to define the bargaining unit and decide which union or unions should be given negotiating rights in it (applications initially through Department of Employment Officers).

Longer term assistance with policy questions or review of practices

Conciliation and Advisory Service   The possibility of assistance from these officers at times when there is no crisis but an attempt is being made to review, improve or up-date policies and practices in industrial relations are shown in Figure 5:3. Where crises have occurred or continue to occur, the Secretary of State may intervene, as shown at the bottom of the chart:

1   A *Court of Inquiry* may be set up in cases of severe and wide-spread industrial trouble, such as was investigated at GEC by the Wilberforce enquiry in 1971.

2   A *Committee of Investigation* may be set up, such as the Devlin Committee on the docks where a longer term investigation was required

Though in both cases the Secretary of State may take the initiative careful soundings normally take place both on the setting up of either body and on the acceptability of any particular chairman. This is necessary as again the findings are not binding on the parties and, sadly enough, may be ignored in the short term at least.

3   *The Commission on Industrial Relations*   The Secretary of State may refer any question to this body. Specified in the Act are matters of organisation, recognition of unions, negotiating rights, disclosure of information for collective bargaining and facilities for training the negotiating parties. Obviously these are long-term exercises. The Commission will conduct its own investigations and publish findings if appropriate. Some of the reports produced before the Act are interesting reading. The yearly Report of the Commission is likely to be required reading for those interested in industrial relations since it will by statute include a general review of developments in collective bargaining during the year and draw attention to any trends and problems encountered. Since the National Board for Prices and Incomes' Reports have now ceased and the Department of Employment does not publish

a report, the CIR reports should be useful to managers as well as students.

The Office of Manpower Economics   This newly created body appears likely to carry on some of the labour and remuneration studies done by the defunct NBPI and to publish reports from time to time.

The Conciliation and Advisory Service[4]   The staff of this service command between them a fair range of skills which they can draw on to advise organisations. There are industrial relations and personnel specialists together with recruits from industry and commerce with experience of other management skills, for example financial accounting, work measurement and method improvement, etc. The career civil servants working in the service may nowadays have had secondment to industry as part of their training. The work they do may be illustrated by following an imaginary though realistic problem through the stages indicated in Figure 5:3.

Example of problem

In North West Widget Company Ltd, which is federated and unionised, a team of skilled men servicing and maintaining the assembly line complains of the low level of their earnings compared with those of the unskilled assembly line workers. They see their foreman (largely as a formality, unfortunately) and their shop steward and subsequently the management, so putting the agreed disputes procedure into motion. (Had this been a small non-federated and/or non-unionised firm, the Department Adviser might agree to act at this stage if trouble appeared likely.) The local trade union officer happens to see this officer or one of his staff at a meeting and discusses his fears that some of his members may take unofficial action in order to put pressure on the company. The final stages of the disputes procedure[5] do not produce a settlement, nor does reconsideration at any level, and the men down tools. The company contacts the Department Officer who, after satisfying himself that all stages of procedure have been used and every effort made to reach a solution, may suggest a conciliation meeting or series of meetings *if both sides are willing*. The dotted direction lines in the chart indicate the purely voluntary nature of the arrangements. The possible results of the meeting are shown as:

1   Settlement with no further action from the exhausted parties but the possibility of further unrest

2   Arbitration as outlined on page 73—*Arbitration*—leading to settlement and no further action for the present

3   Industrial action leading eventually to the withdrawal of one o r both parties from the positions taken, the exhaustion of resources or patience of either or both, outside intervention as outlined on page 73—*Industrial action, industrial tribunals* or *the National Industrial Relations Court* . . . This dispute will figure for its duration on the weekly report sent direct to St James's Square by the Regional Department of Employment

4   After 1, 2 or 3, the organisation may decide or be willing to receive suggestions that its procedures and practices need review, and the departments advisory services may have the opportunity to give basic long-term assistance

No indication is intended that there must be trouble before the service will advise. A good deal of preventative work is done. In this and in the example quoted, the advisers might carry out a diagnostic survey of the wages systems and the firm's internal negotiating procedures. Possibly the two groups of workers concerned belong to different unions and relationships between them, including their place in the bargaining procedure, may have to be sorted out. Possibly also the grievance procedure functions too slowly. Staffing ratios may need review and training facilities are possibly inadequate, making for a good deal of extra maintenance work, with absence and high labour turnover contributing to discontent if they mean frequent unwelcome moves of job.

The advisers may assist in in-plant training courses or co-operate with other bodies in external courses if the need for these is shown during their day-to-day contacts. Their job is not to do management's or trade unions' work for them but to provide outside informed and impartial assistance in their efforts to resolve their differences. The role is not an easy one. As a noted Permanent Secretary once said—advisers must walk a tight-rope between the two sides while yet keeping their feet on the ground. The job can be very demanding since surveys may have to include the night shift and conciliation meetings may go on till the small hours. This is particularly likely with the big national negotiations at headquarters where officers may have to sleep on the premises and brave the press, TV and radio reporters encamped around

D

the door. Nevertheless advisers seem to find the job interesting and rewarding.

References
1 *Department of Employment Gazette*, February 1972.
2 TUC reported to favour separate Conciliation and Arbitration Services, financed from public funds. (*Guardian*, 10 March 1972).
3 The Commission on Industrial Relations is working on a report.
4 Formerly Manpower and Productivity Service.
5 Nowadays procedures may be national, industry-wide, company-wide or relating to one plant only.

Locations of Departmental Advisory Services

Conciliation and Advisory Service
Department of Employment

NORTHERN:
Wellbar House, Gallowgate, Newcastle-upon-Tyne NE1 4TP
Newcastle-upon-Tyne 27575

YORKSHIRE AND HUMBERSIDE:
City House, New Station Street, Leeds LS1 4JH
Leeds 38232

EASTERN AND SOUTHERN:
Bryan House, 76/80 Whitfield Street, London W1P 6AN
01-636 8616

LONDON AND SOUTH EASTERN:
Hanway House, Red Lion Square, London WC1
01-405 8454

SOUTH WESTERN:
The Pithay, Bristol BS1 2NQ
Bristol 21071

MIDLANDS:
Five Ways House, Islington Row, Birmingham 15
021-643 9868

NORTH WESTERN:
Sunley Building, Piccadilly Plaza, Manchester M60 7JS
061-832 9111

WALES:
2-4 Park Grove, Cardiff CF1 3QY
Cardiff 45231

SCOTLAND:
13 Bath Street, Glasgow C2
041-332 6981

6

Employers' Associations and Trade Unions

Rachel Naylor

Lecturer, Department of Management Sciences, UMIST

This chapter is inevitably a largely historical survey with comments, relying heavily on the references given at the end. Writing in the Spring of 1972 in Manchester, one is well aware of an unprecedented rate of change in industrial relations institutions and their operations. In December, 1971 the Engineering Industry Disputes Procedure disappeared; there is heavy union pressure in the Manchester district for plant agreements; there are numerous sit-ins; firms who worked hard to establish joint industrial councils are now withdrawing from them 'the better to negotiate with their own employees'; employers' associations and unions merge and change.

Nevertheless the institutions of industrial relations continue to exist and agreements are still sought. The previous history of industrial relations has certainly not been forgotten and this chapter recalls some of the incidents which may be considered to have a bearing on present-day attitudes and comments on the working of the current systems.

The institutions in the negotiating field are considered under three headings:

1 Employers' Associations
2 Trade Unions
3 Procedural Agreements

The emphasis throughout is on the services each can provide toward the improvement of relationships in the working situation.

Employers' Associations

This section is particularly concerned with those employers' associations which deal with industrial relations.

The history of employers' associations still remains to be written a the Royal Commission Report points out, but the evidence is that their pre-1914 innovatory role was subsequently lost to either the governmen or to large firms which might or might not be in membership. The pioneer work done on codifying practice and improving relationship by Sir Alfred Mond (later Lord Melchett) and his chief labour officer Richard Lloyd Roberts, was done largely outside the framework o any employers' organisation.

The existence of an employers' association covering an industry i necessary for national collective bargaining to exist. Agreements thu arrived at often provided at least protected minimum rates and con ditions for workers and thus also safeguarded employers against th commercial advantages which might have accrued to some of thei competitors who otherwise could have paid less than minimum rates

Until fairly recently employers' associations seemed mainly intereste in procedural questions arising from these agreements or substantiv questions, for example pay, hours, holidays, etc. Their resistance to th infringement of managerial prerogatives was made clear on man occasions. H. A. Clegg[2] gives a number of these in his chapter o employers' associations. The Secretary of the General Builders' Asso ciation told the 1867 Royal Commission on Trade Unions that: 'A an association we object to trade unions under three heads; first tha many of their objects are improper and contrary to public policy; i the second place that those objectives which may not be improper an contrary to public policy are pursued by them by improper means and thirdly . . . they exercise coercion over both masters and men and tend to separate both masters and men.' The engineering industry also has had its share of strong words from employers. It has sometimes in the past appeared that the Engineering Employers' Federation's views on labour relations were to be permanently shaped by their experiences with the militant shop steward's movement during the 1914 war. This is now not the case but it is likely that the views expressed by Sir Allen Smith, who dominated the Federation in the late twenties, and reflected by A Shadwell in *The Engineering Industry and the Crisis of 1922* (1922) still cast their shadow. The engineering workers, Shadwell says, were responsible for 'a policy of interference, urged on by the unions and encouraged by war conditions . . . with a view to shifting the frontier into management's territory . . . Complaints of obstacles placed in the way of executing orders poured into the Employers' Federation from all quarters.'

Many employers' associations have appeared much attached to the traditional modes of conducting industrial relations affairs and unwilling to proceed beyond the pace at which the slowest member could keep up. Although there were far-sighted employers amongst their members, very often it appeared that their influence was not predominant in association affairs. Possibly they would have found the demands on their time and energy too great. Some firms did not become members because they were not willing to bind themselves to agree to the terms agreed by the associations. Others, perhaps smaller in size, were unwilling to pay the membership fee. Others again withdrew or did not join because too rigid an adherence to industrial general agreements precluded innovatory experiments on questions of hours, holidays, bonus schemes, etc. Renold Chains Limited is an example of a firm which has withdrawn a number of times on this type of issue.

Services provided

Associations vary in the range and quality of the services provided and in the type of service members require and are prepared to pay for. At one time it appeared that the demand was largely for imaginative commercial services and skilful presentation of the industry's case to government. Little lead was given on industrial relations or personnel policy, indeed association scepticism of the latter seemed as great as that of trade union officials, and perhaps for the same reason. The retention of managerial control and a cautious use of time-honoured practices seemed the main guides to action, perhaps because member firms were often only too willing to leave industrial relations to the 'specialists' while they got on with 'the main business of the company.' These specialists did indeed develop considerable practical expertise. What they did not always do was to develop the skill of their member firms either in bargaining or in the analysis of their problems. This was perhaps particularly true of the local associations.

Fortunately there has been much change. Associations have recruited to their staff more analytically minded men with much more specialist knowledge. These may include negotiators, training officers, work study and financial control experts, and legal advisers to assist with the work of the association centrally and to advise individua firms. For years the textile employers have had, for example, the services of work study experts to assist with wages system installatior and maintenance. The reported advantages of membership are set ou in Figure 6 : 1 (from research for the Donovan Commission).

BENEFIT	WORKS MANAGERS (*per cent*)	PERSONNEL OFFICERS (*per cent*)
Collective action/uniform decisions	28	24
Technical information	28	15
Advice on trade union matters	25	28
Representation/liaison with government and trade unions	24	35
Advice on wage rates	19	19
Advice and information on government or local authority regulations/price policy	16	27
Advice on training schemes, etc.	5	8
Advice on holiday arrangements	2	3
Other answers	12	7

Figure 6:1   Employers' views on advantages of federation

Source: Government Social Survey. *Work Place Industrial Relations*. H.M.S.C (1968)

A useful service which may be offered is insurance for damage to members premises and work in progress by, for example, fire or flood or against damages claimed at common law for injury to employees in the course of their work. Insurance against loss through industrial action appears rare in this country.

Many of the associations visited for the Royal Commission's survey were running training courses or conferences. Some had their own training establishments. The Engineering Employers' Federation is one of many which have run seminars on, for example, productivity bargaining which is a far cry from their earlier national agreements. It has been suggested that there is here an important role for employers' associations to play in educating their own members in the prevention and control of inflationary wage-drift.

The Confederation of British Industries

The Federation of British Industries and the British Employers' Confederation merged in 1965 (with the National Association of British Manufacturers) to form the Confederation of British Industry. The CBI admits to membership employers' associations, trade associations, individual companies in production industries and transport, whether members of their associations or not, and the public corporations administering the nationalised industries.[4] Banks and insurance companies may become 'commercial affiliates.' The Royal Commission found that 108 associations were in membership, the Confederation claiming that they covered more than three-quarters of all employees in the private sector and in transport. It is in the 108 important member associations that the CBI's strength lies. This is a more significant figure than the 1150 or so listed unincorporated associations of employers, some of whom may, in effect, be unregistered trade unions.

The CBI is an advisory body with no formal control over its members, though it may influence and advise and is consulted by government. Recently the CBI has attempted an unusual initiative in appealing to members to withhold price increase for a period in an attempt to halt the wage/price spiral.

Trade Unions

In The Royal Commission Report, the Industrial Relations Act and the Code of Industrial Relations Practice there is support for the view

held by many practitioners that management's responsibility is heavy
for the achieving of reasonable working relationships with the trade
unions in the factory situation. For this it is needful to recall certain
events in the trade union history, to realise and accept the present
position of trade unions in our society and to remember something of
the way unions are organised. These are discussed below; this
section ends with a list of points for consideration during negotiations

Events in trade union history which are likely to influence current attitude
Even the much condensed story of the unions' past brushes with the
law (in the *Industrial Relations Handbook*) shows clearly the reason
for them to be wary of it. Having had their existence and function
legalised in 1871 after a protracted struggle, they then found their
operations restricted again by an Act passed in the same year. This
later Act remained in force until 1875 when the Conspiracy and Pro
tection of Property Act gave protection against indictment for act
which would not have been 'criminal' if done by individuals, and
allowed peaceful picketing. The only areas excluded from the
de-restrictions were the public utilities where strikes might be danger
ous or injurious to others or to the public.

Trade union finances have suffered on three well-known occasion
due to the intervention of the law. In the *Taff Vale* case, the Amalga
mated Society of Railway Servants was liable, according to a judgmen
of the House of Lords (1901), to pay heavy damages to the Taff Val
Railway Company which claimed to have suffered considerably becaus
of a strike. The Trade Disputes Act 1906 was passed to protect, it wa
thought, union funds. In 1964, however, the Draughtsmen and Allie
Technicians Association found itself liable when judgment went again
it in the *Rookes* v. *Barnard* case.

In 1909 the *political levy* was found to be *ultra vires* in the Osborn
judgment; the trade unions moreover were not to take part in an
local or national political activity—after having in effect created the
Labour Party to represent their views in Parliament and to the public
The Trade Union Act 1913 restored the legality of the political levy
provided that members had the facility of contracting-out. The *Trade
Disputes and Trade Union Act 1927* nervously passed after the General
Strike replaced 'contracting-out' by 'contracting-in' and caused a size
able drop in Labour Party funds. Other clauses in this Act prohibited
by law all strikes designed to coerce the government and made criminal

proceedings possible against any who took part or incited others to do so; civil servants were prohibited from joining affiliated unions and the law on picketing was made more rigid and severe. Not until 1946 was 'contracting-in' again replaced by law with 'contracting-out.'

Union members did not always behave like model citizens. Scenes of violence did occur and there was always the fear in some minds that growing industrial power would be used for subversive political ends. In times of depression when workers fear for their livelihood and managements for the viability of their undertakings relationships easily become strained. The unions' experience seems to be that in such times repressive legislation may be passed. It is likely then that trade-unionists may oppose *any* legislation since they feel it will curtail their ability to carry out the functions for which they consider they exist! They even oppose an Act which has in it so much for them (the Industrial Relations Act, 1971) and which, for example, gives unions the opportunity to force recognition on an employer for the first time in the history of the UK.

Present position of the unions

The figures available in the Autumn of 1971 show the number of trade unionists as some ten millions out of an employed population in this country of about twenty-three millions. The trade unionists are organised into 508 unions. This is a considerable reduction from the 651 operating in 1959, mainly due to amalgamations and other joint agreements. Vic Feather, General Secretary of the Trades Union Congress, said recently: 'We're doing pretty well at reducing the number of the unions—and how well are the employers doing with their associations?' He did not wait for an answer, since if all associations are counted, the figure is apparently much greater than the number of unions (see page 85), and in any case is difficult to quantify exactly. Perhaps the new Act will make this easier. Mr Feather's comment was obviously made in answer to the complaints of problems caused by multi-unionism in this country where, for example, the Ford Motor Company negotiates with some twenty unions but in its West German plant, with one manual union; there are only sixteen unions in that country. In Britain industrial unionism has been canvassed from time to time but does not seem a likely possibility. The powerful unions are interested in many industries.

Trade union administration; Shop stewards; The TUC

The government and administration of unions is well shown in B C Roberts' charts[5] which clearly indicate the 'outside' position of the shop steward in many unions; with considerable authority deriving from the members electing him but no really formalised or well-controlled place in the union hierarchy. They show too the different ways in which unions have sought to make their officials the servants of the membership in fact as well as in theory. Sometimes they elect officials for life but make sure that the executive committee seats are held by laymen. Some unions ensure that officials have to seek re-election at three or five-year intervals so that the membership may have an opportunity of signifying approval or disapproval of the policies followed. Industrial relations scholars have written much on this. The manager needs to be aware of the arrangements in the unions he deals with, using the knowledge to assist his understanding of union behaviour and the stresses which union officials work under. Trade union links with the Trades Union Congress are discussed in the references listed at the end of this chapter. They all stress that the TUC has *moral authority* only over members who guard their autonomy carefully.

As at December 1970, the 508 registered and unregistered unions were linked with the TUC in 142 single or jointly affiliated bodies. Eighteen trade groupings were represented on the General Council, which is still well known to be dominated by the traditional manual workers' unions though the white collar unions show the greatest membership increase. The TUC's voluntary machinery for settling inter-union disputes and the Bridlington Rules allowing for the investigation of 'poaching' complaints will presumably still continue in the age of the Industrial Relations Act. Whether the initiative which the TUC was beginning to take to sort out inter-union problems will continue is open to question.

Points for management's consideration in negotiations

This list has been compiled from various texts, from experience and from interviews with managements in the course of work at the University.

1 Multi-unionism creates problems for both management and unions. A number of firms are attempting to prevent any increase in the number of unions with which they deal. The incursion of the Association of

Scientific, Technical and Managerial Staff into the field perhaps traditionally occupied by the Amalgamated Union of Engineering and Foundry Workers has caused difficulties. So has the possible differences between the white collar section of the traditionally manual unions such as the Transport and General Workers' Union and other white collar unions. It is thought in some quarters that the Act will give an opportunity for such a union to gain a foothold where a small group of members is dissatisfied with the existing arrangements and certainly this would be something for management to watch. There is a fair amount of evidence to which a recent report[6] from a plant in America adds that unions often think in terms of the greatest good for their particular members rather than in terms of worker solidarity as a whole, except in times of crisis such as the threat to close the shipyards on the Clyde.

2   The changing pattern of employment has decreased the status of the craft union member who may look with a jaundiced rather than a 'brotherly' eye on advances in pay and status by unskilled workers and on the increasing importance of white-collar unionism.

3   Problems of union organisation may mean that the centre appears remote from the periphery on the factory floor. Communications may be poor, with union branch attendance figures at no more than 2–7 per cent of membership unless, as in mining and printing, meetings occur at the work place. In other circumstances, the assessment by management of union members' knowledge of and commitment to the line being taken or the proposed agreement becomes increasingly difficult. If communication within the union is poor the union official is likely to lack information concerning the actual situation.

4   Into this vacuum may step the shop steward . . . until he too becomes part of the establishment, the last one out of the factory at a walk-out, saying over his shoulder, 'I tried to stop them but they wouldn't listen.' It is important to remember, as Saif Choudhri found,[7] that shop stewards are elected to represent, not to co-operate with management.

5   Comparisons of terms and conditions and support for any member in trouble is officially channelled through the Branch or District Committee. It may be that the shop steward in a multi-union plant may find himself in effect representing his union in a joint shop stewards' committee at the plant. The link with the officials of the union may be very tenuous; the officials are in any case few in number,

on average about one to every 3800 members. In engineering they are even fewer: one to 6800 members. Many surveys, including those done for the Royal Commission[8], found that managers mainly preferred to deal with their stewards rather than with the full-time officer.

6   The combined committees which have been formed by stewards in multi-plant companies such as British Leyland or Dunlop Rubber Co, are not only completely outside the official union structure but often in rivalry with it.

7   Union finances are usually inadequate for their present job. This means, amongst other things, that office help in sifting and organising the evidence to prepare a case for negotiation is not always available; perhaps paradoxically it may be wise for management to allow for this rather than take advantage of it if a long-lasting bargain is sought. Moreover, training schemes to assist officers particularly in their early days may be good or faulty dependent on the time and money the union has allotted to them.

8   It is essential for management to know the point at which decisions are taken on policy matters and on routine practices; this varies from one union to another.

9   The union presentation of cases has begun to acquire some sophistication with the presentation to Ford of an economically well-documented and well-argued case prepared, with the help of friendly academics, by the TGWU. Research effort at both TUC and union head offices is still small but likely to make an increasing contribution.

10   It is impolitic to assume that shop stewards, particularly convenors (or senior stewards) are less sophisticated than trade union officials. Both of these may be knowledgeable and skilled bargainers. Generally speaking, it may also be unwise to assume that all shop stewards have good relationships with their officials (witness the Ford story). Furthermore, allowance needs to be made for more detailed and slower communication with stewards who are new or are pushed into this difficult job because no one else will take it.

Agreements

The usual national union-management agreement in this country is concerned with minimum terms and conditions, holidays and holiday pay, disputes procedure, overtime and shift premiums, work study, co-operation in plant changes, guaranteed working week. It often seems to have been designed for manual workers only in spite of the increases in other forms of (unionised) employment. It is not usually legally enforceable. It may well be that this last characteristic will remain in spite of the Industrial Relations Act. No adequate sampling of opinion or practice has been possible at the time of writing (August 1971) but there are certainly some recent agreements which have the permitted clause stating that they are *not* legally binding.

For purposes of illustration this section looks critically at two disputes procedure agreements, one in engineering and one in rubber. These are set out for comparison in Figure 6 : 2. In both, the man with a grievance should according to the agreements consult first his supervisor. This is a very sensible step—and one which is ignored in many a firm in both of these industries. It has apparently been felt that the risks of allowing the foreman to have any part in the procedure, except perhaps to know that the worker has gone off to see someone else, are too great. Isolation of the foreman from important decisions in the organisation is understandable in view of past errors on his part, but has led to cases of complete withdrawal by foremen from an important part of their function or, in some cases, to a demand for unionisation at their level, 'so that we can have a say in things that go on,' as a group of foremen on a recent course said. It is interesting that the Code of Industrial Practice, with the apparent concurrence of all, stresses the key position of the supervisor and his need for adequate training in industrial relations.

In both industries, the worker may consult his shop steward, who may assist him in presenting his case. If there is no solution reached, the grievance or dispute then begins its journey up the chain of command. Often, however, this is not the *line* command. The worker and/or his shop steward may go straight to the Personnel Office. The Personnel Department's role in ensuring equitable treatment is extremely important, but their role should be seen to be that of advising, with as much force as is necessary. This department should monitor rather than control the administration of grievance procedure; not have this thrust upon them because of their skills or the lack of these skills in others. In the past it has not been appropriate in industry for central guidance to be given on codifying the points at which action should be taken internally. Also, companies have not been encouraged to agree disciplinary procedures and penalties. Such codification must now be undertaken to comply with the Code of Practice. A number of difficulties

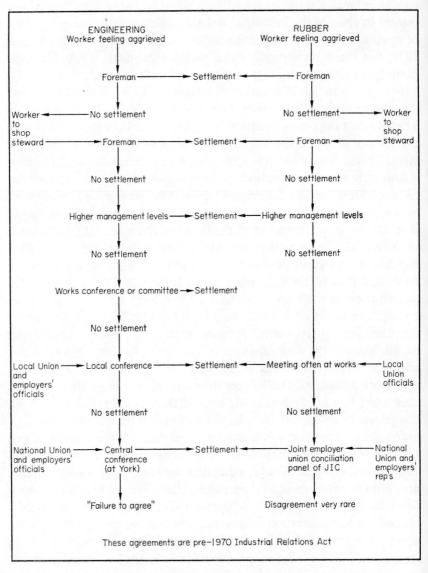

Figure 6:2   Dispute procedure agreements

should be obviated thereby. A recent investigation by a student in a rubber firm showed that although there was in fact an agreed disciplinary procedure, few of the foremen or the shop stewards were clear about its provisions and on the factory floor confusion reigned concerning the level of penalties incurred for various breaches of discipline. Some employees thought the penalty for spoilt work was suspension. Others thought that a friendly warning was the more likely outcome. Given problems of standardising interpretation, such wide differences seem likely to exacerbate disputes rather than to resolve them.

Both agreements were based on the assumption that the majority of day-to-day affairs would be resolved by contacts and discussions within the plant at the appropriate meetings. Clearly the Industrial Relations Act and the Code of Practice support the creation and maintenance of comprehensive internal procedures which will be able to handle most grievances. Neither agreement gives guidelines on the facilities which worker representatives need if they are to function effectively nor is the importance of communication stressed. It appears to be assumed that the problems of worker representatives in the representation of their numbers are not serious and are of no practical concern to management. In fact, of course, a number of firms have given facilities for representatives to consult their members and to report back to them. It is difficult to know what proportion of firms pay for the time so spent. Some certainly do.

When the dispute cannot be settled within the firm and moved into the further stages of procedure, there was a difference in the two agreements. The rubber industry has an agreed conciliation procedure. In engineering, a dispute which could not be resolved at factory level might be passed to local conference where, theoretically, the experienced officers of the employers' association and very likely the more senior District Secretary or Divisional Organiser of the union might find further possibilities of settlement. Professor Turner's researches[9] among others show that in fact a declining number of settlements were made at this level. The dispute might then go to the Central Conference at York, no industrial action on either side is to take place while the process continues. Criticisms continued to be made particularly from the trade union side that the whole procedure was dependent on the goodwill of the employer for its functioning, that it allowed the employer to institute changes which were not agreed and must be retained until the unions had won their case against them and that the whole procedure was too cumbersome and lengthy. Professor Turner gives the usual length of time as thirteen weeks. Finally, in December, 1971, the unions withdrew altogether from the procedure.

Unresolved disputes in the rubber industry go to the Joint Industrial Council conciliation panel. On the whole decisions made by the joint conciliation machinery have been loyally accepted except in some well-publicised instances. The machinery has felt the strain of our current inflationary situation of course. But it has worked at least as well as the arrangements in the more traditional industries, and thus justified the enormous effort which was put into formulating it. These procedures also suffer from the defect of slowness. This is perhaps inevitable where non-professionals—or rather part-time members of the various bodies—have to fit this work into their normal programme. It does not, however, assist with the prevention and resolution of conflict which was the reason for their existence. Whether the JIC system will be affected widely by plant bargaining and the new legislation is not known at this moment.

A section on agreements would be incomplete without mention of the recent developments away from national agreements which have often left important questions such as the determination of piece-rate standards to local or plant negotiation. The concepts of productivity or efficiency bargaining and plant agreements are dealt with elsewhere. The points to be made here concern the length of time the agreement will run, the problems of piece-meal bargaining at different times in the year and the difficulty of achieving any sort of uniformity in timing.

As the conclusion of an agreement is time and effort consuming, a number of trades made an attempt in the mid-sixties to introduce three-year package deals, rather than engage in the yearly marathon. These deals might cover rates, hours, holidays, guaranteed week, etc., all of which had previously been bargained about singly. Often an attempt was made, sometimes successfully to impose conditions, such as the abandonment of restrictive practices, in return for concessions. Some unions felt that their members were thus safeguarded for at least three years. The employers' view was that their labour costs could be predicted for three years. Such deals were inevitably very complex and because of increased inflation did not always cut out interim claims. The presence or absence of inflation appears to be significant in determining the length of time an agreement should run. A number of both unions and companies in the north-west at least now review the situation annually.

At the same time some managements are making headway with grouping their negotiations at least if they cannot achieve the same date line for all of them. This may make the performance even more stressful for managements but assists them in seeing the pattern as a whole. For unions it diminishes the possibility of 'leap frogging' claims but allows them also to see that their members do not get far behind.

Again in many north-west firms, textiles apart, such negotiations are likely to be with the shop stewards.

In any investigation of industry's liability to strife, it soon becomes clear, however, that it is not the *type* of agreement to which the firm is a party which is the deciding factor, but the interest shown by management and reflected in trade union attitudes. In increasing managements' sense of responsibility for the quality of industrial relations, the Act and the Code of Practice should help, particularly if attention is focused on the actual causes of discontent and ways of removing them.

References

1 *Industrial Relations Handbook*, HMSO, 1961
2 *The System of Industrial Relations in Great Britain* by H A Clegg, Blackwell, 1970
3 *Concise Guide to Industrial Relations* by T Wylie, University of Aston, fifth edition, 1968
4 *Royal Commission on Trade Unions and Employers' Associations*, report Cmnd 3623, HMSO, 1968
5 *Trade Union Government and Administration* by B C Roberts, Bell, 1956
6 *Human Resources Administration* by Wasmuth, Simonds, Hilgert and Lee, 1970
7 *British Workers' View of Industrial Relations* by S R Choudhri, unpublished MSc thesis, UMIST
8 *Shop Stewards and Workshop Relations*, Research Paper No. 10 by W E J McCarthy and S R Parker, *Royal Commission on Employers and Trade Unions*, 1968
9 *Labour Relations in the Motor Industry* by H A Turner *et al*, Allen and Unwin, 1967

7

Sources of Information

D P Torrington

Senior Lecturer in Industrial Relations, Manchester Polytechnic

The industrial relations practitioner is constantly seeking out information that will help him do his job more effectively. He is in a dynamic situation where practice is continuously developing, bringing new opportunities and fresh problems. He is also in a competitive situation, needing to attract and retain employees while others may be offering more tempting terms and conditions of employment.

There is a steadily-growing volume of knowledge about human behaviour, an understanding of which may assist in determining the practices that are to prevail in the future. Also the practice of industrial relations is set about with extensive statutory obligations, ignorance of which could lead to difficulty.

Types of information

In this chapter there is a consideration of the types of information that might be sought, and then suggestions on where it may be found.

Rates of pay

Managers have a continuing, urgent curiosity about the going rates. With manual work it is important to know what is being paid by other firms for comparable work, both in the area and within the industry generally. This enables them to assess how rates inside the organisation compare with those outside. This may be used to refute contentions in collective bargaining, or it may be a form of index that the organisation can use as a general yardstick for up-dating, aiming to keep domestic rates at the average for the district, or in the top 10 per cent, or whatever other point is chosen.

A similar exercise may be required for white collar employees, to measure the realism of union claims and to assess the competitive situation. Perhaps because of the lower level of union representation among white collar staff, or perhaps because of comparison difficulties, rates of pay seem usually to be more varied and difficult to compare than in the blue-collar field.

The need to compare managerial salaries is also developing, although this is presumably more to ensure the acceptable competitive situation than because of industrial relations pressures.

Prevailing practice

If there is curiosity about what other people are paying, there is equally curiosity about what they are doing; what Bruce Williams described as industrial folklore. Many managers review and up-date their procedures and strategies as a result of looking over the fence to see what someone else is doing rather than thinking a new procedure through from first principles. This saves the intellectual burden of starting from scratch, and gives some feeling of confidence in that someone else has done it first and proved that it works.

This can be dangerous if a practice is transplanted to a situation for which it is inappropriate, or where there is not sufficient management expertise to make it succeed. After the Fawley Agreements there were some attempts at following that experience that were successful: there were many more that failed.

Whatever the dangers it is unlikely that managers will stop doing this, and it will remain one of the main ways of learning.

Agreements

A specialised type of practice is the plant agreement, copies of which are eagerly sought by industrial relations practitioners with plant bargaining responsibility. The well-known productivity agreements of the sixties were reproduced many times over and examined with great care.

Research

A smaller number of managers attempt to keep in touch with the findings of the many different research programmes which are conducted in areas having a bearing on industrial relations. This enables the organisation to plan industrial relations policies and practices not simply on the basis of what other people have tried and made to work, but on the basis of what new evidence is coming forward in the behavioural science field which can then be used to develop original thinking on policy and practice.

Information from governmental, professional and similar bodies

The sources of the information the industrial relations practitioner needs are more varied than the types of information he may be seeking. Much of it is available from agencies of the government, professional institutions and similar organisations.

Department of Employment

The Department of Employment has a number of industrial relations officers, or conciliation officers, stationed throughout the country, and this service is being expanded with the passing of the Industrial Relations Act. These officers, within the Manpower and Productivity Service of the Department, can provide official guidance and assistance, as has been mentioned by Miss Naylor in Chapter 5, which also includes the regional addresses of the service.

The Department of Employment produces a number of invaluable publications. Recently they have produced a series of Manpower Papers, each dealing with a particular topic, such as manpower planning. In these they draw together some of the different lines of industrial practice being pursued in the topic, and present them in a way that can easily be followed and copied. The explanatory booklets produced by the Department on the Industrial Relations Act are probably the best guides to the Act that are available—and they are free.

Commission on Industrial Relations

Information or advice from the CIR might be sought by, or imposed on, managers in certain specified situations. There is already in existence a number of reports produced in the early days of the Commission, when it was investigating various industrial relations problems, mainly problems of recognition. They have also had a series of specific references on matters such as the facilities to be accorded to shop stewards and industrial relations training. The annual report which they are to produce in the future will include a general review of collective bargaining in the United Kingdom during the year.

Office of Manpower Economics

At the time of writing the Office of Manpower Economics is still a relatively new body, but promises to be a helpful source of information. It is in some ways the successor of the National Board for Prices and Incomes, which ceased to exist in 1971. The NBPI did sterling work during its career and the reports of its investigations remain model presentations of the facts in a particular industrial relations situation. They also produced a series of guides—which are not yet too dated—on such matters as job evaluation and payment by results.

Courts of Enquiry

From time to time the Secretary of State orders an enquiry into a dispute. The *ad hoc* court hears evidence and produces a report with recommendations. The reports frequently contain detailed evidence and analysis of the evidence that led to an agreed recommendation. The reports are published and may be helpful reading.

Professional Institutions

At least two professional institutions provide industrial relations information. The British Institute of Management has a large library and publishes a series of checklists and information papers for their members. Many of these are free of charge. They also have an information service for members, who may pose specific queries. The BIM, in addition, organises a range of courses and conferences at which aspects of industrial relations are discussed.

The Institute of Personnel Management issues publications and arranges conferences and courses specifically to deal with industrial relations.

Both professional bodies have many local branches, and active membership of the local branch can be helpful to the practitioner both from the point of view of the industrial folklore he can acquire through meeting other people with similar problems, and from the branch activities themselves.

A slightly different body is the Industrial Society, which produces some of the best practical guides on techniques that are available in the country, as well as running conferences.

Information from employers' associations and trade unions

The next group of sources to consider are the employers' groupings and trade unions, although trade unions may at first seem an odd source of information for managers.

Employers' associations

The manager whose organisation is a member of an employers' association will readily obtain information from its officials. A telephone call or letter should produce advice on the interpretation of government legislation or policy. Equally it could produce guidance on the interpretation of the national agreement for the industry, and it is in this area that the employers' association will speak with unique authority, as the association will have negotiated the agreement. Unlike most bodies to whom the manager might turn, the official of the employers' association is under an obligation to give *advice* as well as information, if a member seeks it.

Such advice could well extend to suggesting how a dispute should be handled, and the official may be involved in coming to the plant and helping the local managers decide what to do and how to do it. Depending on the size and organisation of the association, they may be able to supply information on prevailing rates of pay in the locality, as they will probably elicit such information from their members from time to time, and will be willing to pass the results of their enquiries on to individual members providing that company identities are not revealed.

The association will disseminate information on certain developments as a matter of course, so that member companies are kept up-to-date on progress in the negotiation of national agreements, and of issues in procedure.

The Engineering Employers' Federation produce a useful monthly pamphlet that is circulated throughout their membership entitled *EEF News*. This sets out to summarise general developments in industrial relations within the industry, recent legal cases of interest and a series of indicators: wage rates, strikes, prices and unemployment.

The CBI provides a similar publication that may be of value to the practitioner, although the information is essentially more general, due to the wider coverage of the CBI.

Both individual employers' associations and the CBI publish occasional booklets on particular matters they feel to be of use to their members.

Trade unions

Some information is also available to the manager from trade unions on industrial relations matters, either unofficially or officially. Trade unions sometimes publish booklets which may find their way into the hands of managers here and there, and the manager can see the expression of a trade union point of view on an issue.

It may be a heretical statement but some managers try to obtain a copy of their national agreement produced, with interpretation and guidance, by the union, as they find it easier to follow than the version produced by the employers.

Quite recently there has been a new source of trade union information. Partly as a result of a research grant from the Transport and General Workers' Union to Ruskin College, Oxford, a number of wage claims have been submitted to employers supported by a wealth of detailed argument and analysis. Apart from being supplied to the appropriate officials, copies of the claim can be purchased from the Publications Department of the TGWU at very modest prices. Currently there are three such claims available: Ford Motor Company, Local Authority Manual Workers and ICI.

The TUC has a series of publications that are on general sale. Some of these are of general interest only, such as the list of affiliated unions and their membership figures, but there are also some of specific interest and value to managers.

Information from other employers

Thus far this chapter has looked at sources of information that are more or less readily available. Specific information from other employers can be helpful, but has to be rooted out with more initiative. Usually this information is on comparative rates of pay. How can it be obtained?

One way is to ring someone up and ask what you need to know. Most people will readily divulge the information you seek, although there are obvious taboo areas of inquiry, and there may be some reluctance to divulge information if the person at the other end of the telephone feels that he is competing with you for employees.

More systematic information can be collected by sending a detailed questionnaire of all the information that is needed. This is best preceded by an exploratory telephone call or face-to-face conversation, and almost always the person receiving the questionnaire will expect to hear at least as much about the details in the enquirer's firm as he is being asked to provide.

A more elaborate device is to initiate a meeting among several employers in a conurbation to discuss rates being paid in the various companies for specified jobs. One assumes that the information given at these conclaves is accurate, although presumably nobody wants to emerge as the poorest payer, and one wonders whether earnings levels are occasionally presented with some imagination, designed more to impress than to inform.

It is obviously important to know who to approach in the first place, and active membership of the professional institute may help.

Although it might be regarded as time consuming by the busy manager, perhaps the most effective way of gathering useful information from another employer is to go and get it in person. If you want to know how company A operates their ingenious system of consultation or wage payment, it is worth ringing up and asking if you can come along for a few days to watch it in operation; or if you can send someone to watch it in operation. This has advantages over simply reading the company's hand-out material, as you can see with your own eyes and ask all manner of questions that you would never think of unless you were there on the spot to get the feel of the situation.

Such an approach might not succeed. Company A might not wish to waste their time or divulge their secrets to that extent, but many companies—particularly the pace-setters who introduce new ideas—are quite ready to offer such a facility to a genuine enquirer.

Information from the academic world

In the opening of this chapter one of the types of information a manager might be seeking was mentioned as being the results of the latest research. This is eventually available in printed form, unless it is inconclusive or extremely esoteric, but it may not be easy to understand, and the manager will almost certainly not have the time nor the inclination to read through all the appropriate learned journals.

It might be worth making a contact with a member of the academic world, who could let you know when anything that might be interesting appeared in print. With the right academic, this type of service could extend further, so that you could put specific questions to him when particular problems arose: 'What does Programme Evaluation Review Technique mean?'; 'What is our convenor getting at when he talks about Rookes and Barnard?'

This might extend to asking him for recommendations on specific matters: 'How much should a company of our size pay the Personnel Manager?' The important thing is to seek out an academic with whom the management of the organisation can work effectively, and in whom you can have confidence. Such a person may be hard to find and harder to attract. The usual methods of finding the right person include using the o.b. network, seeing who writes readable and sensible books, looking to see the regular performers at management seminars and courses, and asking young members of staff whom they found to be effective lecturers on the courses you have compelled them to take.

If the company is fortunate enough to find itself a potentially useful academic adviser, one way to make use of him is to invite him to lunch and use the time to discuss a problem that is facing the organisation at the time. It plays havoc with the digestion, but can be a practical way of getting people together for an exchange of ideas.

The use of publications

The amount of useful information that is systematically gathered and presented is steadily growing in the industrial relations field.

Government publications

There has already been reference to the agencies of government that produce information valuable to the manager. A monthly publication with up-to-date statistics on earnings levels, employment, stoppages and associated data is *The Employment Gazette*. There is also *The Directory of Employers' Associations, Trade Unions, Joint Organisations*, etc. It will presumably become more important to read *Industrial Court Awards* and *Industrial Tribunals Reports* as the amount of legal precedent steadily builds up. All of these are published by the HMSO.

Information services

There are one or two organisations supplying information of current industrial relations developments, but leading the field are *Incomes Data* and *Industrial Relations Review and Report*. Both are invaluable reading, as they are detailed and thorough in their coverage and present their material in a way which is easy to assimilate quickly. The format of the two publications differs, but they set out to do two things: first to survey the news of recent days on the industrial relations scene; and secondly to set out some of the details of recent settlements. The news sections frequently include articles by major figures. Both publications are available monthly or twice monthly to subscribers only. *Industrial Relations Review and Report* is appreciably the costlier of the two at £40 per annum, but all subscribers are eligible to use the publication's free enquiry service.

Professional journals

The Institute of Personnel Management has a monthly magazine, *Personnel Management* that frequently includes items on industrial relations. The Institute has recently launched a new quarterly journal, *Personnel Review* which is a more heavyweight publication, concerned more with reporting on the progress of research and associated matters than on day-to-day practice.

The British Institute of Management publishes *Management Today* monthly and the Institute of Directors have a monthly journal, *The Director*. Both have occasional articles of interest to the industrial relations practitioner, and they—like the IPM publications—are available on subscription to non-members of the particular institute.

BIM also publish *Management Abstracts* for members, which is a series of digests and reviews of books and articles which have appeared on management topics, as well as an account of current management research.

There are many other professional bodies that publish magazines or journals with occasional articles of industrial relations interest. Again mention should be made of the Industrial Society and their monthly publication, *Industrial Society*.

Learned journals

The leading British learned journal is the *British Journal of Industrial Relations*. A recent addition, not to be confused with it, is *Industrial Relations Journal*. Occasional articles of use are to be found in *Occupational Psychology*. Under this general heading it is worth mentioning *Index to Theses Accepted for Higher Degrees in the Universities of Great Britain and Ireland* as a means of finding out the areas under research still to be published. It does not include research being done other than for a higher degree, but it is nevertheless a substantial proportion of the whole. Some of the bodies undertaking research publish their own lists of work underway, the main institution in the United Kingdom being the University of Warwick.

Earnings surveys

Government statistics, provided mainly through the *Employment Gazette*, cover many needs of the industrial relations practitioner, but there are various other surveys that can be useful, mainly in the salary-earning field, where government information may not be analysed in the way the manager needs.

Associated Industrial Consultants produce an annual survey of executive salaries under various functional headings, comparing firms of different sizes according to both turnover and the number of people employed. Mainly this deals with personnel beyond the range of collective bargaining, but it can provide certain useful yardsticks for interfirm comparison.

Cornmarket produce a quarterly survey of the earnings levels among qualified men, classified according to the discipline in which they took their qualification. One of the most comprehensive salary surveys to be had is *Clerical Salaries Analysis*, published by the Institute of Office Management.

Part Two

THE COMPANY FRAMEWORK

8

Management Responsibility

L F Neal

Chairman of the Commission on Industrial Relations

As long as man has been in paid employment there have been industrial relations problems. They arise, inevitably, from the conflict of interest between the employer and the employee, as each endeavours to maximise income. Employee discontent, of which direct pressure to increase pay is only one manifestation, is inherent in our social and economic system and is at the same time a main agent in modifying the system. It has been the causal factor of such legislation as the nineteenth-century Factory Acts and present-day equivalents and an important consideration in social security legislation. It was, and remains, the main driving force of the trade union movement.

Balance of bargaining power

The present prominence of industrial relations problems and their significance to the well-being of individual enterprises and the national economy is a twentieth-century phenomenon which has particularly developed in post-war years. It stems from a marked shift in the balance of industrial bargaining power in favour of the employee and against the employer. The shift in bargaining power has been caused by many factors working in combination.

E

They include:

1   The expansion and increasing power of organised labour. Membership of trade unions has increased from 2 million to 10 million since 1900. In the same period the number of unions has halved, indicating a growing concentration of power. Many agreements made by trade unions control the pay and working conditions of non-members, as well as members, so augmenting the sphere of Trade Union influence. In this situation overt industrial relations are mainly conducted by the employer not with the individual employee (who still has in general only a limited bargaining power) but with his representatives. Within the trade union movement itself there has been a further shift of power to workplace or shop floor representatives and away from the permanent trade union officials; in the process many existing industry-wide bargaining procedures have been undermined or set aside.

2   The growth in size of the individual firm or organisation through expansion and amalgamation. Technological progress and the economics of large-scale production have acted as catalysts in this process. Given the existence of organised labour this means that industrial discontent can spread rapidly amongst a large internal labour force and have widespread repercussions on the other organisations because of the interdependence of production processes. To these tensions has been added the fact that the communication process has lengthened and become more complex.

3   Technical progress has often been accompanied by job fragmentation which tends to reduce work satisfaction and foster discontent. Successful operation of production lines is dependent on co-operation of many individuals and small groups of key workers are able to create major dislocation if they so choose. The pursuit of efficiency through extreme forms of work specialisation has led to a de-humanising of work itself and is rapidly becoming counter-productive.

4   The influence of improved educational standards in the community as a whole. The growth of further education and the impact of the mass media have made the employee increasingly aware of the shortcomings of his working environment; of alternative job opportunities and of his bargaining strength. Our industrial society has, in consequence, become more questioning and challenging. A new social, economic and political awareness has brought the old institutions of

control and authority into positions where respect and acceptance is by no means automatic.

5 The effect of a lengthy period with low rates of unemployment together with greatly improved social security benefits has been to lessen the importance of poverty as a deterrent to industrial action; the workforce has been able to assert its economic freedom without fear of the consequences.

This is not the place to argue whether the shift in power has been for good or ill or whether it has been hastened by action or inaction on the part of employers. It is an accomplished fact and points to a need to re-think the whole approach to industrial relations.

Recognition of this developing situation led to the setting up of the Donovan Commission on Trade Unions and Employers' Associations. Their report[1] was critical of employers' associations and of managements for failing to adjust bargaining procedures to meet changing requirements, and also of the general absence of positive employment policies. This is not a sphere of activity which it would be practicable or desirable to govern by statute, but the Industrial Relations Act 1971, Sections 1(1) and 2(2), leaves no doubt as to where future responsibility lies:

'1(1)   The provisions of this Act shall have effect for the purpose of promoting good industrial relations . . .'

and, with regard to the draft code of practice which he was required to produce

'2(2)   . . . the Secretary of State shall have regard to—
   (*a*) the need for those who manage undertakings to accept the primary responsibility for the promotion of good industrial relations, . . .'

The onus is clearly with employers and their associations to take the initiative.

Responsibility for industrial relations

In general terms management is responsible for industrial relations, but this raises the problems of deciding how the responsibility should be allocated within the organisation and how the work involved should be approached.

Industrial relations is an integral element in business management, not something set apart. Satisfactory industrial relations is a prerequisite of efficient management and neither legislation nor any amount of patching by personnel experts will help solve industrial relations problems which will arise from bad management. Employees can only appreciate whether management is efficient if they know what managers are doing. This emphasises the need for good communication and consultation, a point touched on at some length in the Code of Practice, which is made infinitely more difficult by the growth of large/scale organisations.

Industrial Relations Policy

Policies and objectives for industrial relations (forming part of a total personnel policy), should be laid down by the Company Board or top management group. They should also define the responsibility for implementing the policies and monitor performance. The industrial relations policies and objectives must be consistent with commercial and investment policies and should be designed to foster 'good' industrial relations.

Industrial relations policies should cover four main aspects:

1   The basis of the relationship with employees including the attitude towards trade unionism
2   Systems for deciding wages and salaries
3   Principles of employment—recruitment, training, promotion and redundancy
4   Principles of procedural arrangements

Policy can be expressed in general terms but detailed and specific procedures are needed, within the policy framework, for:

1   Consultation arrangements and communication
2   Negotiating arrangements
3   Arrangements for review of salaries (or wages) not subject to negotiation
4   Disciplinary procedures
5   Grievance procedures

6 Dismissal procedures
7 Method of notifying terms of contracts of employment

All of these will need to be ironed out and agreed in discussion with trade union representatives where unions are recognised. Additionally, the arrangements for recognition of shop stewards and facilities provided for them need to be defined.

Procedures

The procedures, when agreed, should be made known to all affected by them, both management and employees. All levels of management who have a major responsibility for collective bargaining should be adequately instructed and trained in industrial relations matters. The procedures will only gain respect if they are applied objectively and consistently; senior management should take steps to ensure that this is done. The supervisor, as the representative of management with whom employees have most contact, plays a vital role in industrial relations, and the Code of Practice stresses the importance of careful selection and adequate training of supervisors.

Rule-making

These proposals may appear to be obvious, but experience suggests that they are not quite so obvious and widespread throughout industry. The principle of *joint regulation* that lies behind this argument relies on the theory that two sets of unilateral, but independent, approaches to rule-determination is the very heart of our new socio-industrial problem. Since the industrial revolution, employers and, latterly, managers have claimed as a management prerogative the right to make the rules themselves. The growth of trade unions has largely occurred for the purpose of eroding this right of management to make, unilaterally, the rules of work. The consequence of this has been the production of two or more sets of rules about the same activity which all miss out on the grounds of:

1 Appropriateness to the situation they are designed for
2 Self enforcement

Joint rule-making must, at the very least, have a better chance of giving effect to these two principles.

Allocation of responsibility for industrial relations

The industrial relations task facing management is a major issue, but there is also the related question of who within the organisation, or industry, should be allocated the responsibility for industrial relations.

In the archetypal small business of the early industrial age this would have presented no difficulty. The all-purpose management would have taken in the task along with other facets of their work: but in practice the need did not arise because of the direct relationship which existed between employer and employee and the fact that organised labour as known today did not exist.

Effect of trade union development

As industrial units grew rather larger in size and trade unions gradually developed, the first reaction of employers was to form associations of businesses engaged in particular industries or trades to regulate, amongst other things, the rates of pay and hours of work of employees by presenting a common front. The trade unions marshalled their forces similarly so that industry-wide negotiations could take place. This principle of fixing the rates at the same levels for the same types of work irrespective of the locality was accepted with equal force by both sides of industry.

Absolved from direct responsibility for negotiation with their employees—at least over basic rates of pay—many employers gave much less attention to industrial relations matters than would have been necessary had they acted in an individual capacity. The growth in size of industrial units itself tended to make for increasingly impersonal relations between employers and their workforce and also made necessary a subdivision of the management functions and the creation of complex administrative organisations.

Negotiations and agreements

It was in this atmosphere that the personnel specialist emerged from embryo along with many other specialists. Initially, the purpose of the personnel specialist was to look after factory welfare and to tidy up the local problems left over from the application of industry-wide agreements made by the employers' associations. In some businesses personnel people have continued to play this confined role; looking after staff records, selection, training, welfare and so forth. In other

hey have come to be regarded as professional negotiators and con-
ductors of consultation with trade unions and are largely left with
these tasks in isolation from the mainstream of management action.
Employers have clung to the principle of industry-wide negotiations
beyond the time when this was appropriate. The reality of the current
bargaining situation is that in many industries the balance of power
has changed in favour of shop floor representatives who have succeeded
in undermining the system by securing local agreements for supple-
ments or bonus payments additional to the rates of pay agreed for the
whole industry. In this they have been aided by the pressure created
by full employment. Many companies have not re-deployed their
managerial resources in order to meet this changed circumstance, and
those which have did so more as a rearguard action than as a positive
approach to industrial relations.

This state of affairs is illustrated by the following extract from the
Donovan Report[1]—

Para. 84:

'Most companies do not have comprehensive and well-
ordered agreements for regulating the employment of
labour within their factories over and above the minimum
conditions laid down in industry-wide agreements. Generally speaking only non-federated concerns negotiate
with the unions as companies. Federated companies generally leave negotiations to their factory managers, but
comprehensive factory agreements are as rare as comprehensive company agreements. Factory managers may
enter into written settlements on some issues to supplement industry-wide agreements, but on other matters
there will be oral undertakings and on still others each
workshop will have its own practices.'

Paras. 94–95:

'If companies have their own personnel specialists, why
have they not introduced effective personnel policies to
control methods of negotiation and pay structures within
their firms? Many firms have no such policy, and perhaps
no conception of it. . . . Even if a personnel manager has
the ability to devise an effective personnel policy, the
director responsible for personnel (if there is one), or the

board as a whole, may not want to listen to him. Many firms had acquired disorderly pay structures and unco-ordinated personnel practices before they appoint a personnel manager, and the burden of dealing with dis-putes and problems as they arise has absorbed his whole time and energy.'

Donovan recognised that there were exceptions; companies which had taken positive steps, often in association with productivity agreements to introduce rationalised pay structures and an improved approach to industrial relations problems. Special mention was made of Esso Mobil and Alcan. Since the report was published many other organisa tions have followed suit; they were encouraged to do so by the Prices and Incomes policy pursued by the Government during 1966–9 and by the views expressed by the National Board for Prices and Incomes

Positive approach to industrial relations

Even if the employers' associations continue to agree industry-wide conditions which govern such matters as minimum rates of pay, work ing hours and holidays—and there are many instances where this can be advantageous to both sides of industry—there is still a need for organisations to adopt a positive approach to industrial relations. In most organisations it is only at company or plant level that a real link between pay and productivity can be successfully established. Develop ment along these lines requires a great deal of managerial effort and employee co-operation, and it can only be successful if it is part of an overall policy of good industrial relations.

In the larger public service organisations and in the nationalised industries there is an equal need for a positive approach to industrial relations on the part of management, partly for the practical reason that they compete in the same labour market, but also because their efficiency cannot be achieved by any means which relies on the ex ploitation of labour; the public sector cannot afford to be left behind as an employer.

Line or staff

The need for management to give effective attention to industrial relations is clearly established. To recapitulate points already made:

1 Management is responsible for industrial relations
2 Management should take the initiative towards improving industrial relations
3 Industrial relations policies should be an integral part of overall business policy
4 Individual organisations need to allocate adequate managerial effort to industrial relations even if they are members of associations which conduct industry-wide negotiations on their behalf

Against this background, mention has been made of the growth of specialist personnel management.

Personnel specialists

There can be little doubt that personnel specialists are necessary especially in sizeable companies/organisations. Quite apart from the increasing complexity of collective agreements there is a need for an expert approach to such matters as recruitment, selection and training, management development and manpower planning. It is significant that the Code of Practice, although keyed to the Industrial Relations Act, mentions all of these other aspects of personnel management. This suggests that industrial relations must be seen in the round and not in the narrow sense of cross-table bargaining only.

Personnel specialists are needed but problems surround their status and function within the organisation, and the question of whether they should take ultimate responsibility for decisions on personnel matters. In the 1930s Lloyd Roberts of ICI was already promoting the philosophy that every firm should have an industrial relations policy approved by the board which should govern the work of personnel or labour managers. This same line of thought is reflected in the Code of Practice; the Code indicates that the policy should be agreed at the top but begs the question of who should draw up the details of the policy and who should make the consequent decisions in the process of implementing the policy.

Industrial relations policy

In some organisations there is a Director or Board Member with special knowledge of and responsibility for industrial relations and other personnel matters. He is able to influence and advise the Board or top management group both in the process of framing policy and setting objectives within the industrial relations field. He is also abl to ensure that possible industrial relations repercussions are taken int account in making other business decisions.

The work involved in drawing up the details of industrial relation policies and procedures falls properly to the *staff* personnel group. It i vital, however, that in the process of development there is full con sultation with line management and others within the managemen team, and with trade unions where they are party to the procedures The result is the joint product and responsibility of line and sta management, an essential prerequisite if the agreement is to hol respect throughout the organisation. These comments apply to what ever levels are appropriate for policy setting. In some organisation this will be at 'national' level, in others it may be that Group, Compan or Factory policies are required; alternatively, subsidiary Company o Factory policies may conform to general frameworks set at a highe level of management.

It is in putting flesh on the policy skeleton that problems of respon sibility really begin to arise. Most organisations clearly define personne specialists as *staff*, with no responsibilities only for the work of thei immediate specialist group. Decisions on personnel matters are th responsibility of *line* management, who are in the direct chain o command from supervisor to board, on the grounds that line manager and supervisors are dealing with employees all the time and they shoul be seen to be the effective management in industrial relations as i other matters. These decisions should of course be taken within th personnel policy and with expert advice from the personnel specialis who should be available at each line management level.

Whatever the organisational chart may depict, the realities of th situation are usually less clear cut. In practice, line managers are onl too willing to pass their personnel responsibilities, particularly fo industrial relations, to the personnel specialists. In the process the have in many cases avoided taking on a vital element of their prop role in leadership. Flanders[2] expressed the following criticism of th common situation:

> '. . . confusion over the role of personnel management can produce a compromise that gets the worst of all worlds. In major areas of labour relations policy—such as employ-

ment, negotiations, communications and training—line management may shed all the details of administration, while retaining ultimate authority and an illusion of responsibility.'

This is particularly true within the field of negotiations with trade unions. Line managers in many cases lack intimate knowledge of complex agreements and established customs and are eager to leave the job to personnel specialists who in turn grasp the opportunity to extend their authority. There are those who see this to be desirable, arguing that the personnel specialist is equipped for the task and that he should be seen to be involved in difficult and, at times, unpopular decisions; to be more than a smoother of troubled waters and solver of personal problems.

This situation conflicts with the principle of involving management as a whole in its total responsibilities. If line management is to have precise obligations concerning costs and profits then it cannot opt out of its involvement with labour—employment, pay and performance. If, on the other hand, the personnel specialist confines himself to a purely *staff* role there is the danger that he will only be called in by line management when crises arise, to help prevent a fire which already exists.

The right approach probably lies between the two. It is for the personnel specialist to play the staff role but to be available for the line manager to include him as a participant in decision making. His job is then to interpret personnel policy and suggest approaches to problems which are anticipated. There will be occasions, particularly at the higher levels in very large organisations, where it is necessary for personnel specialists to take on the mantle of general or line management, particularly in leading discussions with trade union officials of similar status. When this is necessary there should still be agreement with line management on the course to be pursued, and the outcome of meetings should be reported back. At no time should industrial relations be allowed to run as an independent and self-perpetuating business.

The evolution of industrial organisation and changes within the economy and social fabric have all tended to increase the importance of labour to the extent where it is vital that management should treat it as an equal with other elements in total business policy. Management must take primary responsibility for the promotion of good industrial relations; this is now endorsed in the Industrial Relations Act 1971 and the Code of Practice. Industrial relations should be seen as part of a wider personnel policy covering all aspects of employment. The growth in size of businesses has led to the emergence of personnel specialists who can do much to further a positive approach to industrial relations. Director responsibility for industrial relations should rest with line management, but they can be greatly assisted in carrying out this responsibility by effective personnel specialists who should be involved in and be a party to industrial relations decisions.

References

1 *Royal Commission on Trade Unions and Employers' Associations* 1965–68, report, Cmnd 3623, HMSO
2 *The Fawley Productivity Agreements*, p 254, by A FLANDERS, Faber and Faber, 1964

9

Plant Agreements

D P Torrington

Senior Lecturer in Industrial Relations, Manchester Polytechnic

Plant agreements have been with us for some time, but only since the 1960s have they been widely known, and usually in a fairly crude form. During the currency of the prices and incomes policy of the Labour Government from 1965 onwards, there was a rash of plant agreements, usually referred to as productivity bargains. This was an attempt to break the cycle of straight wage-bargaining that had developed with its emphasis of initiative from the unions and grim resistance from the employers for as long as possible. Instead, managements seized the initiative and offered bigger-than-usual wage increases in exchange for more economic ways of working.

With the incomes policy biting hard, both managements and some unions preferred the productivity bargaining approach with the result that wage-bargaining was supplanted in some areas by wage-work bargaining. In many cases the opportunity was used to go beyond the straight trading of more money for more efficient working. A number of managements took the opportunity to rationalise the whole area of management/employee relations by negotiating a regular, well-thought-out treaty with extensive coverage; putting working relationships on a more satisfactory basis.

The productivity bargaining concept was welcomed by the National

Board for Prices and Incomes, which encouraged unions and managements to think in terms of this concept for conducting their affairs and stemming inflation at the same time. Even more weighty endorsement was to come with the publication of the Donovan proposals which suggested that factory-wide agreements could provide the remedy for many of the defects of the British system of industrial relations, viz:

> 'Factory agreements (with company agreements as an alternative in multi-plant companies) can regulate actual pay, constitute a factory negotiating committee and grievance procedures which suit the circumstances, deal with such subjects as redundancy and discipline and cover the rights and obligations of shop stewards. A factory agreement can assist competent managers, many current industry-wide agreements have become a hindrance to them' (Royal Commission on Trades Unions and Employers' Associations Report, para. 1020)

Although the Donovan Report describes a full-scale factory agreement, it was the productivity strings that appealed to management and most managements saw themselves buying labour-cost effectiveness, rather than clearing the decks for a fresh start.

By the end of 1970 the popularity of productivity agreements was beginning to wane, principally because the effect of inflation was bringing wage increases of 10 per cent and more without any productivity conditions. Also, there was a chastening experience in the application of Devlin recommendations in the docks, which sometimes caused efficiency to get worse rather than better: productivity became a dirty word. The 1971 Act gives a central place to plant agreements in the legislation on collective bargaining. The productivity emphasis has been dropped to be replaced by thinking along the Donovan lines.

In this chapter we shall consider plant agreements under four headings:

1 Agreement strategy
2 Procedural content
3 Substantive content
4 Other contents

It is assumed that readers will be familiar with the section of the Code of Practice on Collective Bargaining, particularly paragraphs 71 to 98.

Agreement strategy

If we start at the point where there is an agreement on what the bargaining unit is and who the bargaining agent is; how does the management approach the setting up of a plant agreement?

Selling the idea

The first step is for the appropriate management official with responsibility for industrial relations to sell the idea of a plant agreement. He has to sell it to his board and to his managerial colleagues—all of them—and then he has to get concurrence from the bargaining agent.

The appropriate management official will usually be the personnel manager, as he will have the industrial relations responsibility in the management team. In selling to his board the validity of the idea he will have a useful instrument of persuasion behind him in the Code (paragraph 2):

> One of management's major objectives should . . . be to develop effective industrial relations policies which command the confidence of employees

The board may agree with this in principle but he will probably find it harder to persuade his Board to be enthusiastic about a plant agreement as this inevitably reduces the notional freedom of action of the management. Much has been said and written about the reluctance of trade union officials to get involved in legally binding agreements and long-term commitments. Many company directors are equally reluctant to commit themselves to this type of obligation. If there is an agreement, the terms of that agreement have to be met even if the market does suddenly turn sour or a key supplier becomes bankrupt. The line of argument used to persuade the board and senior members of management must be that a sound agreement will improve industrial relations in the plant and create a more constructive working environment. This, in turn, will lead to greater profitability and predictability of operations.

Other members of management may readily accept the idea of an agreement, as they may think in terms of a panacea for all their managerial problems. They need to understand, however, before negotiations begin, that an agreement can come only as a result of bargaining, which is an open-ended process. The personnel manager cannot guarantee in advance the contents of the agreement that will be negotiated. There are two parties to the bargain and both parties are seeking different objectives. The personnel manager will not be imposing terms; he will be negotiating an agreement on behalf of the management with an autonomous agent of the employees.

The difficulties involved in negotiating with the bargaining agent and the employees will vary according to the unions that are concerned and according to the industrial relations history of the plant. Normally, the agent will willingly open negotiations with the management on an agreement. The personnel manager may need to make clear his position at the very outset of negotiations on whether or not he sees the eventual agreement as being legally binding; this may inhibit the bargaining agent from even coming to talk.

It is principally the responsibility of the bargaining agent to communicate and consult with his members on the implications of a plant agreement and its progress. Management normally assists in this job of communication by allowing use to be made of the house magazine, notice boards, letters to members of the bargaining unit, arrangements for meetings of employees and so forth. The personnel manager and his colleagues can help the bargaining agent and stewards in the task of communication and consultation but he must avoid two dangers. These are

1 *He must not abrogate their responsibility.* If it appears that the personnel manager is trying to get at the lads behind the backs of the stewards he is heading for trouble. If an item of his appears in the house magazine there should also be an item written by the convenor or chief shop steward, to give it credence. Letters to union members about proposals should be from the stewards.

2 *He must beware of raising false expectations.* Few things are as intriguing as novelty and nothing spreads faster than rumour, and the most elaborate rumours can develop on the basis of what has not been said. The biggest danger is in cash expectation. Employees will automatically smell money in the deal. If the object of the agreement is

merely to regularise working relationships (arrangements about wage increases being made separately) this needs to be spelled out clearly and early. If there is to be a 'biting on' or a 'greasing in', then the likely value of this can be established in the early stages. Negotiations can break down or get needlessly bitter because employee expectation has outstripped any possible management offer. The longer the management delays making its first cash offer the more highly exaggerated will be the amount, by speculation in the canteen and by individual flights of fancy.

Agreement programme

Negotiating an agreement is hard work which requires painstaking application and patience. It is easy for negotiations to be in the doldrums after an initial strong puff of wind of enthusiasm. Once in the doldrums it is difficult to start moving again and there is a danger at this stage that the attempt at reaching a plant agreement has to be abandoned because the whole operation is in disfavour. This will worsen the industrial relations climate within the plant (and will speed the departure of the personnel manager to join the ranks of the unemployed). To avoid the doldrums, a programme can be agreed which includes target dates for the completion of the different activities that are necessary to make up the total agreement package. All those working on the agreement can then work within these deadlines to get the work done.

Critical path programming can be used but may be thought to be too sophisticated by some people and shop stewards might regard it as an attempt to baffle them with management guile. A simple, and quite adequate, method of programming is to prepare a table showing the breakdown of all the different jobs to be done with the target completion dates and the names of the individual people responsible. An example of part of such a programme is in Figure 9:1. The programme sets out a timetable to be followed, and followed it should be, even if it means persisting with an especially difficult set of negotiations until late in the evening. If there is pattern established whereby deadlines are met they will continue to be met. Once that pattern breaks down it is very difficult to re-establish it. At the same time there will inevitably be occasions of force majeure which cause unavoidable delay. In these cases the programme will need to be modified by reducing the time allowed for a subsidiary part of the work so that the final target date is not missed.

WEEK NO.	ENDING	ACTIVITY		RESPONSIBLE
Ten	8th Oct	14	Job Evaluation Phase I begins	Smith
		15	Phase I of Agreement Negotiation	Jones
Eleven	15th Oct	10	Work Study Phase I complete	Robinson
		16	Progress Report to Management and Works Council	Smith
Twelve	22nd Oct	17	First draft of Plant Agreement	Jones
		18	Work Study Phase II begins	Robinson
		19	General Information Session for employees	Smith, Jackson
		20	Newsletter on progress compiled and distributed	Smith, Jackson
Thirteen	29th Oct	14	Job Evaluation Phase I complete	Smith
		15	Phase I of Agreement Negotiation complete	Jones
		216	General Review of Progress and Up-dating of Programme	Smith, Jackson
Fourteen	5th Nov	22	Job Evaluation Phase II begins	Smith
		23	Second draft of Plant Agreement	Jones
		24	Progress Meeting with T.U. full-time officials	Jones, Jackson

Figure 9:1 Plant agreement programme

The preparers of the programme must guard against the danger of setting dates that establish expectations that have to be changed because of delays.

Status of the agreement

There are basic questions that must be considered before the agreement can be negotiated. How important is the agreement which is being negotiated? Is the firm opting out of a national agreement? Is it to cover all aspects of working practice in the plant or is it subordinate to an industry-wide national agreement? Is it to be legally binding? Does the bargaining agent intend it to be legally binding?

The Code of Practice makes some suggestions about the relationship of a plant agreement to a national agreement for the industry (paragrap 94):

There is advantage in agreeing at industry level as much as is suitable for adoption over the industry as a whole; including:

1 Terms and conditions of employment suitable for general application;

2 General guidelines for negotiating at a lower level matters which cannot be decided satisfactorily at industry level;

3 A procedure for settling disputes, either for the industry as a whole or as a model for individual undertakings to adopt by agreement.

The actual practice will vary from industry to industry and will develop in the future. There seems to have been a significant shift away from total dependence on industry-wide bargains in recent years and there is no set pattern at the time of writing.

Some managements have already opted out completely from their appropriate employers' association and national agreement. Others have partly opted out. Others have never opted in but still follow the general guidelines of national level bargaining. In most cases, there is a mixture of both with national agreements being the basis for determining the length of the standard working week, the number of days annual holiday, the number of days of statutory holiday, the standards for shift working and overtime working, and a procedure for settling disputes when they are taken outside the plant. In addition there may still be regular gladiatorial combats at national level to determine cost-of-living increases that will apply to all employees within member firms. The scope for the plant agreement will be to agree on all the details of working relationships that apply to that particular plant only; working practices, methods of payment and incentives, work measurement, job evaluation, holiday periods (as opposed to the number of days), and so on.

The legally binding aspect of agreements is one on which the Act is quite clear. Unless the parties include an escape clause every agreement made in writing shall be 'conclusively presumed' to be intended to be a legally enforceable contract. Leaving the question of legal enforceability on one side, the following section might be a useful sample:

> 'This agreement covers those members of the Unions employed at the . . . site of the Company, and cancels all previous agreements between the parties applying to those employees, other than those negotiated between the two national bodies of which the parties are members (Confederation of Shipbuilding and Engineering Unions, and Engineering Employers' Federation). The parties will also be bound by future agreements between those two bodies, made during the currency of this agreement'

Negotiation of the agreement

The negotiating team for the management needs to be chosen with some care. Normally, the personnel manager will lead the negotiations. He is the industrial relations professional with knowledge of the existing agreement, industrial relations legislation, negotiating expertise and behavioural science. Also, he is the company executive with the overall responsibility for industrial relations and personnel matters within the organisation. In many undertakings the lead in negotiation is taken by a line executive on the basis that as he is responsible for production, or another function, he must lead negotiations which affect his operating performance. The drawback with this arrangement is that—unless he is the managing director or general manager—he will be responsible for only a part of the business. Negotiations with one group of the employees will always have repercussions among other groups and the personnel manager is in a position to judge the likely side-effects and try to keep all sectors in balance.

There will obviously need to be line executives present and taking a major part in the decision-making because they will have to live with and work within the parameters determined by the negotiations. For this we need line executives present who are people with authority and responsibility, so that the management's negotiators are not seen as people who merely carry messages.

An official who seldom takes part in negotiations, but who perhaps will be needed in the future, is the company secretary. This is because industrial relations now come within a more precise legal framework. The wording of agreements and the consideration of legal obligations is a necessary field for the company secretary, even though he may be bewildered by the specialised way in which such bargaining is carried out.

A final thought about the negotiating team is to ask whether first-line supervision should be represented. As a general practice they are not represented partly because there is usually not room for them because so many line managers claim a place, and partly because negotiations cover a wider field of activities than that of any individual supervisor. Nevertheless, the first-line supervisor should not be by-passed. If a representative of the supervisors can be included in negotiations, there is advantage to be gained from his particular point of view and expertise, as well as partly avoiding the by-passing charge.

The agreement needs to grow, section by section, rather than be modified piecemeal. It is not a parliamentary bill which is presented in its entirety with subsequent detailed argument and debate about the different clauses, until an adequate compromise document is produced. In industrial terms that is a consultative rather than a bargaining process.

In collective bargaining to produce a plant agreement, it is necessary to start with a rough framework of the topics to be discussed. This will usually be a brief set of headings worked out by the management with one or two additions from the stewards of other topics they wish to include. Thereafter, the agreement is built up section by section with detailed discussion of what is to go in each, and tentative agreement being reached that the section contents are right before going on to the next section. This method helps people to follow and to absorb the substance more easily than being confronted with a complete document at the beginning. Also, it allows more effective development of material to be included from both sides without one side constantly being in the position of making suggestions while the other side is constantly finding fault. At the end of each stage the agreement is *tentative* and does not bind anyone at all. Later difficulties may cause one side or the other to wish to withdraw their earlier tentative agreement. Nothing is finally settled until both parties give assent to the completed document. Before that stage, there are a series of working agreements for the sake of making progress.

There is no need for the sections to be negotiated consecutively, and both sides will doubtless favour an arrangement whereby some of the easier bits are dealt with first no matter where their place will be in the final version. If some easy material comes first it enables both parties to have some practice in negotiating. Also, it helps to establish an atmosphere of agreement and mutual understanding before they reach the really tough sections, where agreement will be very difficult to reach.

Although it is suggested that the agreement is built up in stages, the stages should be logical and thoughtfully worked out so that topics are grouped sensibly together, despite their potential difficulty in negotiation. For example, a company might find it harder to get agreement on arrangements for the annual holiday than it does to get agreement about the exact days on which statutory holidays are to be taken. In this situation it would be pointless to deal with statutory holidays early and annual holidays late as they are subjects to be taken in conjunction.

Sometimes the wording of a clause in an agreement can cause greater difficulty than the settlement the wording is attempting to convey. If a particular sentence or paragraph is offensive to one party, it should be withdrawn and re-worded. The company secretary always checks the wording to make sure that it is appropriate.

Feedback

The personnel manager needs constantly to check the available feedback on how things are going. The management negotiators need to know what the reaction to their proposals are, not only from the bargaining agent negotiators, but also from the rank-and-file members themselves. These are the people who ultimately have to accept the agreement and make it work. The personnel manager and his colleagues have to reassure themselves that the right understanding is being generated.

To get the right feedback there is no substitute for walking round the plant, talking to people, listening to what they have to say and endeavouring to judge the feeling and reaction. This is a fundamental part of personnel practice and at a time of negotiating an agreement of great potential significance, it is important to do it constantly.

Occasionally, an aspect of what is under negotiation will be either misunderstood at the bargaining table or misunderstood in the re-telling. A single thoughtless remark by a management negotiator can be misinterpreted and start to develop inaccurate expectations that can spread rapidly around the plant. There can even be difficulties with language. On one occasion a management negotiator used the phrase 'That will be for the benefit of *the personnel*'. He meant that it would be for the benefit of the employees but his listeners understood him to mean 'Personnel Department'.

In walking round the plant information can be obtained on how understanding is developing and immediate action can be taken to correct any real and serious misunderstanding before it becomes an *idée fixe* in the minds of employees.

Procedural content

The parts of the agreement that deal with matters of procedure seek to regulate the procedures which the two parties to the agreement will use to settle differences between themselves and to interpret and apply the substance of the agreement. Paragraph 91 of the Code of Practice is helpful here.

Recognition of trade unions and shop stewards

A trade union is recognised when the management agrees to bargain with it in relation to the working conditions of a particular group of employees. In the 1971 legislation the process and conditions of recognition are considered in detail and a formal procedure is intro-duced to deal with situations where there is disagreement between management and unions on the question of recognition. For negotia-tions, the terms 'bargaining unit' and 'bargaining agent' should be used.

The Code of Practice has several sections dealing with shop stewards and the CIR have produced a report on the position of stewards in the collective bargaining process.

It is normal for agreements to open with a clause stating which unions are recognised to bargain on behalf of the particular group of employees covered by the agreement. Preferably, this clause should also include a statement of willingness to bargain and an acceptance that this will benefit both the management and the employees.

The agreement normally specifies the number of stewards who are to represent the bargaining unit, together with a note on the sections of the unit they will represent and the means whereby they are appointed. Appointments will presumably be by election, and on their election most unions will issue to the management a formal letter of credentials for the stewards. The letter will confirm that they have been elected to this position and will ask for management to provide him with the appropriate facilities. It is less common, but desirable, for the management also to accredit the steward thereby formally acknowledging his position.

With large bargaining units there will be senior stewards or convenors who will have slightly different responsibilities from the bulk of stewards. These differences can be included in their credentials and in the agreement.

Constitution and scope of joint negotiating bodies

Having established who will be recognised and how the recognised bargaining agent will be represented the agreement sets down how the negotiating bodies will be constituted.

Negotiating bodies are set up as means of resolving the inevitable conflicts of interest, that will or do exist in any organisation, between employees and management. The priority interest for management will be efficiency, output and profitability, and they will also be interested in working conditions, job satisfaction and so forth. The priority interest for employees will be the level of remuneration, the length of the working week, the degree of job satisfaction and the nature of the working environment. Employees will also be concerned about the efficiency of the organisation. The priority interests of the two groups are different but both have equal importance. It is important to the employees that the management runs the organisation efficiently and profitably because this will ensure that the organisation continues as a viable unit and that they will be associated with the success of the undertaking. Equally it is important to the management that employees are paid the right amount for working in acceptable conditions at work which they find satisfying. Otherwise, the long-term prospects of the organisation will be adversely affected.

A joint negotiating committee provides the machinery for these differing interests to be resolved. There will be one senior committee, frequently called the Works Committee or Works Council. At this committee, negotiations take place on behalf of all members of the bargaining unit or on behalf of several bargaining units. If there are several bargaining units there will be various subsidiary committees to deal with differences of interest on localised issues. The plant agreement needs to specify the scope of matters to be covered by the main committee and the negotiating scope of the subsidiary committee. Unless this is agreed, and rigorously made to work, there is likely to be a tendency for everything to be referred upwards—this is the same situation as one in which an executive does not delegate and the main committee becomes bogged down in interminable discussions of detail difficulties. These discussions are made more interminable because the people present do not know anything about the situation; supervisors are frustrated, individual stewards are not given a proper chance to do their job, and the effectiveness of the negotiating procedure is undermined.

The agreement also needs to specify the number of representatives on each committee. The danger is size. The optimum number to transact business productively is probably between three and seven. There is, however, a tendency for the numbers to swell, particularly if representation on either side is not effective. If the number does swell it becomes much more difficult to reach sound agreement.

Matters to be bargained about

The section in the agreement which states the matters on which the parties will bargain is usually brief. The previous section has laid down the scope of the negotiations and in this section the substance to be negotiated is agreed. This follows from the agreement mentioned earlier in this chapter on the status of the agreement; what will be negotiated within the plant and what will be left to national industry-wide negotiations.

Agreement term and means of termination

When the substance of the agreement has been negotiated there are two major aspects of those terms to be considered: how long will they last and how can they be re-negotiated if found unsatisfactory in practice.

If the negotiated terms cause higher costs, following increases in rates of payment, shift and overtime premium, holidays and fringe benefits, management will make plans for the future knowing that the increased level of these costs will remain the same for a predictable period. Management will, therefore, want an agreement which stipulates that there will not be further increases in labour cost for a stated period; twelve or more months.

On the other hand both sides to an agreement may be uneasy about making a firm agreement on any matter which has not been proved in practice. This is most common where there is to be a change in working practice as a result of the agreement, such as a reduction in the number of mates or the removal of a protective/restrictive practice. It is not in the interest of either side to get shackled with aspects of an agreement that might not work.

It is, therefore, necessary to have both an agreed term for the agreement to run and an agreed method of re-negotiation. A typical clause might contain the following:

> 'The agreement shall initially operate from the date of signature for a minimum period of twenty-four months. Rates of pay will be reviewed after twelve months.
>
> 'If the Company or the Union wish to vary the terms of this agreement during its currency they shall give two weeks' notice in writing to the other party, specifying the changes wanted. The other party should then give notice of agreement or disagreement within two weeks. Any disagreement should be resolved through the negotiating procedure set out in this agreement. If there is eventually failure to agree, then either party may give one month's notice of a desire to terminate the agreement'

Settling collective disputes and individual grievances

The Code of Practice (paragraph 126) distinguishes between two kinds of dispute:

1 Disputes of right, which relate to the application or interpretation of existing agreements or contracts of employment
2 Disputes of interest, which relate to claims by employees or proposals by management about terms and conditions of employment

It is not only a means for employee representatives to raise claims, it is also machinery to allow management to initiate proposals for change. A suggested system is:

1 Supervisory Level. An issue is raised within a department by the steward on behalf of a group of employees or by the supervisor on behalf of the management. It is raised in the department first as this is the most appropriate level at which it can be settled. If there is no satisfactory settlement after two working days a procedure report is made out on a standard form and signed by the supervisor and the steward. The form specifies the issue and the reason for failure to agree and is sent to the departmental manager, with a copy to the personnel manager.

2 Managerial Level. The departmental manager will try to resolve the matter with the supervisor and the steward. If there is no satisfactory settlement within two working days, a further procedure report is made out and the matter is referred to the plant negotiating committee.

3 Plant Level. When the matter is discussed at the plant negotiating committee it has gone as high as it can for settlement within the confines of the plant. The meeting should be held within five working days of the failure to agree at managerial level. If the matter is still not settled in plant level discussions, either side can register failure to agree.

When these steps have been taken without satisfactory result there are two alternatives available. Either, the matter can be referred to the disputes procedure for the industry that has been agreed between the employers' association and the trade union, or it can be referred to independent conciliation and/or arbitration. Usually this means asking for the assistance of a Department of Employment industrial relations officer to come and attempt conciliation between the two parties. As a safeguard there should be a clause included in the plant agreement which precludes any industrial action by either side before the procedure stages have been formally completed.

Individual grievances will usually follow a similar pattern, with the person suffering the grievance being involved with the representative in the discussions.

Trade union activities in the plant

Trade union representatives need to hold meetings amongst themselves and with their members for communication and consultation. The plant agreement should include the arrangements for such meetings when they are to be held on company premises during working time.

Redundancy, lay-off, discipline and dismissal

Probably the most serious penalty that an employee can suffer in the course of his work is to lose his job or to lose part of his earnings through external factors or disciplinary proceedings. When there is a redundancy situation or short-term lay-offs there is a high emotional temperature and a crisis. It is almost inevitable that there will be argument as there is a clear conflict of interest. Any attempt to resolve that conflict of interest at that time will be jeopardised by the unfavourable industrial relations climate. For this reason it is advisable to plan at a relatively calm time for possible situations before they happen. In this way, procedures can be agreed for handling such matters in a way that is most appropriate for the particular plant.

With discipline and dismissals there is now the possibility of unfair dismissal followed by reinstatement or compensation. This means that the ways in which disciplinary action is to be taken, and by whom, has to be treated with great care by the management. The details of the arrangements need to be included in the plant agreement.

Consultative committees

Distinct from negotiation there is consultation. Negotiation recognises conflict of interests but consultation is discussion of common interests. In consultation, the management is not a party in negotiations, but, instead, is seeking counsel and comment from employees. There may also be consultative committees on which decision-making is fully shared with stewards.

The most common types of consultative committee are:

1   Safety Committee
2   Canteen Committee
3   Suggestions Committee

Each committee deals with matters on a joint basis. The terms of reference of these committees, as well as their constitution and scope, are included in the plant agreement.

A more important consultative committee is the Works Council which is sometimes referred to as the Joint Production and Consultative Committee. This is a body on which the most senior managers and the most senior stewards sit and it has the objective of informing employee representatives of how the company trading position is developing. Management use the experience of stewards to test the wisdom of proposed changes in management policy, systems, etc., and to give stewards an opportunity to comment on any aspect of the company's business. Strict terms of reference are needed with rigorous discipline to ensure that this council does not change into a negotiating body.

Substantive content

The substantive content of an agreement has been described as 'How much, and how much for it'. It is all those matters which determine how much time should be spent working, how much people should earn for their work and what the arrangements about working practices should be. The variation in matters, from plant to plant, is so great that it is difficult to include much that will be of any value to managers. The Code of Practice limits comment on substantive provisions to thirty-three words! Nevertheless, some of the major substantive aspects are covered elsewhere in this book; in the chapters on payment, shift-working, racial integration and the employment of women. A few brief additional comments may be useful here.

Payment

The intricacies of payment are usually left to industry-wide agreements with the plant agreement determining only the actual basic rates of pay (as distinct from the nationally agreed basic rates). Most plants appear to stick firmly to industry-wide agreements on holiday pay, shift premium, overtime rates and the main outline of national agreements on incentive payments. The plant agreement determines the rate and the national agreement determines the application of that rate in the whole gamut of varying working situations.

Hours of work

It is unusual, but not unknown, for individual plant agreements to depart from nationally agreed rates for premium payment. It is even more rare for them to depart from national agreed levels of hours and holidays. The number of hours worked in a standard working week varies very little from one plant to another within each industry and the number of days holiday varies very little. The only major differential is that which obtains in many companies whereby staff employees work less hours than manual employees.

What is open for local negotiation and agreement is the question of when the work will be done, rather than how much of it. Among the many ways in which a forty-hour, five-day week is worked are these:

1	8.00–12.00	13.00–17.00
2	7.30–12.00	13.00–16.30
3	8.00–12.30	13.15–16.45
4	7.45–12.30	13.30–17.00 (16.00 on Fridays)

This also extends to arrangements for shift-working where there are innumerable variations on a nationally agreed theme.

Holidays provide an essential plant bargaining point in most industries. The national agreement specifies the number of days for each year and leaves local negotiations to settle when the days are to be taken. The problems which arise can be quite exasperating, particularly in trying to settle the question of Christmas and New Year where there frequently seems to be a need for an extra day from somewhere.

Working practice

If management is to obtain the maximum benefit from plant agreements it should use such agreements to introduce changes in working practice. This may be the scrapping of time clocks; or the withdrawal of a protective/restrictive practice; or the introduction of job evaluation; or a fresh incentive scheme; or a new manning agreement. Management negotiators should take the opportunity, when initiating or re-negotiating a plant agreement, to do as much re-trimming of the sails for the future as possible. Change is in the minds of people on both sides and a great deal of thought is being given to aspects of working relationships. It is a chance to have a major overhaul and re-fit.

Other contents

Negotiators will concentrate first on procedural and substantive content but there are other matters which may be included.

Fringe benefits

The Code of Practice urges managements to extend or introduce fringe benefits and steadily to eliminate the inequitable differentials in conditions that may exist between white-collar and manual employees. Principally, these are sick-pay and pension schemes. Many plant sick-pay schemes could do with being carefully overhauled as they may not have been looked at since the introduction of earnings-related supplement by the Department of Health and Social Security. As some schemes are out of date, it is now quite common for employees to receive more money when sick than when fit and working.

Check-off

The practice is growing of companies operating a scheme in conjunction with trade unions of deducting trade union subscriptions from wages and making a lump sum repayment of these to the union. This is a great help to the union and some unions will pay the management a fee for doing it.

Information

With the new strictures in the Act and the Code of Practice on the disclosure of information to employees, it may be appropriate to include in the agreement a note on what information is to be given and how.

10

Communications Structure

R G Jeffrey
Management Consultant, North, Paul and Associates Limited

Christine Howarth
Research Officer, North, Paul and Associates Limited

'Speech was given to the ordinary sort of men, whereby to communicate their mind; but to wise men, whereby to conceal it' (Goldsmith).

The jaundice which provoked this view is today still shared by many managers and shop stewards. They remain, however, persistently optimistic that commands will be understood, that consultative procedures will become more effective and less tedious and that negotiations will be increasingly concerned with the positive hopes offered by the future rather than with the misunderstandings of the past. Why is it then, that with such high aspirations and undoubted effort we fall so far short of what we feel we ought to achieve? Many problems in industry today are blithely labelled 'communications problems' but despite the undoubted acceptance that the word 'communications' has achieved in management parlance today does it not conceal, beneath its simplicity, a complexity which is rarely admitted, much less understood?

'Communications' can be quickly and easily defined as the imparting or exchange of information. But to stop here is to deny the complexity

F   141

of a process which is both linguistic and behaviouralistic, and dependent on ambiguous interaction processes between individuals and groups. It is just this complexity and ambiguity that makes the discussion of communications processes and structures so hazardous. Is therefore our competence in the field of communication unequal to the complexities with which we are confronted? Or are there certain fundamentals which need to be considered for effective communication to take place at all?

This chapter considers the different ends served by communications within an organisation and the varying, and at times conflicting needs that require to be satisfied. These needs arise from two sources—those of the organisation and those of the individual. They are at the same time both interdependent and different, possibly even to the point of conflict. As the requirements of the organisation and of the individuals within it are different, different types of communications processes and structures are necessary for the two sets of needs to be adequately satisfied. Four principal structures are required, which are:

1 The Command Structure
2 The Consultative Structure
3 The Negotiating Structure
4 The Grievance Procedure

The effectiveness of communications will also be influenced by other factors such as the clarity of message, management credibility, the preconceptions and self-interest of the audience. It is evident then that any system of communications must be seen in the total sociological, organisational and psychological environment in which it operates. This can best be understood if the purpose of communications is considered first.

Why communicate?

It was calculated in 1962 that more than one third of the industrial disputes which have occurred in this country since the Second World War have been due to inadequate communications. There is a substantial body of evidence which suggests that more effective communications between management and worker might have avoided some of their more serious confrontations. This emphasis on the avoidance, or mitigation of industrial conflict has led people to underestimate, if not ignore, the more positive benefits that an effective exchange of information can bring about.

Such exchange is a necessary preliminary to the development of a thorough appreciation of company policies, practices and objectives. It should lead to the creation of an environment of mutual understanding in which employees are able to participate in the achievement of the company's objectives, in which means of improving productivity and efficiency might be freely explored, in which employees feel free to make suggestions and to innovate without anxiety, and in which they are encouraged and able to use their abilities to the full. A good communications system is, in fact, an important way of maximising the efficiency of an organisation.

Positive proof of the material benefits gained by good communications is difficult to come by, but there is some proof in the experience of several companies in different industries in the United States as illustrated in Figure 10 : 1. This table shows a comparison of absentee rates before and after the introduction of joint consultative machinery (JCM) during the Second World War.

TYPE OF COMPANY	ABSENTEEISM RATE (%)	
	BEFORE JCM INTRODUCED	AFTER JCM INTRODUCED
Oil Refining	5.3	3.3
Ship Building	7.0	5.3
Iron Founding	8.0	4.0
Electrical Manufacturing	10.0	1.0

Figure 10:1   Benefits of good communication through
joint consultative machinery

These considerations, however, are principally concerned with the requirements of the organisation and its objectives of efficiency and profit. The picture can only be completed after consideration of the needs of the individual within the organisation.

Formal and informal organisation structures

An organisation cannot operate efficiently without the clear exchange of the information through which it is directed and co-ordinated. The view that it is equally important in terms of organisational efficiency to meet employees' needs to give and to receive information may be the subject of more serious debate. Experience shows, however, that it is equally important to satisfy both organisational and individual needs and any communications system must take this into account. An organisation can only be efficient if mutual benefit both for the individual and for the organisation is derived from the industrial situation.

A communications system can promote this mutual benefit in two important ways:

1   In a motivational sense
2   In reducing rumours and inaccuracies

Motivation

The work of Herzberg and others has shown that an individual's performance is strongly influenced by the amount of satisfaction he derives from the work he does. Without a realistic definition of his role; without sufficient information to enable him to carry out his role properly; and without a system into which he can feed his ideas and feelings about his job and company procedures and policies it will be difficult for him to find the satisfaction that is a prerequisite of good performance. Thus communications policies and system have an important role in the motivation of employees.

Reducing rumours and inaccuracies

To illustrate the second point, the results of an opinion survey conducted recently is included—Figure 10 : 2.

These were typical of the responses received in similar surveys, describing a situation in which in the absence of official channels the 'grape-vine' had developed with all the risks of rumours and inaccuracies inherent in it. The need which the official communication system had failed to satisfy was now being satisfied through unofficial channels. A study of the transmission of rumours confirmed this picture by suggesting that people will spread rumours when they are

STATEMENT	RESPONSE		
	AGREE	NEITHER AGREE NOR DISAGREE	DISAGREE
1 The Company keeps us well informed	37%	16%	47%
2 I get enough information for the needs of my job	43%	6%	51%
3 I get information through the grape-vine before official sources	71%	9%	20%

Figure 10:2   Results of an opinion survey

short of real information, and when they are confused and unclear about what is happening in an attempt to give meaning to an unstructured environment.

In the situation illustrated above, the formal and informal communications structure operated in an environment of mutual tolerance. In some situations, however, the formal communications are so unsatisfactory that they are not only replaced by but come into conflict with the informal structure. In these situations group cohesion will break down and sporadic outbursts of unofficial action—such as sudden 'blacking,' overtime bans or wildcat strikes—will occur.

Effects of organisation structure

Different types of communication structures are necessary not only because of the different requirements of the formal and informal sections of the organisation but also to meet a variety of corporate objectives. A structure for example that is effective in an army platoon is not one which is likely to be effective in a research establishment. In the first, one would expect to see a short, clear, command structure, a strongly centralised network; in the second, a less clearly defined structure which encourages greater freedom, flexibility and the development of initiative, a decentralised network.

The two types of structure are compared in Figure 10 : 3.

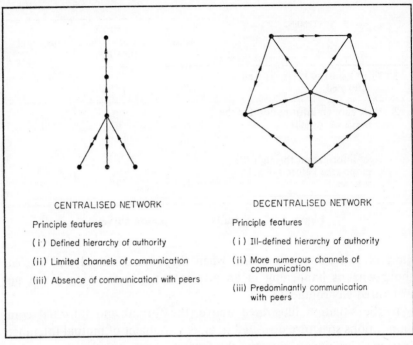

CENTRALISED NETWORK

Principle features

(i) Defined hierarchy of authority

(ii) Limited channels of communication

(iii) Absence of communication with peers

DECENTRALISED NETWORK

Principle features

(i) Ill-defined hierarchy of authority

(ii) More numerous channels of
communication

(iii) Predominantly communication
with peers

Figure 10:3   Comparison of centralised and
decentralised networks

In a comparison between the two structures, laboratory experiments have drawn the following conclusions:

Centralised networks

The work of centralised networks has fewer errors, and members within them are quick to react to instructions. Such networks generally facilitate the efficient performance of routine problem solving. They also have the characteristic of imposing clear-cut organisation on the group, defining each person's job, and strengthening the leadership position.

Decentralised networks

Whilst their members are slower to react to instructions and produce work with a greater number of errors than that done in centralised networks, the members making up such networks find greater satisfaction in their relationships and roles within the structures. Such structures appear to facilitate the handling of ambiguous and unpredictable situations and group members tend to be more imaginative and innovatory in their approach to problems. Multidisciplined teams formed to undertake a specific project are perhaps the commonest example of the type of group well suited to this structure.

The comparison of these two types of network emphasises the necessity of considering the functions of the different types of communication necessary in an organisation. The centralised structure fulfils the executive requirements of the organisation but provides little satisfaction for the individual; whereas the decentralised structure falls short in some command situations but provides much greater satisfaction for the individual. To be comprehensive, therefore, the communications system needs to take into account

1 a variety of organisational needs
2 the needs of the individual within the organisation
3 the interdependence of both.

Communications structures

The exchange of information that goes on within an organisation cannot be effective if only one type of system is used. A comprehensive communications structure comprises four parts:

1 The Command System
2 The Consultative System
3 The Negotiating System
4 The Grievance Procedure

Each system operates differently and is designed to serve a different purpose. Within a production unit, for example, there will normally be first the aim of achieving a prescribed level of output within defined cost and quality parameters—this would be carried out through the Command Structure. Equally, there will be the need to undertake discussion in those areas where close co-operation between the organisation and the employees within it is of mutual benefit—this would be through the Consultative Structure. There will also be the need to resolve conflict between the organisation and the employees within it—this would be through the Negotiating and the Grievance Procedure.

Command structure

The purpose of the command structure should be to make clear to employees the objectives of the organisation and their role in achieving them. These will be expressed in terms of production programmes within defined limits of cost, quality and quantity. Authority will be exercised through the hierarchy of the organisation and role specifications will prescribe the authority and the different responsibilities of employees within the organisation.

Such structures are usually of the centralised type described above. Other common characteristics are short, direct lines of communication frequently made possible by the separation of the staff and executive functions as illustrated in Figure 10 : 4.

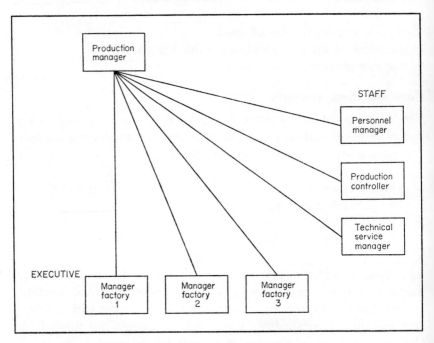

Figure 10:4   Organisation structure showing separation
of staff and line functions

In this type of structure the flow of communications is usually along a closely prescribed course but it has the advantage of speed and clarity. Such a structure will adequately meet the organisational need for execution but will provide little opportunity for the exchange and exploration of views. Where this failure to satisfy the communication needs of the individual is further emphasised by a situation in which the work itself is also highly prescribed, as in the case of a mass production line, at the best, apathy and lack of initiative and at the worst, tension and outright conflict will result.

Consultative structure

It is frequently possible and necessary to fulfil within the Consultative Structure many needs which remain unsatisfied by the Command Structure. The principal function of the Consultative Structure is advisory and deals with those areas where co-operation between company and employee is of mutual benefit.

It is often difficult to distinguish between what rightfully falls into the sphere of consultation and what falls into the sphere of negotiation. There are those who would maintain that all matters between employer and employee are a matter for negotiation. There are others who would maintain equally strongly that some matters can only remain a matter for consultation. The distinction differs from one company to another and is largely determined by the negotiating tradition. The trend for negotiated agreements to become increasingly comprehensive is already established and items such as pension schemes, profit-sharing schemes, which were more often than not outside the competence of negotiations some ten years ago, now figure increasingly in Company/ Trade Union agreements. The distinction between consultation and negotiation does not depend on subject matter but on its purpose. Negotiation is concerned with the resolution of conflict; consultation with the process of discussion and joint problem solving leading to jointly agreed action. There are, therefore, some areas where there is interaction between the organisation and the employee(s) which are nevertheless unlikely ever to fall into the field of negotiation—such are the Suggestions Scheme, Charity Schemes, Safety, Canteens and Transport.

The consultative structure should be based on the natural operating unit, for example a production unit, plant or works, a sales force, or a research department and should include representatives from both the staff and line functions within that unit. The composition of a con- sultative committee from a typical manufacturing department is illustrated in Figure 10 : 5.

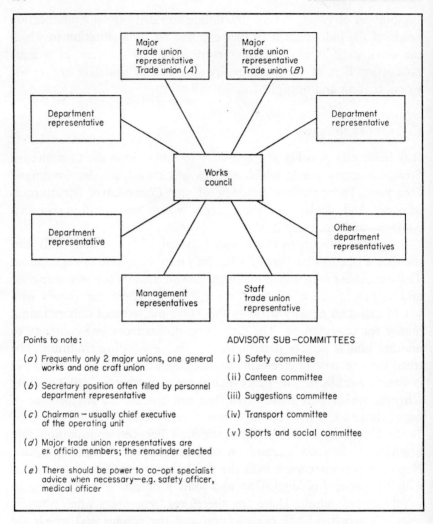

Points to note:

(*a*) Frequently only 2 major unions, one general works and one craft union

(*b*) Secretary position often filled by personnel department representative

(*c*) Chairman – usually chief executive of the operating unit

(*d*) Major trade union representatives are ex officio members; the remainder elected

(*e*) There should be power to co-opt specialist advice when necessary—e.g. safety officer, medical officer

ADVISORY SUB–COMMITTEES

(i) Safety committee

(ii) Canteen committee

(iii) Suggestions committee

(iv) Transport committee

(v) Sports and social committee

Figure 10:5   Composition of typical works council

The *purpose* of such a committee is twofold. It provides a forum in which:

1 The appropriate authority may dispense information which falls outside the scope of the command structure and yet which increases the knowledge of the environment in which the organisation is operating. Examples of this are information concerning the company's trading position, or a new technological development

2 Employee representatives within the operating unit may discuss proposed practices and policies. This might well concern the operation of security precautions, safe working practices or the organisation and execution of work itself. On occasion the need will arise to appoint a project team from common interest groups within the unit to report to the consultative body on proposed solutions to a problem affecting the operating unit as a whole

The *constitution* of a consultative council will vary according to the size and disposition of the operating unit concerned. Below are some guide lines which have been found to be useful in practical application:

1 Size of Committee. The most successful size of committees is nine persons, with a maximum of twelve members, each with their own constituency

2 Size of Constituency. A desirable number is between thirty and forty constituents. This is likely to be a practical limit for constituencies in which members are scattered or where shift-work is involved

3 TU Representation. In some companies there is sometimes a problem of distinguishing between the sphere of negotiation and that of consultation which is further compounded by differences between the consultative and negotiating representational systems. One way of overcoming such problems is to legislate in the constitution for *ex officio* representation from the major trade unions

4 Communication of Business Transacted. Many consultative systems have been prejudiced by the failure to make adequate provision for communication between the representative and his constituents. In addition to the prompt circulation of meeting summaries, provision must be made for the attendance of constituent observers and for regular meetings between the representative and his constituent

The *advantages* of a consultative body are that:

1   Employees within a given consultative unit are better able to comprehend the operation of their unit in the wider environment of the company, the industry and the economy, and their place within it

2   In addition, management can take into account employee reactions and ideas from a representative sample of the constituent interests within his organisation before taking a decision. Such decisions may then be based on improved information. Such communication is essentially multi-directional, allowing for transfer outwards from the organisation centre, inwards towards it and also horizontally between its various component groups

3   Consultation will give the employee the chance to influence and to become involved in those decisions which affect his job and his environment. In giving him the opportunity to put forward his ideas and opinions with the assurance that they will be given real attention, job satisfaction and, with it, job performance will improve.

The negotiating structure

The purpose of the negotiating machinery is the resolution of the conflict of interest that inevitably arises in any organisation. It is natural therefore in an economy with a capital base that the share of wealth forms the area in which conflict most frequently takes place. The recent Fiat negotiations which included provision for a study on the organisation of work at the assembly line, are as yet exceptional but are likely to become increasingly the rule. Although it is quite possible for more effective work organisation to be successfully devised through the consultative machinery, it is never possible for the wealth that accrues from it to be divided between the employee and the organisation through other than the negotiating machinery.

Until relatively recently negotiations have been principally preoccupied with the field of wages and hours of work. Only of late have they entered the wider field of sickness schemes, pensions, and preparation for retirement, to quote some examples.

In contrast to the consultative structure, whilst representing the confrontation of two common interest groups the negotiating structure need not be based on the natural operating unit. For example the terms and conditions of many employees are regulated by National

Joint Industrial Councils, or agreed on an industry-wide basis between a trade union and an employers' federation.

In order to resolve conflict negotiating machinery will need to possess the following characteristics:

1 *Negotiating Procedure.* The prompt resolution of conflict requires a defined framework within which such resolution may take place. This is characterised by formal and highly prescribed procedures which provide a framework within which the resolution of conflict may take place, and which specify each stage in procedure in the event of failure to reach agreement. This procedure would need to include

(*a*) a definition of the parties bound by the agreement

(*b*) the topics on which it is competent to decide

(*c*) a constitution of the negotiating group and the procedure for election to it

(*d*) the authority possessed by representatives at the negotiations

(*e*) the procedure for settlement in the event of failure to reach agreement

(*f*) agreed time-limits for each stage in the negotiating procedure

2 *Authority to Decide.* Where conflict has arisen it can only be resolved by a modification of the views of at least one of the two parties in conflict. That each party needs the authority to change his position is self-evident. In spite of this so many negotiations are still entered into where, on the one hand trade union representatives are unwilling or unable to make a decision on behalf of the membership they represent or on the other hand managers take part in negotiations without having the authority to modify the company's position. Considerable time might have been saved by ensuring that negotiations took place only when the parties have full authority to make decisions on behalf of those whom they represent.

Where the size of the company is such that more than one tier is necessary in the negotiating structure the areas in which each tier is competent to negotiate should be clearly delineated. A typical division of authority between two tiers of a negotiating structure is shown below:

National Negotiations	*Local Negotiations*
Basic rates	Implementation of job
Overtime and shift rates	grading scheme

National Negotiations	*Local Negotiations*
Length of the working week	Plant incentive schemes
Grade differentials	Productivity agreements within a national framework
Bonus percentages	Demarcation disputes
Statutory and annual holidays.	Local and individual grievances.

3 *Small Negotiating Committee*. The constitution of the negotiating committee and the framework within which it operates should assist in the clarification of the points at issue. Simplification assists in this and one way in which this might be achieved is the constitution of a small but powerful negotiating committee. Size and disposition of the operating unit will strongly influence the size of its negotiating committee. It is not infrequently found that in manufacturing units of 1200–1500 employees' negotiations could have been adequately undertaken by a negotiating committee of two management and three trade union representatives.

Whilst it is not customary to find negotiating committees as small as this it is quite usual to find that negotiating committees will work through a principal spokesman for either party. Some negotiating procedures have even formalised this to the point where negotiations are concluded by one representative for either party whilst all other representatives are present only in the official capacity of observer.

4 *Representation Machinery*. Whilst small negotiating committees such as those illustrated above facilitate negotiations they can only be as effective as long as the agreements they conclude are acceptable to their members. The very smallness of these committees increases the authority vested in each member and as a result increases the danger of alienating the committee member from those whose interests he represents. In order to maintain the authority of the trade union representatives it is essential that adequate provision is made for elections to the negotiating committee and for consultative meetings to take place before and sometimes during negotiations. This will ensure the presentation of a representative point of view. Union branch meetings are most frequently used for this purpose but it is all too common that attendance at them is too low to ensure the presentation of an opinion which is representative of the branch as a whole. This is particularly true of craft unions where membership is more often

based on the area in which its members live rather than the place at which they work. Whilst it is recognised that some managements oppose union meetings on company premises as a matter of principle it is in our experience preferable to allow them to take place particularly where matters of crucial importance to the company are concerned.

5 *Feed-back*. At the conclusion of negotiations, or at any stage of them, it is necessary to provide prompt and accurate information concerning the outcome. If, as in the case of a serious dispute there is keen interest in the result, failure to provide the information will provoke irritation and rumour. In order to prevent this the publication of a jointly agreed statement is to be recommended and in cases where more comprehensive information is required, an information meeting with a joint presentation should be arranged.

6 *Failure to Reach Agreement*. All negotiating procedures should provide for the failure to reach agreement after the final step in the procedure. This should take the form of a voluntary arbitration procedure, of which the principal features are enumerated below:

(*a*)   that it is voluntary

(*b*)   that it may not be invoked until all other means of settlement of the dispute have been exhausted

(*c*)   that the arbitrator(s) be acceptable to both sides in the dispute

(*d*)   that the arbitrator(s) decision is final and binding.

Grievance procedure

This procedure is also used for the resolution of conflict. It provides for those circumstances in which an individual or a minority group wishes to protest or appeal against treatment which he or they consider to be unjust. Most grievances can be settled between the employee(s) and the first line supervisor. The grievance procedure is devised for those that fail to be settled at that level.

This procedure needs to be considered alongside the negotiating procedure. The requirements are similar and it is necessary to specify procedural requirements and in particular the maximum periods of time that may elapse between stages in the procedure. In theory it may allow for a succession of appeals through succeeding levels in the hierarchy of the organisation until the appeal is placed before the chief executive. In practice provision should be made for such disputes to enter the negotiating machinery at an early stage. A convenient time is when the parties have failed to reach agreement either on appeal to the foreman's immediate superior or after two weeks from the time at which the action causing the grievance took place. This course of action has the advantage that the more extreme reactions resulting from what are often emotional issues are more easily controlled.

Factors essential to communication

We have discussed so far the structural requirements that are necessary for a communications system to meet the needs of the organisation and of its employees. There are also other factors which are an important influence on these considerations, such as clarity, credibility and the preconceptions and self-interest of those receiving the message. There are certain factors which must be borne in mind when considering any of the various types of communication, whether command, consultation, negotiation or grievance procedure.

Clarity

Whilst it is a statement of the obvious, a communication must be understood. But this task is often made more difficult by variations in the intelligence, abilities and interests of those at whom the message is directed. Precautions need to be taken against the distortion of a message during its transmission and one way of achieving this is to transmit it by several routes, for instance, through the foreman as well as the shop steward; by several means, that is verbal as well as written, and with adequate coverage.

Promotion of self-interest

People will communicate, or fail to communicate, in order to achieve some goal or satisfy some personal need. In the execution of their job employees will communicate with those who serve to achieve their goals and resist communicating with those who serve to work against them. For example an employee will quite readily turn to his supervisor if it is he who is in the best position to assist him. However, if the supervisor does not have the authority to assist he will be ignored and the employee will turn to him who can—this may be a colleague, or shop steward or the supervisor's immediate superior. Lack of authority amongst supervision and junior management is frequently at the root of why so many industrial relations problems end on the desk of the chief executive.

Trust

For communications to be effective, it is essential that the audience trust the communicator. In one case where the effectiveness of communications was compared between two identical departments the difference between the two was traced to the degree of trust that the subordinates had in their superior. Consistency of decision taking and plausibility of motive are both essential to the establishment of trust between the communicator and his audience. We are aware of one situation where a strike occurred because the trade union membership mistrusted the ease with which management, out of character with their previous behaviour, had made a major concession.

Preconceptions

The process of giving and receiving information is notoriously subjective. There is a strong interest in information which refers to the receiver personally who usually wishes to have at least some of his preconceptions confirmed. This is illustrated by an extract from a survey which was conducted on the dangers of smoking:

Opinion of Respondents Concerning the Link Between Cigarette and Lung Cancer

Category	Proved	Not Proved	No Opinion
Non-smokers	29	55	16
Light smokers	20	68	12
Moderate smokers	16	75	9
Heavy smokers	7	86	7

This is a topical illustration of some of the difficulties which face communicators whose message conflicts with the preconceptions of the recipient. Such is the strength of preconception that more information will not necessarily bring about closer agreement or a reconciliation of views which are at variance. Some studies which have been carried out would suggest that increasing contact between people who are in disagreement might only serve to confirm their different opinions.

In discussing the prerequisites for information to be efficiently exchanged within an organisation the most important consideration should be that any act of communication cannot be separated from the total environment in which it takes place. It is ineffective to consider merely 'doing something about communications' *in vacuo*. The organisation structure and management style are the first considerations. The construction of a sound communications system will certainly require a review and perhaps even a revision of the structures through which it is expected to operate, of the relationships between the people in their structures and, even more basically, of the whole philosophy of the company's management. It is only then that the mechanics of transmitting information can become fully effective.

11

Methods of Payment

D H Langton

Manufacturing Manager, Oldham and Son Limited

An incentive is an objective goal which is capable of satisfying what we are aware of subjectively as a need, drive or desire.

'If money is all that a man can get from his work, he will take any means possible to get all that he can.'

J A C Brown
The Social Psychology of Industry

The aspect of remuneration is possibly the most important point in relationship between employer and employee. It is the chief reason, though certainly not the only reason, why people work. The way in which remuneration is determined is, therefore, very important in maintaining good relations. It must at once satisfy the economic requirements of the organisation and the personal expectations of the individual.

This chapter considers methods which can be used to meet the problem in all employment conditions arising in the industrial environment. In some cases traditional attitudes to payment may affect the attitude at the workplace. Generally, however, the payment system should be geared with a combination of measured performance and payment levels to provide the incentive where this can be effective. In areas of work where the individual has little or no control personally over the pace of output, payment schemes at shop-floor level with a variable incentive element can, if applied, fall into severe disrepute.

Payment by results schemes should never be regarded by management as an instrument which will automatically do management's job; they are not means whereby management can abrogate its responsibility for control of output and costs.

For staff, the problem usually is to demonstrate a reward for effective contribution to the organisation. This may be completely impossible to measure in terms of profit. In cases other than the salesman in the field or the executive whose decisions may have a directly measurable effect on the organisation performance, a graded salary scale and thorough routine appraisal scheme usually achieve the most satisfactory results.

Payment of manual employees—selecting a system

Although payment of manual employees in certain cases through a bank may become more accepted in the future, for the purposes of this chapter it will be assumed that manual employees are paid weekly in cash.

	TYPE OF WORK	
1	Man Controlled	
	i Short Cycle	Batch Assembly
	ii Long Cycle	Batch Assembly
2	Machine or Process Controlled Batch Work	
	i Short Cycle	
	ii Long Cycle Process	
	iii Long Cycle Engineering	
3	Machine or Process Continuous	
4	Team Control	
	i Mass Production Assembly	
	ii Process	

Figure 11:1 Main categories of work occurring in industrial activity.

Figures 11:1, 11:2 and 11:3 list the various parameters which come into consideration in operating a payment system. Figure 11:3 shows the various manning arrangements which are used.

The method of payment which is adopted should be carefully selected, chiefly according to the nature of the work, as illustrated in Figure 11:1.

Although payment systems will vary according to the nature and organisation of the work as well as local factors, the following principles, as noted in the Code of Industrial Relations practice, should apply:

1 A payment system should be as simple as possible
2 Differences in rates should be related to the requirements of the job. The job should be assessed and agreed by objective methods. All the judgements should be justified
3 Pay structures and job descriptions must be reviewed when there are changes in the work or job requirements
4 Piecework, incentive bonuses or similar payment must be determined against standards obtained by some form of recognised work measurement

	PAYMENT SYSTEM
1	Fixed Weekly Payment based on industry national agreement
2	Fixed Weekly Payment using Job Evaluation and a locally agreed Graded Wage structure
3	As in 1 or with measured day work
4	As in 1 or 2 with a production incentive bonus based on work standards
5	Schemes as in 3 or 4 operated on a co-operative or pool bonus basis
6	Plant-wide bonus schemes of the Rucker or Scanlon type

Figure 11:2 Main categories into which payment systems fall.

	TYPE OF MANNING
1	Normal 40-hr week (overtime as necessary)
2	Rota Work means, whereby a normal 40-hr week is spread to extend the manned hours and increase, for example, maintenance cover
3	Shift Rota Work outside 'normal' hours to: i Increase the utilisation of capital; ii Meet the demands of the process Examples of Shift Rota extend from 5-day 'Double Day Shift' to 24-hr working throughout seven days

Figure   11:3   Manning arrangements.

Further general principles which may be difficult at times to maintain but in the long run will prove to cause far less trouble are that:

1   Personnel concerned with collecting and issuing data for work values, that is Work Study Officers, should not be concerned with monetary values
2   Bonus payments based on simple quantity or production should not be considered
3   Manning bonuses should not be used
4   The illustration of a Wage Structure shown in Figure 11:4 is one way in which an organisation can provide a rational progression for shop floor employees and it is only in the context of the basic rates in such a structure that negotiation for pay and differentials should occur

Man-controlled operations

Short cycle batch assembly   Payment for work where the speed of operation is entirely controlled by the operator should be based on either measured day work or a proportional incentive scheme. It is vital

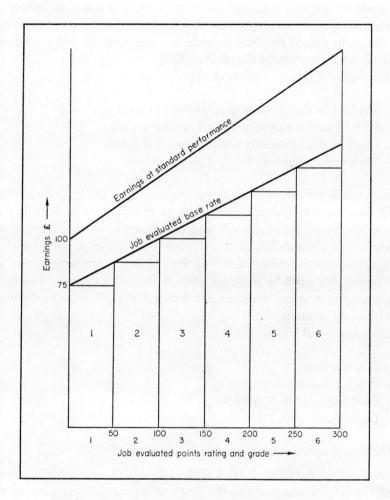

Figure 11:4 Wage structure based on six job-evaluated grades and proportional standard performance incentive bonus

that the scale of payment is based on reliable and correct work standards and desirable that it is superimposed on a 'Job Evaluation' scheme. Although measured day work could be used for this type of operation, in areas of difficult relations there may ensue a constant review of performance to maintain the standard set. In this case a variable bonus, at which the agreed standard provides a bonus element, which is 25 per cent of total earnings, is the ideal method.

Examples of this type of work are:

1   Welding or metal burning operations in small assembly
2   Manual packing of routine and repetitive nature
3   Small manual assembly such as electrical goods
4   Sheet metal working

Long cycle batch assembly   The payment method for long cycle work will, to some extent, depend on the length of cycle time. It is likely that the work differs for each cycle and consequently work standards are awkward to set and difficult to maintain. For long cycle work which is repetitive incentive bonus methods may be useful and satisfactory, or measured day work be more suitable. If the work cycle is variable, a fixed weekly payment based on Job Evaluation is likely to be the most satisfactory solution.

Examples of this type of work are:

1   Shipbuilding
2   Process Plant Fabrication
3   Civil Engineering Contracting
4   Dock Work

Machine- or process-controlled batch operations

Short- and medium-length batch cycles   For both operations involving batch work, in which either the machine or the process controls the speed of output of each unit of production, the operator will have under his control only the time in which the plant is not operating to specification; that is during turn round, when operating outside specification or during essential attention to plant. The proportion which the time of non-production, or outside time, is of the total operating time will obviously vary according to the process. Clearly, for maximum efficiency the proportion of outside time should be the lowest possible, strictly controlled and the subject of continued scrutiny for reduction. It will normally be between 10 per cent and 25 per cent of the total time. From the payment aspect either fixed weekly payment or a straight proportional incentive scheme may be applied. The effect of an incentive scheme for this type of operation is unlikely to be great when the outside time is a low proportion of the total time on the grounds that the operator has very little control over output. The most effective method is likely to be measured day work with measured performance maintained.

Examples of this type of work are:

1 Repetitive casting operations
2 Batch process work
3 Dyeing
4 Plastic sheeting and upholstery material

Machine-or process-continuous operation

The very nature of continuous operation means that the operator, while having some control over the rate and quality of output, has not, as an individual, a highly significant effect. His role is likely to be one substantially of surveillance requiring vigilance. The output rate will have been fixed by the designer of the process. Indeed there may even be requirements in the process limiting output on grounds of either safety or quality. For work of this type a fixed weekly payment based on job evaluated scales and industry or locally agreed rates is the most satisfactory method.

Examples of this type of work are:

1 Printing
2 Spinning
3 Continuous chemical reaction and distillation
4 Oil refining

Team control

Mass production assembly The production of an assembly line is governed by the operation taking the longest time. It is important, however, in designing the work for the line that the times for each of the operations are as near equal as possible. It is possible on this basis, with standard manning to operate an incentive scheme taking the time for the longest operation as a basis for the standard. However, this type of operation is ideally suited to measured day work and use of this payment system may save a lot of unrest in some areas where there is local rivalry or where there are inadequate standards in operation.

Examples of this type of work are:

1 Vehicle assembly
2 Consumer goods assembly
3 Battery assembly

Process Team work in this case will be closely similar to the work described in the previous section and as such a period of weekly payment based on job evaluated scales and industry or locally agreed rates is the most satisfactory method.

Payment systems

Figure 11 : 2 lists various payment systems which are in use. It is almost essential in a modern organisation to operate a job evaluation scheme for semi-skilled manual employees. The method of Job Evaluation is less important than the principle that a systematic assessment of all aspects of a job is collated with other assessments and all jobs in the evaluation scheme are ranked according to the assessments. However, all combinations of the payments methods in Figure 11 : 2 are in use in different organisations.

National agreement fixed weekly payment

Where an employers' organisation and the relevant trades unions have reached a national agreement which applies to an industry and where payment is at fixed levels the rates provided in the agreement may apply. Such a policy will allow for no differential payment other than between the labourer and semi-skilled employees.

Graded structure at local agreement rates

The generally accepted principles of Job Evaluation can be used to develop a graded structure, as illustrated in Figure 11: 4. Such an approach, however. will usually mean that the rates of payment and differentials between grades must be settled locally, either with employees or local trades union officials. There should normally be between five and eight grades in a wage structure of this type. The principle can be used with either measured day work, fixed weekly payment or incentive bonus schemes. The Code of Practice is one of a long list of publications advising the adoption of Job Evaluation for classification of semi-skilled jobs. The institution of Job Evaluation can be expensive when undertaken from a situation of random payment based on traditional individual rates. However, a graded structure of the type illustrated provides, on the one hand, a progressive opportunity for operatives and, on the other, a basis for common knowledge of the earnings associated with each job in the organisation. The differentials can be justified by the data used for evaluation. Adoption of a graded structure must be accompanied by agreement to negotiate the grade payments as a total exercise and will eliminate perpetual individual negotiation at random. Job Evaluation analyses the requirements of manual work under four main headings:

1 Training
2 Acquired skills and job knowledge
3 Physical and mental requirements
4 Working conditions

There are various methods of completing the analysis. Whichever method is used the objective is the same; that is to complete a list of jobs in ranking order with as much supporting objective data as possible.

Measured day work

Sound and reliable work standards are essential for the satisfactory operation of a measured day work scheme. The principle is that a fixed weekly payment is established equated to an agreed performance level range, say between 95 and 105 on the BSI work study scale. Any persistent lower performance is examined and discussed with the operators according to a previously agreed procedure. If performance is not maintained within this range the payment level falls in fixed amounts related to achieved performance until the output is restored to standard.

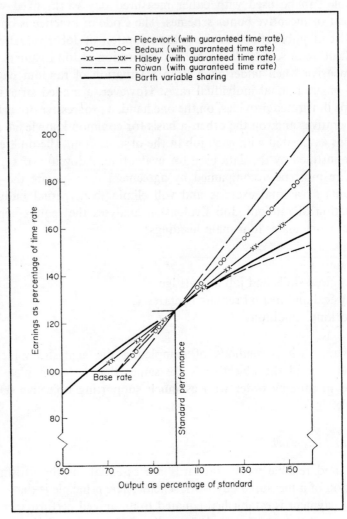

Figure 11 : 5 Earnings under various payment by
result systems

The advantages of this method are:

1. Wage calculation is greatly simplified
2. Product costing is simpler
3. Uncertainty of earnings for employees is less than in the use of bonus schemes

Incentive bonus schemes

There are several variations in method of calculation of production incentive bonuses. Figure 11:5 shows certain schemes which have been developed and used. As with measured day work, the operation of schemes of this type demands completely reliable work values.

There are systems in which earnings vary proportionately:

1. Less than increased output
2. At the same rate as increased output
3. More than increased output
4. Differ at different output levels

Most of the schemes are applied with a guaranteed time rate, which in the case of Figure 11:4 could be the Job Evaluated Base Rate, and the bonus level which is earned is one third above the base rate.

Earnings proportionally less than output Systems embodying this principle are often applied where it is difficult to set standards or measure output accurately. The basis for calculating the bonus is based on the time saved against the standard time. The variations are dependent upon the proportion of saved time paid as bonus. This varies from 30 per cent to 70 per cent and is usually about 50 per cent. Under these systems, unit direct labour costs about standard output are lower than under straight piecework. As, however, the same work is worth different values to the employee, depending on when it is produced, these systems can lead to malpractices such as delayed booking of work until some problem prevents achievement of standard performance. For similar reasons, these methods can also be restrictive to output at higher performance levels. Figure 11:6 shows comparative earnings for the four systems based on the example data given.

Halsey (50–50 Time Saved)	Rowan % of Time Saved at Time Rate	Barth	Bedaux 75% Time Saved
$8 \times 0.75 = 6.00$	$8 \times 0.75 = 6.00$	$10 \times 8 \times 0.75 = 6.71$	$8 \times 0.75 = 6.00$
$1 \times 0.75 = 0.75$	$20 \times 6.00 = 1.20$		$3 \times 120 \times 0.75 = 1.13$
	$\overline{100}$		$\overline{4 \qquad 60}$
Payment $= 6.75$	7.20	6.71	7.13

Standard Time = 10 hrs. Hourly Rate = 0.75 units
Achieved Time = 8 hrs. Time Saved = 2 hrs. (20%)

Figure 11:6 Comparative earnings; bonus varying proportionally less than output

Earnings proportional to output It is particularly important that wor standards are extremely accurate. This system either as straight piece work or as 'Standard Time' is one of the most used methods of produc tion bonus payment. A Standard Time is determined for a specified jol Completion in this time is paid at time rate. In the example in Figur 11:6, however, payment will be ten times the hourly rate, that is 7.5 units. The systems both reward employees in direct proportion t output and therefore work at whatever time is always worth the sam There is consequently no need to retain work for slacker occasions.

Earnings varying proportionally more than output Labour costs und such a system, that is high piece rate, increase for output levels abov standard. Earnings increase in proportion to output but the incremen is greater than under the standard hour basis. The principle of calcula tion is, however, the same.

Earnings varying differently at different levels of output There are man payment systems which are of this type. The main principle is the larg increase in payment earned upon achieving a given level, or levels of output. For example, in one scheme there is a 6 per cent increase in bonus for the final 1 per cent production achieved to reach standard. Such schemes can create as many problems as they attempt to solve and the distortion of the earnings curve to emphasise achievement of the task levels should not be seen as an alternative to bad management and administration.

Examples of systems are:

1 The Gantt Task System
2 The Merrick Differential Piece Rate System
3 The Taylor Differential Piece Rate System

Payment reflecting effort in more sophisticated terms

There are two well-known plans, Rucker and Scanlon, which originated in the United States but which have been used elsewhere.

The Rucker Plan This plan is based on a calculation of the ratio between wages and the value which has been added to materials within the company, known as the production value. This is obtained by deducting the cost of materials and supplies (plus any other goods or services bought outside) from the sales value of production. The ratio should remain constant unless a major revolution in production technique occurs. It is based on an examination of the company's accounts for at least six preceding years. The bonus depends on a company's employees obtaining greater output for the same amount of materials or by using materials more efficiently. The bonus is calculated by working out the base ratio figure of the month's production value and subtracting the actual factory payroll for the past month from this. The surplus is distributed to employees.

The Scanlon Plan This plan is based on a less rigid set of rules than the Rucker plan but it does have a basic formula. This relates labour costs to sales value of production and uses this ratio to determine any saving in labour costs which forms a bonus. A proportion of the bonus is paid to employees. The base ratio is less stable than that of the Rucker plan as it can be affected by the introduction of new machinery or substantial changes in material prices.

Profit sharing

Distribution of a portion of company profits as a share of prosperity bonus or as a profit share is adopted by some organisations in efforts to let employees share in the success of the relevant period of trading.

Effectiveness of various methods

A Payments-by-Results system can be a useful tool in increasing or assisting to maintain effort in situations of low performance. It can also be used as a device to raise performance over a short period with the intention of changing to a more stable system later. Claims are made that the installation of payment by results will provide considerable savings and the initial impact is likely to increase productivity by something in the region of 50 per cent, increase earnings and reduce unit labour costs.

Where payment by results has been used for a long time, however, and control is inadequate the cost effect can be significantly unfavourable. In addition, the costs of operating a scheme may be considerable both in the simple administrative tasks and in measuring, maintaining and discussing measurement and standards of work. The contrasting human relationships which two payment systems can generate is illustrated by a case where in two similar departments two foremen worked, one with payment by results, the other with measured day work. In the former case, it had become the foreman's major task under production pressure to settle disputes over standards quickly at the expense of costs. In the latter, the foreman's main responsibility was to see that the department was well supplied, working to schedule and adequately trained. He was held responsible for any decline in performance.

Organisations will normally have a proportion of employees engaged in service work of some description. Such work, normally referred to as indirect work, for example stores, maintenance and boilers, does not readily lend itself to incentive payment. Incentive schemes are used in maintenance work. However, as a general principle, payment for indirect work should be based on a fixed rate at manning levels determined by work study. Should some form of incentive payment be considered essential, the bonus for service department employees should be based on the total organisation performance determined by combining the performance of all production departments.

Payment of staff employees

Staff fall into four broad categories for payment considerations and will normally be paid through a bank account:

1 Junior Staff; office, supervision and clerical employees
2 Staff; superintendents, technicians, administrators and middle management
3 Salesmen
4 Executive managers

The two levels of staff cannot normally have a measurable effect on the success or profits of the organisation. While essential to the work, their activities may be concerned with future developments (research) or with communications (secretarial). Salesmen can be assessed to some extent directly by the level of sales in their area. Commission payment can thus reasonably form part of their remuneration. Executive managers, by definition, are at a level of responsibility and authority at which there is a direct influence on profits. A form of profit sharing is therefore a justifiable incentive.

Staff grading

Unlike shop-floor employees whose work can be measured, although techniques are now being developed to measure office work, payment of all levels of staff should be on the basis of a graded salary structure. Staff incentives can be diverted into effort for career progression and this should be seen as the reward for effective work. Clearly the time scale is the longer the higher the level of responsibility.

A staff grading and salary structure is made up of three main items:

1 Staff grading
2 Job specification and evaluation
3 Personal performance appraisal

The aim should be to ensure the economic and efficient employment of personnel with an equitable reward.

Staff grading A staff grading scheme should be fair and be seen to be fair. It should take account of variations in both individual respons-

G

ibilities and individual performances. It must be simple to allow for the publicity of grades and scales and provide a framework for staff careers. Rewards must be comparable with market values and equitable between subordinates, equals and seniors. The scheme must also provide for a systematic review of jobs through job descriptions and appraisal of individuals by use of objectives. Salaries will not look after themselves. Increases at lower levels will create pressure at management levels. Although salaries should be somewhat flexible to retain 'high flyers' there must be recognition of comparative levels and the total salary bill must remain within the organisation's economic capacity.

Job specification and evaluation   A salary should be made up of the following:

1   Base rate for job worth
2   Personal performance payment
3   Acknowledgement of age within the grade scale

The base rate is the most important element and should represent some 75 per cent of the total. The first step in determining a base rate is the completion of a job description.

Evaluation follows the completion of all job descriptions. There are various methods of job evaluation, and for setting up an evaluation for staff jobs it may be desirable to use two methods side by side.

Evaluation methods are:

1   Ranking
2   Points rating
3   Factor comparison
4   Paired comparisons

Upon completion of the evaluation, a market survey is necessary. Several well defined jobs should be selected and a survey completed of salaries for jobs in the categories selected. Although wide variations may be found for apparently similar jobs, the median figure of the survey will provide a guide. The relative importance of these jobs within the organisation will then confirm the scale.

Personal performance appraisal   Correct performance appraisal, although difficult for many managers to do, is extremely valuable. It is a

STAFF REPORT   *Strictly Confidential*   Name and Initials ....

	A	B	C	D	E

Year ....

Report on................Date of Birth................

Position and Date of Appointment ....

Salary Grade................Date of Joining ....

Overall Rating of
Effectiveness in Job

To be completed by the departmental or
equivalent manager

Assessment of effectiveness in present job

a)

		Assessment	Degree of Importance to Job Performance
1	Knowledge of Function		
2	Effective Output		
3	Analytical Ability		
4	Initiative		
5	Leadership		
6	Co-operation		
7	Development of Personnel		
8	Co-ordination		
9	Acceptance of Responsibility		
10	Reporting		
11	Other Characteristics		

b) Other Comment. (To be completed in all cases. Is there anything of significance which has not been included in (a) above? Health? Interest in extra official activities? Appearance? Highlight strength(s) and weakness(es).

c) The Interview given (Date) .... by................ Signature of First Assessor ....

Position................ Date ....

Signature of Second Assessor ....

Position................ Date ....

Figure 11:7   Staff report

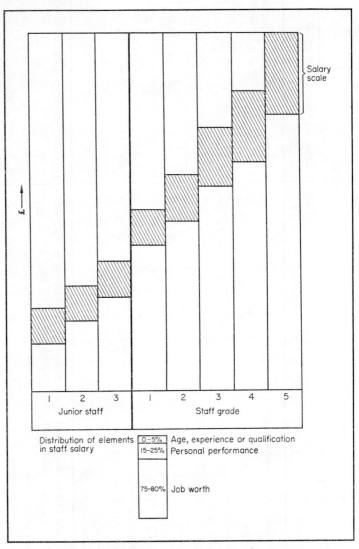

Figure 11 : 8   Staff salary structure

vital tool in improving supervision and selection on the one hand and establishing training needs and career progression on the other. There are many ways of conducting appraisal schemes. The staff report form Figure 11: 7 is an example. If used correctly, such a form can provide a guide, through the overall rating figure for the performance award element of salary.

Figure 11: 8 shows the build up of a company salary structure, and the elements within the salary.

Sales staff

Although a graded salary structure, as shown in Figure 11: 8, is applicable equally well to sales staff in the field, it is common practice to use payment of commission as a way of applying incentive and increasing effort. Commission in this case is a fourth element in the salary block shown in the Figure below. The percentage of total income which is represented by commission varies very widely and may be held to be the essence of a salesman's earnings. However, in the context of a graded salary structure it should not represent more than 20 per cent. Hence, if the sales are budgeted to be 1000 pieces for a salesman per annum equating to commission of 400 money units, and 1200 pieces are sold then commission will be 480 money units and total income to the employee will rise from the 2000 budgeted to 2080, as shown:

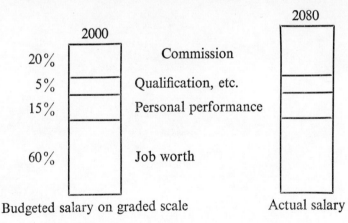

Budgeted salary on graded scale   Actual salary

Executive managers

Given the definition of this grade to include a close influence on the success and profitability of an organisation then there is a case to provide for some share in profitability as an incentive to continued progress. The share of any profits to executive managers is mainly a matter for the board of directors. Once again, however, the total proportion of earnings paid from profit sharing should not be higher than 20 per cent of total salary and may, of course, vary from year to year. Any profit share should be related to the profit in that period only and each period of profit calculation should be taken independently when considering distribution under this heading.

12

Shiftwork

Robert Sergean

Industrial Psychologist

This chapter discusses the practical problems and social responsibilities facing managers who are concerned with multiple shiftworking. Inevitably, in the space available, it does so in fairly broad terms since shiftwork is a highly complex and extremely varied feature of working life.

Difficulties presented by shiftwork are not entirely new. Shiftwork is part and parcel of a much wider problem area—that of the length and arrangement of working hours in general. For a century and a half men have been concerned with what should be the length of the working day and working week, and with how work and leisure time should be related. Shiftwork, as an extension of conventional daywork, brings a new dimension to an existing problem. Whatever economic or productive benefits the introduction of a particular type of shiftwork may offer, these will inevitably be accompanied by new administrative headaches for personnel and production staff, and fresh problems of adjustment for the men and women who have to adapt to unaccustomed hours of work and free time.

Although multiple shiftwork in certain sections of industry has a long history, the demands of the postwar period have seen it practised on a far wider scale. Its expansion during the 1950s and 1960s has resulted from a variety of economic, technical, and social factors. It has been introduced into industries and occupations where it was previously unknown. As a result of increased mechanisation and use of the computer, shiftwork has penetrated into white-collar activities. New categories of workers have been affected. Geographically it is now accepted in areas which were previously purely daywork in character. Not only is shiftwork found in an increasing number of units, not only are more and more people paid on a shift basis, but there is increasing variety in the pattern of shiftwork used and in the way in which working and leisure hours are arranged. Experiments with a growing range of permutations are a feature of the current industrial scene, and such developments will continue to be of special interest to both employer and employed during the 1970s.

A brief word is advisable at this point on what is meant by 'shiftwork.' While in localised conditions it may be taken to refer exclusively to a particular type or system, in its broadest sense it is concerned with shifts of any kind which are used in addition to, or as an alternative to, a main single shift operating in the hours of daylight. This is the only realistic way of defining shiftwork since *any* departure from a single conventional dayshift must inevitably create fresh problems for management in the organisation of manning over an extended period of time, and for shift personnel in the formation of new habits of work and leisure. This applies as much in the case of a double-day shift or a split daytime shift as it does for regular nightwork or continuous round-the-clock working over seven days.

The nature and scale of shiftwork problems will vary from situation to situation. They will vary according to the pattern of shiftwork in use, the particular demands imposed by this, and the particular constitution of the workforce concerned—whether it is predominantly male or female, young or old, staffed by volunteers or by those for whom shiftwork is a condition of service. They will vary according to whether 'abnormal' hours of work are the rule or the exception in the particular workplace and in the wider social environment outside.

Practical problems for management

Four main practical decision-making areas for management will be defined:

1 Whether to introduce multiple shiftworking at all, or to make a major change from one form of shiftwork to another
2 What detailed pattern of shiftwork to adopt
3 How to introduce change in the arrangement of hours
4 How to handle the variety of day-to-day problems which arise in the administration of shiftwork

The decision to introduce shiftwork

Whether to make use of shiftwork at all is often a question which does not arise because its use is already determined by the nature of the production process (for example in continuous process industries), or by the nature of customer demand (as in catering and transport), or by the perishable nature of the commodity (for example bread baking or newspaper production).

In other cases, where work has been conducted on a day basis, a variety of circumstances may arise to make shiftwork worth consideration. Cost of new capital equipment may be so high and technological development so rapid that investment is only justified as an economic proposition by intensive use. In other circumstances shiftwork may be considered as a means of coping with increasing demand, variable demand, or as a means of exploiting new markets. A choice between alternative courses must be taken.

It is sometimes suggested that companies in such situations turn to shiftworking as an act of faith rather than on the basis of detailed costing, and that they start with a basic assumption that shiftwork must bring benefits. While it may be true that forecasting frequently leaves something to be desired, it is only fair to say that such prediction can never be straightforward. However carefully planning for change in the arrangement of working hours may be carried out, calculation can easily be upset by such human factors as availability of labour, the attitudes of employees to shiftwork, and their performance and behaviour under abnormal hours of work. Such factors are more difficult to allow for, though all too often little attempt is made. The building of more than one new factory, intended to run on a shift basis, has been well advanced before serious thought has been given to the essentials of recruitment and training. In the 1970s it ought not to have to be pointed out that such a major change as that from day- to shiftwork cannot only be considered in technical and economic terms. Shiftwork means people, too.

The type of shift to be used

The broad type of shiftwork to be used may also be predetermined by technical and economic factors outside management's control. In other cases there is again scope for choice. If coverage of only part of the 24 hours is required, should this be done by the use of two day shifts, or by day and night turns? Day and night working, with the possibility of variable overtime between the two shifts may be seen as the more flexible arrangement, yet may not be thought to compensate for the administrative headaches which can be caused by nightwork.

If nightwork is chosen, should this be on a permanent or an alternating basis? Or should there be provision for both? Many managers are opposed to regular nightwork on the grounds that it places one group of shiftworkers permanently out of their control. Recent research on human performance, however, suggests that people may be better able to adapt to a stable pattern which allows them to rest and to be active at roughly the same time each day. There is also some evidence to suggest that, in general, fixed shifts are preferred, and that they are likely to attract a higher proportion of volunteers.

If complete 24 hours' coverage is required, the choice may be between three eight-hour shifts, an alternating double-day shift plus a permanent night turn, or two shifts of twelve hours each. The merits and demerits of these and other main shift arrangements have been discussed in more detail elsewhere.

Where it is decided to have shift crews which alternate or rotate between one shift period and another, the question of frequency of change arises. Traditional argument has favoured change at longer rather than shorter, intervals on the grounds that individual adaptation to working abnormal hours takes some time to achieve. The benefits of such adaptation, once achieved, should therefore be maintained for as long a period as possible. Such an argument only holds, however, if long working periods are uninterrupted by weekends or rest days. Moreover, it now seems doubtful whether individual adaptation is ever completely achieved in the real life situation. A more recent line of thought is to advocate change at much more frequent intervals.

Even wider scope for choice exists when we come to consider detailed features of shift design. These include shift starting and finishing times, length of shift, direction of rotation, the frequency with which weekends occur under a continuous system, variations in weekly hours and weekly pay packets.

From the bewildering range of possibilities, one point at least emerges, that there is no such thing as a 'best system.' The most successful is likely to be one tailor-made for a particular situation, designed to meet the individual needs of one company and one work-force. As these needs change, the shift system, too, may have to be modified. Many factories are still struggling along with a pattern of working hours inherited from the past and quite inappropriate for present-day demands.

The introduction of change in working hours

The actual process of introducing major change is seen by many managers as the most difficult aspect of shiftwork. This is part of the much wider problem of resistance to change generally, of habit formation, and people's tendency to prefer what they have grown used to.

While proposals for any major change in working hours are likely to provoke protest, three points of transition in particular stand out. The first of these obviously concerns the abandonment of daywork for the first time. Objection here relates to reluctance to having to give up 'normal' hours and to adjust to habits of work and leisure quite different to those of family and friends.

But objection may also be associated with fear of loss of earning power, where previous daywork has been combined with regular overtime. The inducement usually held out to dayworkers to encourage them to adopt shiftwork is that of the same, or nearly the same, pay for fewer hours (or more pay for the same hours). Many men, however, prefer daywork with overtime because it gives them greater control over their earnings, and greater control over the hours they spend at work and away from it.

Much the same problem arises where the proposed change is from two- to three-shift working. Much two-shift day and night work is accompanied by additional overtime, and many men prefer the flexibility and optional element in this to a more rigid three-shift arrangement. There is the added problem in this case of persuading men accustomed to two-shift work to accept rotation through three shifts. This is difficult enough where an alternating day and night system has previously been used. Such shiftworkers are now faced with two 'socially dead' weeks out of three (afternoons and nights) instead of one out of two. An earlier start on the day shift will probably also be involved. But change may be even more difficult where a two-shift system has previously been worked by permanent day and night crews. Here the day men may be facing shiftwork for the first time, while the permanent night men face the prospect of losing one of the main advantages of their shift—its regularity and stability.

A third stage of shift development at which opposition is likely to occur involves change from a non-continuous three-shift system to continuous working over seven days. Fears about possible loss of earning power once again arise here, since many Monday–Friday three-shift systems are combined with additional Saturday or Sunday overtime attendance. Even where such fears can be overcome, however, considerable resistance may be met to a proposed loss of the traditional weekend. Saturday or Sunday shifts may have previously been worked on a voluntary basis, but this is regarded as preferable to regular loss of weekends determined by the obligations of a seven-day rota. The advantages of compensating days off during the week have a limited appeal to those who are closely attached to the traditional weekend as the 'proper' time for relaxation. Workers' desire to retain control of their time at the weekend is likely to remain a major obstacle to the extension of seven-day working.

Associated with all such changes from day- to shiftwork, or from one type of shift to another, is the problem of the payment to be made for unconventional hours of work. Difficulties in reaching agreement on the hourly 'compensation' to be made for the inconvenience of a new shift system has not infrequently resulted in the total abandonment of management proposals for change. Particularly where abnormally high amounts of overtime have previously been worked, the size of inducement necessary can neutralise any advantage to be gained for the company.

Shift allowances, of course, are seldom the genuine 'payment for inconvenience' which they purport to be. They measure not so much the inconvenience or hardship imposed by particular types of shiftwork as relative strengths in particular bargaining situations. This is illustrated by the wide range across companies and industries in the percentage payment for any one type of system.

Negotiation of a financial settlement is also made more difficult by changes in arrangements of working hours seldom occurring in isolation. New machines and working methods may be involved, and this means retraining and re-allocation of jobs and places of work.

It is hardly necessary to add that such changes are more likely to take place smoothly where existing working relations are good: more likely to founder where such relations are characterised by misunderstanding and mistrust.

Day-to-day administration of shiftwork

Whatever problems may exist for a manager in relation to a single workforce in attendance at one and the same time, these must be increased by the introduction of any form of shiftwork involving different groups of workers and a longer working period. Nevertheless, such problems are likely to be less acute than those presented at times of change. It is generally considered that departments which have been working on a shift basis for any length of time will raise fewer problems for management; or perhaps it is that such problems seem mild by comparison with those encountered at times of transition.

There are various areas of potential administrative difficulty:

Supervision and control The first of these concerns supervision and control. Since the degree and level of management tends to be lower outside normal dayshift hours—partly a matter of economics, partly of staffing—control of non-dayshift personnel is more difficult. This is particularly so in the case of nightshift workers, and explains many managers' dislike of permanent night arrangements. Such considerations place a special responsibility on first-line supervisory staff who may be required to take decisions and accept responsibility, without reference to senior management, in a way that would not be expected of a dayshift foreman.

Communication and co-ordination Allied to the question of control are those of communication and co-ordination. There is a danger—unless specific steps are taken to avoid it—that communication will be impaired between senior management and daytime service departments on the one hand and night shift personnel on the other. It is very easy for nightshift workers to become isolated in information terms, for them to be neglected in industrial relations matters and their opportunities for training and promotion reduced.

This can lead to a justifiable sense of isolation on the part of night-workers regarding themselves as being less an integral part of the organisation than are dayworkers. From this it is a short step to a state of 'them' versus 'us' and to obstructive behaviour towards the 'Company' and towards those on different systems of hours. Such feelings are not restricted to those on permanent nightshifts. They can develop, for example, among any minority shiftwork group in a predominantly daywork firm.

Provision of supporting services   Another set of administrative problems concern the provision of supporting services to production crews working outside normal daytime hours. Transport, canteen and medical facilities, and arrangements for dealing with personnel matters, may all be less satisfactory for shiftworkers. The amount of technical and maintenance support is also likely to be less. This means that breakdowns at night can take longer to repair, or may have to wait until the following dayshift arrives. Such problems are particularly noticeable in small units which will find it uneconomic to provide anything but the barest of ancillary services. For the larger unit, however, it is likely to be false economy to try to balance the extra cost of nightwork by saving on supervisory and supporting services.

Recruitment and selection   The recruitment and selection of shiftworkers poses some special problems. Not only may the range of choice among entrants be narrower, but the responsibilities involved in the job may call for a higher standard than in the case of dayworkers. Particular care is necessary in the case of men without previous shift experience. Such selection involves an estimate of a recruit's likely adjustment to an unaccustomed living and working routine. More careful medical checks may also be necessary. Bearing in mind possible resistance to change in new shiftworking situations many companies try to recruit new staff from outside rather than transfer existing personnel.

Special groups   Certain special groups such as women, older workers, and the disabled, require special consideration. Although women still account for only a minority of the total shiftworking population the proportion is increasing. Many working women prefer double-day work or part-time day or evening work to normal daywork, since such routines make the tasks of shopping and looking after a house and home easier to cope with. Attention has to be paid to their particular

needs, which become stronger in the case of women on nightwork—
a form of working likely to develop more rapidly over the next
decade.

As regards the older worker, since those above the age of 50 are in
general likely to find it more difficult to adjust physically and socially to
routines involving nightwork, firms adopting shiftwork for the first
time would be advised not to recruit those of this age group. In the case
of an existing shift situation, nightwork ought not to be compulsory
for the over-50s. But transfer of an older shiftworker to days will
involve financial hardship unless the company is prepared to go on
paying him at shift rates.

Something of the same problem arises in the case of the disabled
worker. Men with chronic disabling conditions ought not to be
recruited to shiftwork for the first time, and those already employed
should be able to transfer to daywork if they want to do so. But shiftworkers should not automatically be taken off shiftwork for specific
medical reasons without thought being given to possible financial and
social hardship in individual cases.

Effects of shiftwork The administrator has also to consider possible
effects of shiftwork on job performance and behaviour at work. No
short and unequivocal answer concerning the effect of shiftwork upon
output and quality, and upon the incidence of absence and accidents,
can be given since these are determined by a variety of factors associated
with the individual shiftworker himself, the job he does, and the
physical and social environment in which he works. No two factory
situations are ever precisely comparable, and a unique combination of
circumstances in each is likely to produce effects which are also highly
particular.

One sense in which nightwork can be regarded as less efficient is in
terms of the increased demand which it makes upon the human
organism. To speak of efficiency in this way does not mean that output
will necessarily be lower at night, or that errors will be more frequent.
But though night-time performance may be maintained at its daytime
level, studies which have made use of various psycho-physiological
tests and measures in shift situations—reaction time, oxygen consumption, energy expenditure, and so on—have shown that this is only
achieved at the cost of increased fatigue among the shiftworkers
concerned.

Social implications

So far we have dealt with some of the practical problems facing managers in the introduction and use of shiftwork. Consider now their social responsibilities. To consider these separately, of course, is an artificial distinction made for the convenience of presentation. In arriving at decisions affecting the arrangement of hours of work, consideration of technical and economic necessity, and of administrative convenience, blend with those concerning what is socially acceptable and what is desirable from the point of view of health and safety.

What are the problems faced by those going on to shifts for the first time, or facing a major change in their hours of work? There is probably no other area in which what happens at work and what happens away from work are so closely bound together. Even a relatively minor change in working hours—an earlier starting time or a spell of overtime at the end of the day—automatically and immediately affect travel to and from work, mealtimes, domestic arrangements and leisure activities. The social and domestic effects of a regular shiftwork system will be even more marked.

The nature of these effects will depend first upon the type of system involved. In ascending order of impact they can be listed as:

1 Any departure from a normal dayshift but not involving nightwork
2 Change to any two-shift system involving nightwork
3 Change to a system involving three shift changes in 24 hours
4 Change to a system involving weekend work

Domestic problems

Such stages call for major readjustments not only on the part of the shiftworker himself, but by his wife and family. Shiftwork can place an additional strain upon a wife; her physical relationship with her husband; the extent to which she may have to be alone in the house at night; the special responsibilities it may place upon her in the upbringing of children and the disruption of domestic routine. Difficulties with household chores when the husband is at home and trying to sleep can create particular problems. Attempting to keep young children quiet can also impose strain.

The family and domestic problems involved will obviously depend not only on the particular type of shift but on the particular circumstances of the man concerned. They will vary, for example, not only according to whether he is married or not, has children or not, but on whether he is newly married, on the success of the relationship with his wife, on her attitude to his working shifts, whether she is herself working, the number and ages of his children, his financial commitments, and so on. Some men find their rota a positive advantage in that it enables them to see more of their families than would be the case under daywork.

Leisure and social interests

Regarding a man's leisure and social interests outside the family, the effect of a particular shift rota will again depend upon the nature of these interests and whether they are tied to time-of-day in a way which is determined by a single-shift, daytime economy. Evening activities such as television viewing, and visits to cinemas, pubs and dances, together with Saturday afternoon sport, are those most often quoted as being interrupted by shiftwork. Less affected are such pursuits as gardening, do-it-yourself jobs, car maintenance and fishing. Again, the effect of shiftwork on social life is not uniformly negative. Some men find it a positive advantage in this respect. Shiftwork can enable a man more easily to follow his leisure interests, just as it can hinder him from enjoying them.

Physical effects

Social and domestic effects aside, the other major area where shiftwork can cause problems for the individual is in its physical effects. There has been much speculation in the past concerning the possible adverse health effects of various types of shiftwork. Certain cautions must be given here. Much of the evidence that shiftwork, and particularly nightwork, has an adverse effect on health depends on observations made during the two war periods, when shiftwork was associated with other stress conditions of wartime life. Much of the evidence to support the 'unhealthiness' of shiftwork is also based on subjective reports of shiftworkers themselves: there is little confirmation from more objective sources such as absence or medical records.

An association is often believed to exist between working on shifts and particular forms of chronic disease, but no such association has been established. Shift hours of work may, however, in association with other factors, have an aggravating effect upon an existing condition such as a peptic ulcer. It has even been suggested that long service on shiftwork reduces life expectancy, but a detailed statistical study recently concluded by research workers at the TUC Centenary Institute of Occupational Health failed to find any support for this theory. There is no doubt that a positive association does exist between working on certain shift routines and a range of minor ailments and bodily discomforts. Few shiftworkers appear to escape entirely from such physical repercussions that follow from having to work at unconventional times in the 24 hours, and having to adjust to a succession of different shift periods. Sleeping and eating are the two major problem areas which call for adaptation by the shiftworker.

Complaints about sleep from shiftworkers concern the amount of sleep obtained during the day, which is generally thought to be less than would have been obtained at night. The quality of this sleep is thought to be poorer and affected by noise of various kinds. The effects which follow from difficulties of sleep are feelings of fatigue and of general malaise.

Difficulties concerning appetite and digestion are also commonly reported because of meals taken at unusual hours. These mainly involve loss of appetite and enjoyment of meals, together with such disturbances as indigestion and constipation. Meals often appear to be eaten hurriedly and to be less balanced. Consumption of alcohol and tobacco may also be more erratic.

More information based on careful research is certainly needed about the differential effects of various types of shift rota, for example on the extent to which sleep is curtailed. More information is also required about the factors involved in one man's capacity to adapt to changed hours of work and another man's failure to do so.

In the meantime certain elementary safeguards can be taken by the shiftworker himself, in adopting regular and reasonable patterns of rest-sleep-activity in off-duty periods. The employer could take safeguards by arranging rotas so as to allow adequate time for rest and recovery between shifts worked at 'abnormal' times. A minimum of 24 hours after a full night shift, for example, is recommended. There are various reasons why such a standard may not be achieved in practice. One is the preference on the part of many shiftworkers for concentrating their duties in solid blocks of time, in exchange for extended free periods. The other is the tendency, due to manning problems, for employers to combine shiftwork with overtime working. In theory, shiftwork eliminates overtime: in practice it often only survives because of it, but cumulative fatigue resulting from excessive hours can adversely affect both health and performance.

Organisational implications

There are two ways in which the manager's social responsibilities can be translated into action:

1 Since shiftwork is an aspect of working life where managerial decisions so closely affect the lives of employees and their families, these employees should be involved as closely as possible in the policy and procedural decisions governing the arrangement of their working hours.
2 Since each working routine places certain physical and social demands upon those who must conform to it, and since the weight of these demands differs according to personal make-up and circumstances, as great a degree of flexibility as possible should be built into a company's shift arrangements so as to allow for individual differences in the capacity to adapt.

In any success story involving the introduction of shiftwork, care taken over communication is always apparent. Equally, where negotiation for change has broken down, some inadequacy in the provision of advance information or in the way in which the need for change was presented, can usually be detected. Change of any kind involves a degree of insecurity for those involved, and this is particularly so where change in hours is accompanied by changes in working methods, job allocation, and so on. Bearing in mind the volume of words that has been devoted over the past fifteen years to the need for effective communication, it is astonishing to observe how often its most elementary rules are ignored. 'The first I knew that the motorway was coming straight through the factory,' an aggrieved employee once told the writer, in a London firm whose shift operations were being transferred to a factory in the northeast, 'was when my wife heard it in the butcher's.' Too little; too late; and from the wrong source.

The old maxim that volunteers are to be preferred to conscripts should also be remembered in the context of shiftworking. Shifts are not universally disliked and avoided, and among the ranks of shift-workers are to be found many who are there at their own request. In some cases shifts may be worked because they are genuinely preferred. More commonly shiftwork is accepted because of certain advantages which attach to it, or because advantages outweigh the disadvantages. Since like and dislike are directed not towards shiftwork as such but to particular forms of shiftwork which either suit or do not suit particular needs and circumstances, it makes sense to allow employees as wide a say as possible in the choice of the rota they are to operate. This means taking account of the wishes of the majority concerning shift design, and then allowing as far as possible individual variation within the general rule. Flexibility aids individual adaptation.

Many firms do already arrange for such flexibility to meet individual needs and personal circumstances. In others it is actively discouraged. The principle could certainly be put into practice much more widely than is the case at present.

The most extreme form of flexibility is to allow for exceptions altogether from shiftwork. This is the most difficult provision for a manager to interpret, and the one which is most open to abuse. But there will always be a small minority in any workforce who are psychologically or physiologically incapable of making the necessary adjustment and who will probably be better off on daywork.

Allowing for prior consultation is always time-consuming: an imposed decision is always quicker. Permitting individual choice is administratively inconvenient: it is always easier to administer a general rule than to provide for exceptions. Nevertheless, consultation and choice will be more than repaid in terms of improved employee morale and service. This morale derives in part from the satisfaction that comes from participating in a scheme which employees have themselves helped devise. It also comes from employees' sense of acquiring some degree of control over the way in which their hours at work and their hours away from work are arranged.

13

Racial Integration in Employment

T J Connelly

Chief Conciliation Officer, Race Relations Board

For the purpose of this chapter I have relied on the definition of integration contained in Sheila Patterson's *Immigrants in Industry* (Institute of Race Relations/Oxford University Press, 1968), which describes a situation in which the

> 'immigrant or minority group adapts itself to permanent membership of the receiving society and is accepted by the latter in such universal areas of association as economic and civic life; meanwhile it retains different patterns in some other spheres, such as family, religious, and cultural life, provided that these patterns do not conflict with the basic values and norms of the receiving society'

This differs from assimilation which denotes the complete adaptation by immigrant groups or individuals and their complete acceptance by the receiving society.

The Race Relations Act 1968 signified the intention of Parliament to regard the integration of immigrant settlers and their descendants upon the basis of equality as an important matter of public policy. Although the legislation was originally controversial it has since been accepted by all major political parties and it is reasonable to suppose that it will remain on the statute books until its objectives are achieved.

Apart from the moral issues involved, management consideration of what policies on race should be adopted and implemented within the firm could usefully start from the premise that the vital character of the public policy questions involved will not allow firms to shelve the subject indefinitely. Although the immediate purpose of the Race Relations Act is to prevent persons being treated less favourably on the grounds of race, colour or origin, the primary concern of Parliament was not so much the victims of discrimination as the possible consequences for British life if a situation was allowed to develop in which such victims, belonging to easily identifiable minority groups, existed in significant numbers. The world provides many examples of the dangers that can ensue from the presence of dissatisfied minorities who suffer the injustice of being treated as inferiors and who lack hope of being treated otherwise because of something which they cannot alter such as their origins or the colour of their skin.

These dangers raise basic questions for society. They may involve social instability; they may aggravate crime and delinquency problems and the amount of permanent unemployment. They may create problems in the educational system, in so far as any barriers to achievement created by discrimination lead to frustration and disaffection and increase the *drop out* rate of individuals who might otherwise have achieved a higher degree of educational attainment. They may affect Britain's relations with other countries. The subject of race and community relations therefore poses fundamental issues for society which justify the assertion that Government, in the foreseeable future, will have continuous concern with employer behaviour in this field. No understanding of the significance of the Race Relations Act and other governmental steps taken in this area is possible without a grasp of these underlying social interests. Indeed, it required such considerations to justify the intrusion of the law upon the traditional common law rights of employers in matters of recruitment and promotion, terms of employment, and dismissals.

Employment and integration

What happens in employment is crucial for the whole issue. A person's job and employment prospects obviously determine his current and future material welfare, the well-being of his family and his status in the community. The housing and educational opportunities of coloured workers and their ability to move out of residential concentrations has a vital bearing on the question of their acceptance of integration outside the employment field. An indispensable condition for fuller acceptance is the breakdown of the association between colour and inferiority. If coloured workers are seen mainly in low status jobs and in poor housing, the association will be sustained and strengthened. The more they are seen in higher status jobs, particularly those which involve the exercise of authority, the weaker the association with inferiority will become. The experience of coloured workers in industry will therefore influence crucially the attitudes and behaviour of the host society.

The same experience will be important in the determination of immigrant attitudes towards integration. Acceptance in employment and elsewhere on the basis of merit will tend to create the security and confidence needed if immigrants are to seek social integration. Discrimination and hostility in the workplace will engender insecurity and defensiveness that will increase the propensity to stick to their own national or ethnic groups. If discrimination is general, immigrant groups as a whole may reject integration as a feasible or desirable objective. However, discrimination is likely to produce a variety of reactions both within society and within the firm. It may even be accepted by the majority of immigrants, but it is both reasonable and prudent for a firm to assume that some immigrants will protest against being regarded and treated as inferiors. This is all that is required to create problems for the society and the firm.

Many firms, however, may consider that these social implications relate more to future than to present considerations. In a sense this is true; but delay in the introduction and implementation of the appropriate policies can only lead to problems becoming more entrenched and intractable both for the firm and for society. Although a firm may consider that no serious immediate problems exist, it would be short-sighted not to take steps to prevent their development. This is a lesson that many major US companies learned too late. To cope with problems of discrimination that have been allowed to develop, some have considered if necessary to establish their own equal opportunity divisions operating independently of personnel departments. Too much should not be made of American experience, but British firms which delay the appropriate measures may later have to tackle much more serious problems in a much shorter time.

Immigrant disadvantage

A correct diagnosis of the nature of the elements involved in the subject is an obvious preliminary to such measures. There is a need to distinguish between two separate but related issues. The first is the question of the problems that have a vital bearing on integration, but which do not necessarily involve discriminatory behaviour. In this category are the problems that confront *some* immigrants through being newcomers to British society. *Some* immigrants for some jobs may labour under obvious difficulties associated with language, communications, cultural differences and lack of experience of a modern complex industrial society. With time, these difficulties will diminish in extent and character. They may be classified as problems of immigrant disadvantage. The second issue concerns persons who do not share these disadvantages, but who receive less favourable treatment simply because of their race, origin and/or colour. They may be classified as problems of racial discrimination. (*Racial discrimination* is used here to cover discrimination on grounds of race, colour or ethnic or national origins.)

Overcoming the problems of immigrant disadvantage and those of racial discrimination are both related to the objective of racial integration, but they obviously have separate implications for the firm. Steps to overcome immigrant disadvantage are not legally obligatory, but fall within the area of social obligation. The elimination of racial discrimination is a legal obligation. Discrimination is mainly associated with colour, but of course this is not the only form. A firm may employ coloured workers and discriminate only against particular coloured groups. Research has shown a bewildering variety of preferences for particular racial or ethnic groups. (See *The Coloured Worker in British Industry*, Peter L Wright, Institute of Race Relations/Oxford University Press, 1968.)

Discrimination of this kind is strictly based on origin rather than colour. Of course it is not only coloured groups who face this problem. Discrimination may occur against European workers or the Irish. Even English, Welsh and Scottish workers are not entirely excluded from behaviour based on preconceived negative ideas about the characteristics of their national groups. The unenviable distinction for coloured groups is that they suffer as a group from such irrationalities and prejudices to an immensely greater degree because of the wide and deep associations of colour with inferiority and are not victims of some individual eccentricity or quirk.

It is not possible here to cover the many aspects of the problem of overcoming immigrant disadvantage. Needs will vary with firms and sections of firms. There are, however, some general points which can be made. It should not be assumed that all newcomers of a particular group are at a disadvantage. There are, for example, many Indians and Pakistanis who can speak English and communicate very well. The needs should not therefore be identified with a group, but with individuals within a group. Some examples drawn from experience may help to clarify this point. Many firms, in order to surmount language, communication, training and supervision difficulties with Asian immigrants, have tended to segregate Asians either geographically or to confine their employment to particular shifts. Segregation based on these factors has sometimes facilitated the adjustment and increased the effectiveness of Asian workers and has minimised the adjustment to the newcomers required of management and indigenous workers. Being able to work with immigrants from their own country has contributed to the psychological security of many immigrant workers at a stage when such security can be of great importance to them. There are therefore several self-interest factors which involve everybody concerned which may create and sustain segregated work groups that have nothing at all to do with our discrimination. (The Department of Employment has issued a number of pamphlets connected with this subject. The Department also employs at regional level race relations advisers who will help firms to deal with specific problems.)

There are, however, obvious dangers to be guarded against. Although originally segregation may be based on the genuine needs of many immigrants and also meet the needs of the firm, there is a serious risk that with time the segregated situations may become identified not with needs, but with the particular ethnic group, and if the group wholly comprises coloured workers, identified with colour. The longer segregated situations are maintained, the stronger the identification with the group and/or colour is likely to become. If the pattern established is accepted by management and indigenous workers in terms of the group or colour, there may be considerable difficulties in changing the pattern as the needs upon which it was originally based become less relevant or even completely irrelevant. Coloured workers, who may not be newcomers, may be hesitant to seek opportunities in areas in which all the employees are white. White employees may resist alterations in the pattern that they have come to regard as normal. Persons responsible for recruitment may become accustomed to allocating coloured workers to sections or shifts that have become identified largely or wholly with particular groups. While for a time segregation may represent a form of accommodation acceptable by all, if it hardens into a pattern, tensions and conflicts may occur when pressures upon the pattern arise.

Several simple illustrations of this have been provided by firms which introduced separate lavatory facilities for Asians to meet their special needs. When young persons of Asian origin who were reared mainly in this country endeavoured to use the 'white lavatories' they met with resistance from white workers. Strikes have been known over this issue. The lavatories became identified not with the needs in which they originated, but with Asians as a group, and in some instances, with colour. Dangers of a more serious kind can arise when coloured workers seek employment in jobs, departments or shifts, that have come to be regarded as the preserves of indigenous white workers.

These dangers have been avoided by firms that from the start have dispersed immigrants throughout the workforce, although often the ability to pursue such a policy has been dependent on the exclusion of immigrants with language and communication difficulties. It is clearly in the interests of firms not in this category to pursue a policy of dispersal as fast as circumstances will allow. This requires, with recruitment, promotion or allocation of jobs within the plant, that individuals should be judged on merit and should not have any barriers placed upon their legitimate aspirations. On a different level is the widening of the job opportunities of immigrants by alleviating disadvantages which stem for example from language and communication difficulties. Experience has shown that training and language courses provided by organisations outside the firm are not extensively used by immigrants and in conjunction with local education authorities, some firms have provided courses on their premises. Most industry training boards will consider the costs of such courses for grant aid. The effectiveness of these measures is increased if they are allied with instruction of supervisors in the basic language of the immigrants. Very often the value of such instruction is enhanced by the knowledge supervisors acquire of the culture and customs of different immigrant groups. These measures contribute towards the conditions for greater integration and towards the interests of the firm in so far as they raise the skill and ability level of the workforce and reduce the possibility of friction.

Immigrant needs

A distinction has to be drawn between measures to overcome disadvantages and measures designed to accommodate needs which stem from religious or cultural factors and from the fact that many immigrants retain connections with their homelands. This raises the question of the extent to which firms should meet requests based on these considerations. Individual firms should reach conclusions on these matters based on their particular circumstances, but the enlightened firm should be prepared to accommodate such needs provided there is no conflict with production or other essential requirements. For example, where turbans cannot be adjusted to safety requirements or where, in rare cases, beards pose problems of hygiene, a firm would be justified in refusing to employ Sikhs for whom wearing turbans and beards are absolute religious needs. Where no conflict exists between these needs and the job, there is no such justification. Sometimes refusals to employ Sikhs wearing beards and turbans or women wearing saris are cloaks for discrimination on racial grounds, in which case they are unlawful.

Measures to facilitate integration may meet resistance from indigenous workers, including management. Such resistance may be based on straightforward prejudice, but in most cases the resistance is likely to be the result of a complexity of factors. There is usually a close association between resistance and the attitudes of persons in formal and informal leadership positions. The majority of workers are likely to be unprejudiced but will respond to whatever leadership is given. Other factors that can influence the situation are job and earnings security fears; status considerations; the degree of social and personal adjustments involved in particular work situations; the characteristics of informal work groups; the state of labour-management relations; the way any integration measures are introduced. (The importance of these factors for particular employment situations cannot be evaluated in a chapter of this kind. For a detailed study of them, see Sheila Patterson's *Immigrants in Industry*.) There is no general recipe for success. What measures are needed and the method of introduction should be determined after an analysis of particular situations. A common objection, however, to any steps taken to promote integration is that they involve preferential treatment for immigrants. This objection is often based on a confusion between different treatment and preferential treatment. It ignores the fact that the objective of the measures is to remove handicaps not shared by indigenous workers and to facilitate the integration and adjustment of immigrants in the interests of everybody.

Racial discrimination and the Race Relations Act

Although the elimination of racial discrimination and measures to further racial integration can be analysed separately, in practice they often interact. A firm which in the interests of integration ensures that immigrants are given the range of opportunity enjoyed by indigenous workers is combating racial discrimination at the same time. A firm which segregates on the basis of ethnic groups and/or colour retards integration and discriminates unlawfully.

It is appropriate here to state the salient provisions of the Race Relations Act as it relates to employment and the methods used to enforce it. The Act defines discrimination as treating a person less favourably than another person on grounds of race, colour or ethnic or national origins. To segregate a person on these grounds is also unlawful. Provided a person is qualified and the work is available, it is unlawful to discriminate in recruitment or in the terms and conditions offered to applicants; an existing employee cannot be discriminated against in respect of terms and conditions of employment; a person must not be treated less favourably in regard to training, promotion or dismissals. The Act makes the employer liable for the acts of employees done during the course of their employment and for the acts of his agents. It would, however, be a defence in court proceedings if the employer could prove that he took such steps as were reasonably practicable to prevent discrimination by his employees. It is also unlawful for anyone to aid, induce or incite another person to do acts made unlawful by the Act.

Exemption from the Act

Until 16 November 1972, employers with not more than ten employees are exempted from the Act. From that date all employers will be covered. Other exemptions relate to employment in private households, employment abroad, in ships or aircraft, and where national security is involved. An employer, provided it is done in good faith, may discriminate for the purposes of securing or maintaining a reasonable racial balance in his workforce or sections of the workforce. The racial balance clauses are complex, however, and employers who consider themselves covered by them would do well to seek the advice of the local employment exchange or the Race Relations Board. The Board, in co-operation with the Department of Employment, the Trades Union Congress and the Confederation of British Industry, has published guidelines to the racial balance provisions.

Enforcement of employment provisions

Responsibility for the enforcement of the employment provisions of the Act is divided between the Race Relations Board and industry panels approved by the Secretary of State for Employment. Where a suitable industry panel exists, the Secretary of State must refer any complaint related to employment to them. If no panel exists, the complaint is referred to the Board. However, a respondent or complainant aggrieved by a decision of a panel, may take his grievance to the Board, which may then reinvestigate the original complaint or refer it back to the panel for reinvestigation, or decide that it should not be further entertained. A complaint that is referred directly to the Board by the Secretary of State for Employment may be investigated by the Board itself or by one of the Board's nine regional conciliation committees. To ensure the necessary expertise, the Board and its Committees include persons from industry, employers and trade unionists.

Complaints

Contrary to a common misconception, the bodies dealing with complaints under the Act are not judicial nor quasi-judicial. They are investigative bodies, charged under the Act with the investigation of complaints and with forming opinions on whether unlawful discrimination has occurred. An opinion is not the same as a judgement or a verdict. It merely represents an opinion of informed people on whether discrimination occurred. A necessary corollary is that the standard of proof required is certainly lower than would be the case in a criminal offence—proof beyond reasonable doubt. The standard approximates to, though is not necessarily identical with, the *balance of probabilities* which determines the outcome of a civil action. A further corollary is that the *penalties or adverse consequences* that flow for the party against whom an opinion has been formed are limited. The consequences cannot reasonably be construed as punitive.

Settlement

If an opinion of unlawful discrimination is formed, the body forming the opinion is under a statutory obligation to use its best endeavours to secure a settlement between the parties and to seek an assurance from the employer against a repetition of the act, considered to be unlawful, and against future acts of a similar kind. Although the two processes of seeking a settlement and an assurance do not essentially conform with normal conceptions of industrial conciliation, they are regarded as a form of conciliation. An attempt is made to achieve a settlement mutually acceptable to the parties.

The Act does not give powers to compel, for example, the offer of a vacancy to a qualified person discriminated against in recruitment or to secure the reinstatement of a person dismissed. The body concerned may, however, suggest such steps to the parties, but it is a matter of persuasion and not compulsion. The determination of what is a satisfactory settlement is ultimately a matter for the parties concerned. In giving advice on what constitutes a satisfactory settlement, the body concerned is likely to have regard to what might be achieved for the complainant should conciliation fail and the Race Relations Board determine to bring proceedings in court. The Board may bring proceedings where a satisfactory settlement and/or an assurance has not been achieved. If they satisfy the judge that an act of unlawful discrimination has occurred, the judge may award (*a*) special damages to the complainant to compensate for any losses arising directly from the discrimination (these may in some circumstances amount to no more than *out of pocket* expenses) and/or (*b*) damages for loss of any benefit which the complainant might reasonably be expected to have had but for the act of discrimination. Provided the complainant had taken reasonable steps to mitigate his losses (for example by seeking other employment), the second category of damages might involve compensation for loss of earnings that a person would have received had he secured or retained his job. The Board would be likely to consider it unreasonable for a settlement to give less to the complainant than a court would award and would therefore in their own conciliation process advise the parties accordingly.

Written assurance

The securing, where appropriate, of a satisfactory written assurance, is related to the public interest objectives of the Act and is a matter for the Board and the employer who is held to have discriminated. The primary purpose of the Act is to stop discrimination. In giving an assurance an employer promises to do this. If there is a further act of discrimination of a similar kind by the employer that breaches the assurance given, the Board, if it considers that the employer is likely to engage in further discrimination unless restrained by a court, may seek an injunction to restrain the employer, without first going through the conciliation process described. Should an injunction be granted, the employer would be subject to the normal penalties associated with contempt of court if he continued to engage in discriminatory conduct.

Equality of treatment and opportunity

It will be seen from the Act's definition of discrimination that it is about equal treatment for equals, in so far as any inequalities are the result of a person's race, colour or ethnic or national origin. The purpose of an investigation is therefore to discover what equality of treatment is in any particular circumstance, whether a complainant received it, and if not, whether it was on grounds made unlawful by the Act. The definition of discrimination means that the Act does not assist persons to overcome immigrant disadvantages other than the disadvantage of being discriminated against simply on grounds of colour and origin. Nor is the Act concerned with unfair treatment of immigrants which they may suffer in common with indigenous workers. The Board is not there to remedy work grievances unrelated to colour and origin. Moreover, the rights bestowed by the Act are not confined to immigrant workers. Indigenous workers can use the Act if they consider that they have been treated less favourably on grounds made unlawful by the Act. These points confute the frequently expressed objection to the Act that it confers special privileges on immigrants and coloured workers.

Despite the Act, the elimination of racial discrimination in employment will still mainly depend upon action by employers and trade unions. All experience shows that the type of leadership given is crucial and, with some exceptions, it is management leadership, because of the predominant power of management, that is more important. Although in many firms top management may be opposed to racial discrimination this will not always prevent it, upon the part of subordinates, who for a variety of reasons may discriminate. To reduce the possibilities of discrimination, in companies of any size, a firm policy should be laid down and measures taken to ensure that the policy is being implemented. In medium to large firms this is likely to require the keeping of records of persons by country of origin. Objections may be made to such record keeping on the ground that this is in itself a form of discrimination. Record keeping is a form of differentiation rather than discrimination, but even where it is interpreted as discrimination, the justification is in the fact that such records, being essential to the effective monitoring of an anti-discrimination policy, are needed to overcome a more obnoxious and serious form of discrimination.

Like integration, the steps required to combat discrimination may vary with the particular circumstances of a firm and areas within firms. There are, however, some points that are likely to be of general application. In many circumstances, the problem may not be widespread active discrimination against individuals simply because people may be reluctant to put themselves in a position to be discriminated against. Discrimination may be passive in the sense that there is a conscious or unconscious denial of equal opportunity to coloured workers, which is accepted by all concerned, including coloured workers. These workers may not be willing to risk the humiliation involved in being discriminated against. They may fear victimisation or may not wish to disturb the atmosphere by challenging any accommodation reached. Management and indigenous workers may be content, or want, to maintain the *status quo*. It would be wrong to interpret the absence of protest against lack of equal opportunity as the absence of problems. Coloured workers, especially those educated wholly or mainly in this country, will not always be content to be deprived. Their expectations will rise, and if these expectations are frustrated by discrimination the *status quo* will come under increasing challenge. If by then, the patterns of employment based on discrimination have hardened, the provision of equal opportunity will be a more difficult process. Friction and conflict are likely to be on a more serious scale than if equal opportunity is introduced before the patterns become set.

Recruitment and employment practices

A firm can go a long way to avoid discrimination if it reforms its recruitment and employment practices to eliminate all forms of irrational factors, for example sex and age. This has the advantage of not singling out coloured workers for different treatment with all the misconceptions this often entails. But if such extensive reform is not immediately practicable, the implementation of the principle of treating a person on individual merit rather than on colour or origin should eliminate the crude stereotyping of individuals that often forms the basis of selection in some firms. Immigrant groups are by no means the only sufferers of such stereotyping, but they are particularly prone to it. Different managers may have different stereotypes which lead to a variety of contradictory preferences. Some will have positive stereotypes, up to a point, of Pakistanis and negative ones about Indians. For others the reverse will be the case. Some will prefer West Indians and so on. Although in this chapter abstractions like 'coloured worker' and 'immigrant worker' have unavoidably been used, in reality there is of course no such thing. Neither is there a West Indian worker, nor a Pakistani or an Indian worker. There are a variety of workers in these groups, differing in talent, abilities, skills and potential. It is vital to judge them as individuals and not by unsophisticated judgements based on preconceived notions of the characteristics of the groups to which they belong.

Dangers in assumptions

Discriminatory behaviour is often based not on prejudice but on untested assumptions about the reactions of others to the employment of coloured workers in any particular capacity. Frequently, on being tested the assumptions prove false. Such assumptions may relate to worker and customer reaction. A notable example has been provided in retail distribution. Many department stores long opposed the employment of coloured assistants because of anxieties about the reaction of customers. When coloured assistants were eventually employed

H

customer protest turned out to be negligible. Other examples could be quoted of managerial reluctance to employ coloured workers because of beliefs that the workers would not accept them. On being put to the test, the beliefs were shown to be unfounded. In some situations, there may be obstacles in the form of worker and customer resistances. An essential preliminary, however, to the elimination of racial discrimination is the examination and surmounting of obstacles within the managerial structure itself for it will be predominantly managerial decisions which will determine when, how and where coloured workers are employed.

14

Women and Equality

Rachel Naylor

Lecturer, Department of Management Sciences, UMIST

The passing of the Equal Pay Act 1970 marked an important stage in the campaign begun by the TUC resolution on equal pay for women in 1888, although experience in the European Economic Community does not indicate that the passing of legislation disposes of all differentials. The signatories to the Treaty of Rome undertook to ensure 'equal remuneration for equal work' and in 1961 adopted a resolution laying down a three-year plan for eliminating discrimination in stages by 31 December 1964. Yet in 1966 a report by the EEC Commission stated that none of the countries had established equal pay overall in practice, but significant progress had been made in establishing the principle. The problems have been a difference of view on the right of the commission or of the states to interfere in or monitor collective agreements and the near impossibility of interference with payments of a discretionary type, in addition to agreed rates. Such payments may cause inequality under another name. The National Industrial Relations Court will monitor collective agreements in Britain; women considering themselves to have a claim against their employer on grounds of equal pay may appeal to the industrial tribunals. The Labour Government which steered the Equal Pay Act on to the statute book, did not ratify the ILO Convention 100 on Equal Pay; now, however, the Conservative Government has.

This chapter indicates briefly the main points in the campaign to end pay discrimination against women; it considers the most important sections of the Act and discusses some possible problems of implementation and ways in which they may be overcome. It also considers the related issues of women's employment; protective legislation, training and women's attitude to their jobs. It suggests some developments which may take place. The question of costs is touched upon. Lady Seear's paper for the Royal Commission, No. 11, *The Position of Women in Industry*,[1] G J Mepham's booklet *Problems of Equal Pay*[2] and the Employment and Productivity Gazette article *Cost of Equal Pay*[3] all give useful information.

The campaign for equal pay—some important dates

1888   TUC resolution on equal pay.

1919   Atkinson Committee Report; after women had proved their worth in the Ordnance factories.

1919   Sex Discrimination Act.
       Setting up of Fawcett Society and the Business and Professional Women's Association.

1944–1946   Royal Commission on Equal Pay (Cmnd 6937). Women had made a significant contribution in the war effort. The difficulties put to the Commission were the familiar ones: women's physical strength was inferior; their working life was shorter and their absence rate higher; they were relatively inflexible in their response to changing or abnormal situations: women's legal privileges, such as a wife's presumed ability to pledge her husband's credit—still partially true—would be questioned under an equal pay system. The view was expressed that a man's rate should reflect his greater family responsibility. Women were less interested in trade union affairs, it was said, and unlikely to play an important part in them.

1952   House of Commons resolution favouring equal pay for non-industrial civil servants.

1955   Civil Service and teaching profession schemes to establish equal rates of pay for men and women performing equal work; the objective to be achieved by stages over a period of seven years. (The Equal Pay Act 1970 lays down a period of five years.)

1962 TUC again passed a resolution: 'This Congress notes with concern the relatively slow progress made in implementing the principle of equal pay for equal work for men and women. Congress therefore urges affiliated unions to seriously consider adopting a policy of securing equal increases for men and women in all wage negotiations.'

(The mover emphasised that equal increases were no substitute for equal pay.)

TUC General Council found that in the period October 1959 to October 1961 there had been a slightly unfavourable movement, particularly in manual employment; the earnings differential increased by over £1 and the rate differential by only five old pence.

The average earnings of women remained only half those of men.

TUC call for an *Industrial Charter for Women*, the provisions to cover both pay and pensions in addition to training and promotion opportunities.

The call for equal pay was repeated at almost every union conference.

1969 Engineering trade negotiations. Equal pay not conceded.

1970 Equal Pay Act.

Impact of equal pay

Increased numbers of women in employment

The Department of Employment figures showed that women form 37 per cent of the total number employed, 31 per cent of the total in manufacturing industries;[3] the number of married women is increasing, though about $17\frac{1}{2}$ per cent are in part-time work. The Manpower Research Unit Report No. 1 (*The Pattern of the Future HMSO* 1964) pointed out that married women constitute one of the few remaining sources for any required increase in the labour force.

Industries vary considerably in the numbers of women employees and the extent to which the Equal Pay Act will affect them. Figure 14:1 shows the actual numbers and the percentages of the total in thirteen industries selected by the Department of Employment (then the Department of Employment and Productivity) for a study of implementation costs.

	NO. INCL. PART-TIME (000's)	% TOTAL NO. OF EMPLOYEES
MANUFACTURING INDUSTRIES		
Chemical and allied industries	137	27
Clothing	315	79
Cotton spinning (including man-made)	47	55
Engineering and electrical engineering (including ship-building, vehicle building and metal trades)	932	24
Food	283	45
Foot-wear	53	54
Paper	83	36
Pottery	32	53
Soap, candles, edible fats	12	33
Wool textiles	76	49
SERVICE INDUSTRIES		
Hotel and catering	376	64
Laundries	73	73
Retail distribution	1286	64

Figure 14:1 Numbers and percentage of women
employed in thirteen selected industries

Source: *Employment and Productivity Gazette*, January, 1970.

The large concentrations of women employees stand out in the Figure from the points of view both of the employer and the customer, who may ultimately have to pay the bill. As part of the preparation for equal pay it is advisable for firms both large and small to know exactly how many women not yet receiving equal pay they employ. The existing employment records may not be analysed in this way—this obvious step is the first one to be taken.

Women's place in skilled employment

Outside the professions (sometimes inside) women tend to be employed in the lower-rated jobs. Lady Seear, in her paper for the Royal Commission on Trade Unions and Employers' Associations (1968), *The Position of Women in Industry*,[1] estimates the numbers of women working in skilled jobs as 29 per cent compared with the male rate of 49 per cent. In non-manual jobs 86 per cent of women worked in secretarial, clerical or other similar office-type jobs, with only 2 per cent employed as technicians, scientists, technologists and draughtsmen. In the new occupations, such as computer programmer, women have from the beginning been engaged on the same terms and conditions as men. Above the first-line supervisor level women are few indeed, even in trades such as clothing and hosiery which employ large numbers of women. The PEP report 'Women and Top Jobs,' found that only 2 per cent of the Institute of Directors' members are women; and they often have family connections with their firms.

There is then little evidence of either moves by organisations to train and promote large numbers of women, or of tremendous pressure by women for openings. The above figures illustrate the traditional prejudices of both employers and women. The official policy of the Labour Party and of the TUC is that discrimination against women in the matter of pay should go. No surveys are available of union branch committee opinion or the number of times the question is raised by committee members. A guess based on a number of informal inquiries is that it is few. Nevertheless it is likely that differentials in pay will be challenged in future.

Union instructions to trade union members to withdraw from industrial tribunals due to the passing of the Industrial Relations Act may deprive tribunals of an important source of expertise on job content and value when cases under the Equal Pay Act come before them.

Problem of deciding job similarities

There are considerable problems of comparing 'like with like' and the wage comparability situation varies from textiles, where for many years there has been a rate for the job irrespective of the sex or age of the employee, to other industries where the gap may reach 30 per cent of the basic pay and nearly 50 per cent of earnings. Mepham[2] gives examples of a tobacco firm where the women's minimum rate in 1969 was 77 per cent of the men's rate. Incomes Data Services Ltd found in their 1967 survey that women's minimum rate in engineering was, in fact, 92 per cent of the men's rate; this did not, of course, reflect earnings.

Such surveys tend to take the mid-point of any wage or salary band for men and women and compare the two. Problems of straight comparison arise when women work in groups containing no men, for example typing pools or the canteen where the few men are on highly specialised jobs or on general portering duties. Another factor is that within the range of work theoretically open to both there may be clusters of jobs held only by women or only by men. The textile trade has already been mentioned. In the weaving sheds the heavier and higher rated cloth may be woven by men because it is heavier. Another example is the pottery industry, where bigger articles may be 'thrown' at the potter's wheel by men since women's wrists and arms are not strong enough to control the clay. When the Equal Pay Act is in full operation a blind male typist or telephonist will be precluded from a higher base rate for the job merely because he is a man. The effect of the Act on all-women groupings is discussed below.

The point to be stressed is that actual *earnings* may continue to differ widely. The Act says nothing about the equalisation of opportunity or of training facilities offered. But that it is on the Statute Book at all is an important step.

The Equal Pay Act 1970—requirements and implementation

A guide to the Act is available free from the Department of Employment's offices and Employment Exchanges. It is to come into force on 29 December 1975. The Secretary of State may make an order in 1973, if he so decides, to provide for immediate partial implementation, that is that women's rates are raised to at least 90 per cent of those paid to men.

The Act establishes the right of women to equal pay while employed on work of the same or broadly similar nature to that of men, or on jobs which, though different, have been given an equal value under a job evaluation exercise. It gives to the Industrial Arbitration Board the right to remove discriminatory clauses in collective agreements and empowers industrial tribunals to determine disagreements on women's rights in claims against their employers. The Act covers workers of all ages but does not affect the operation of any wage for age scale. For example, a woman between 18 and 20 years old would be paid the equivalent adult male job rate as soon as she showed herself capable of doing the work normally done by adult women. This would apply irrespective of the existence of any male apprenticeship or learning scale for young men of similar age group. The Act does not, of course, abolish learner rates nor age-related payments but may cause a re-examination of these. For part-time workers there appear to be no special provisions.

Job evaluation

The Act refers to jobs which 'have been given an equal value in terms of the demand made on the worker under various headings (for instance effort, skill, decision) on a study undertaken with a view to evaluating in those terms the jobs to be done,' and disallows for the purposes of this Act an evaluation system setting *different values for men and women on the same demand under any heading*, that is the 'plussing-up' of rates to maintain the male differential. Those firms which have already installed a job evaluation system which operates or can be modified to operate in the way the Act requires, can more easily implement it. It appears that some form of grading system will be essential, but there is no legal requirement.

The Act does, however, stress that men and women whose job rates are being equalised *must have the same terms and conditions of employment*, for example if there is a requirement to work overtime or shifts this must cover both men and women in so far as the hours of the latter are not protected by legislation. The overtime and shift premiums must be the same for both. (See later section on *Implementation of the Act*.)

Job evaluation schemes in use in the firms visited were varied. The National Board for Prices and Incomes Paper on *Job Evaluation* (HMSO 1968) indicates the range from simple grading schemes to more complex factor comparison schemes and Hay/MSL type systems. In many of them it appeared that the weighting for physical effort and conditions was fairly low, since management's effort had been directed to improving such factors. Perhaps with the coming of equal pay, male manual trade union members may complain that these factors are rated much too low, and that others such as skill and training are over generously reflected in the overall rate. Certainly adequate investigation and appeals machinery at organisation level will be required, particularly in the early stages.

Area of comparison

Normally, comparisons are allowed by the Act between men and women working for the same employer at the same establishment. They may, however, be drawn with men at another branch of the firm or an associated company, but only *if terms and conditions are common to both*. The *Equal Pay Guide* published by the Department of Employment gives the following two examples:

1   An employer owns three establishments, A, B and C in different parts of the country. In A and B the same job is performed by men and women, but in C by women only. The women in A, B and C have the same terms and conditions. The men in A and B have the same *terms and conditions* as the women, though their rates are more favourable.

Under the Act all the establishments are held to have the same terms and conditions and the women in A, B and C can claim equalisation.

2   If, however, the men in A and B are on different terms and conditions and those of the women differ in each establishment, then these are not common conditions for all three establishments. The women in C, therefore, cannot claim equal treatment with the men in A or the men in B, though the women in A can claim equalisation with the men in A and the women in B with the men in B.

Problems are likely to arise when the state of the local labour market produces different rates in different parts of the country and when there is no centrally controlled and agreed policy on rates. There is no easy answer. Clearly, there is a case for an examination of the rationale for these differences, whether they represent increases or decreases on any company norm resulting from a careful study of job content and of the utilisation of manpower—or womanpower. (London weightings are presumably outside the scope of the Act, in principle.)

There would be the problem of comparing 'like with like'. There may be a significant difference between similar sounding jobs done in the provinces and in London. The girls working in the provinces may not find this very easy to understand. Presumably a common grading scheme for all units, agreed with their representatives and carefully introduced would assist them to do so. But the size of the wage-fixing unit may have developed haphazardly and be subject to still more query than usual after the implementation of the Act.

Reference to an industrial tribunal

Should women feel that discrimination in pay still exists or an employer feel that the situation is not clear, either may refer to an industrial tribunal from December 1975 onwards. Trade unions or employers' associations, of course, may represent their members. A reference may be made up to six months after the termination of the employment concerned and for arrears of up to two years. In such a case the onus is on the employer to prove a genuine material difference in the male job.

Differences in earnings

Differences based on, for example, higher level of output, degree of merit or long-service payments are not, of course, affected by the Act. It is here that inequality may persist if higher-rated jobs are reserved for men by tradition, trade union insistence or lack of adequate training for women applicants. Long-service bonuses may also favour men if women have shorter spells of employment due to childbirth or other family reasons. Few companies allow maternity leave, particularly for manual workers, without a break in service.

Amendments to collective agreements, internal pay structures and statutory wage orders

The Act is likely to cause the disappearance of any provision applying to women only, or indeed to men only. Reference to the Industrial Arbitration Board may be made by any party to the agreement or by the Secretary of State for Employment.

Implementation of the Act

Since information on the extent of implementation is scanty the following points are taken from the references given on page 220 and from contacts made with eleven organisations in the north-west and in short informal conversations with four trade unions. There were no firms with less than 900 employees in the sample. These soundings taken in August 1971 give the following indications:

1 There appears to be a considerable gap between the group of organisations which already have equal pay, have reached agreement which already closes the differential to 5 per cent or 10 per cent or have

committed themselves to do so within the next two or three years, and the group which has scarcely moved from its original position.

2   There was at least one case of a recent agreement where the size of the increase was indeed equal—this is not traditionally the case—but the differential, of course, remained unchanged. This was apparently done without any great reaction from the trade union concerned. This may not happen with subsequent agreements as the implementation date approaches, but it seems to show a lack of heat in the situation at the moment.

The phasing of equal pay

Looking back to the Civil Service move to equality over a seven-year period, one remembers comments heard there from women that the waiting time was long and that the system was unfair to women whose pension rates depended on salary during the last few years of employment. From some women there was a rather traditional lack of enthusiasm for equal pay and from some men a certain amount of thoroughly unfavourable comment to their women colleagues upon the 'unfair' advantages accruing to them whether they had the support of a husband's salary or were single 'with no dependants.'

One of the advantages of a long phasing period is that the yearly increases are smaller. It did not appear in the sample firms that these smallish increases had generated any demand for general increases from the men. Some felt, however, that a sudden large increase at the end of the period might easily do so. Smaller increases were less likely also to upset the relativities of the internal wage scale. They may also be more easily absorbed into general labour costs.

The cost of implementation

The indirect cost of installing a job evaluation scheme if that were thought desirable to form the basis for an equal pay system would be very considerable, particularly in industries employing large numbers of women as listed in Figure 14:1.

An article on 'Costs of Equal Pay' in the *Department of Employment Gazette*,[3] estimates costs based on a survey of thirteen selected industries. The organisations chosen in these industries were asked to supply information on gross earnings of women employees; including basic pay, overtime and shift allowances, bonuses and any other additions. Only adult women were included.

Published figures for April 1970 confirm that men's earnings were still roughly twice those of women, not only in the middle but near the top and the bottom of the distribution. (*Department of Employment Gazette.* November 1970.)

The following points emerged from the January survey:

1   The cost appeared to vary according to the gross number of women employed, not according to the number of women likely to benefit

2   The extent to which semi-skilled men were also employed was a significant factor. Many groups of 'women only' occupations were found

3   There were widely different assumptions on what constitutes 'the same work.' In the soap and edible fats group some lighter packing jobs were considered to be the 'same' as heavier packing jobs. Others in the same group thought them different

4   Where women were already on a rate higher than the agreed minimum, their new minimum could be the men's minimum, *or* that rate enhanced by the plus on their original rate. In the latter case, the bonus would be at men's rate

5   In catering and retail trades some women were already *earning* more than the men's minimum

6   Employers' contributions to employee benefits schemes, such as sick pay and pensions would rise: many firms estimated 2 per cent to 10 per cent *additional* cost to wages bill

7   It was thought that even where women had no claim for equalisation they might have to receive it to preserve relativities within the firm or parity with neighbouring concerns

8   Over one million women already receive equal pay

9   The percentage of women who would benefit from equalisation varied from 1 per cent in paper and board-making to 67 per cent in clothing and 64 per cent in laundries

10   The extent of their benefit might be 100 per cent in some areas such as retail distribution and clothing to 29 per cent in engineering

It was estimated that equalisation would cost about $3\frac{1}{2}$ per cent of the total national wage and salary bill—spread over the period 1970 to 1975.

There was no indication that women might be replaced by men, but obviously their performance will come under scrutiny. This may not be a bad thing.

Equality of opportunity

Without increased opportunity, Lady Seear proclaims that equal pay would be a hollow victory. There is little evidence in the senior civil service or education that many women have moved upwards into the higher income posts in these professions where equal pay has been established for some time. In the hospital service many of the important nursing posts are held by men nowadays and women Hospital Group Secretaries are rare. These are all areas where women have looked for a career rather than for a stop-gap between education and marriage, though there are now fewer spinsters around and married women may have broken service, or other responsibilities which impede mobility and thus promotion.

In the non-professional field, the lack of women in higher earning groups has already been noted. One of the factors stressed by investigators is the lack of adequate training opportunities to equip women for such work. So far the Industrial Training Act has made little impact on this situation. Training is costly and regarded as an investment even though statistics show that many young men are foot-loose and planning a career designed to widen their experience rather than to fit in with the plans of any employer. This applies not only to the young graduate. Male manual and administrative workers interviewed during a redundancy investigation stated that in this time of involuntary as well as voluntary job change it is well to have experience of as great a number of jobs as possible: this they felt eased re-employment.

It would be foolish to underrate the problems caused by established attitudes; for the woman who earns more than her husband or the man who has to reveal that his boss is a woman. Moreover, experience shows that many women do not take their jobs very seriously. (Some of these may not have been designed seriously to interest anyone.) Lady Seear and others reply that irresponsible behaviour, poor time-keeping and high labour turnover are by no means characteristic of all women in all situations. Labour turnover may be as low as 14 per cent in responsible posts as against a national all-employees average of 35–40 per cent. Dr Viola Klein found in her sample of 120 firms that nearly

40 per cent considered even married women's attendance as good or better than men's. Amal Ayoub's comparison[4] of two firms making a similar product and in the same locality found that the company which had a rigid but fairly administered check system on absence, had a daily rate (3.6 per cent) less than half that of the other (8.4 per cent) and that it compared favourably with the rate in male-employing industries in a 1970 Greater Manchester sample (range 2–26 per cent). It is surely also a waste of ability that only 6 per cent of girls go into apprenticeships (mainly in hairdressing) and only 13 per cent into any form of planned training. Offices, so often the job target for the girl school leaver, still release so few for day-time training.

Trade union membership

Tradition has it that women are uninterested in trade unions, although in clothing and hosiery they form 80 per cent of the union membership. They are held to be passive members, and this may be true—except when they are really roused. They might take more part if more branch or other meetings were held at the plant. Senior women trade union officials are few, and clearly exceptionally able and determined to have forced their way in what is very much a male-dominated profession. The unions have campaigned for over eighty years for equal pay. It will be interesting to see how keenly they watch implementation and whether local action at least reflects the apparent ambivalence amongst members.

Future developments after the Act

The future of the Factories Act legislation protecting women seems to be unclear. Views expressed from the organisations contacted were that it had outlived its usefulness; that some unions would be prepared to bargain about its abolition; that others would strongly oppose this. The question of the shift break after four and a half hours' work had already come up in one factory; it was abolished in return for an earlier finishing time. In this factory also the relaxation allowances, which are of course a matter for negotiation, not legislation, were also being reviewed during the fairly rapid progress towards equalisation of pay. These were likely to be stabilised at the lower male rate. In another factory the difference was likely to remain.

Possible pressure for maintenance of differentials in another form

The evidence for this was incomplete and confused. It was thought in some factories that there would be male pressure, through the unions or by direct approach, to increase job evaluation weightings for effort and conditions, skill etc.; also that increased premiums might be sought for awkward hours, nights, weekends and so on.

Replacement of women by men?

This was feared, to some extent, but there was no real evidence of its happening so far. The risk was thought to be that, suitability apart, this action would force up the price of male labour.

In sum it seems that currently some firms are slow in preparing for implementation on the one hand, and on the other that the effect will not be dramatic. Nevertheless, the situation spotlights again the need for good forward planning, a well-considered deployment of the labour force, an adequate means of establishing job content and of monitoring performance in it.

Postscript

Lady Seear secured a second reading of the Anti-Discrimination No. 2 Bill in the House of Lords on 14 March, 1972. Its object is to increase job and training opportunities for women.

References

1 'The Position of Women in Industry' by B N Seear, *Royal Commission on Trade Unions and Employers*, research paper no. 11, 1968
2 *Problems of Equal Pay* by G J Mepham, Institute of Personnel Management, 1967
3 'Cost of Equal Pay', *Department of Employment and Productivity Gazette*, January 1970
4 *Absenteeism amongst Women Manual Workers* by A M Ayoub, unpublished MSc thesis, UMIST

15

Training in Industrial Relations

C V Kettle

Group Personnel Manager, Lankro Chemicals Group Limited

It is widely recognised that good industrial relations are essential if misunderstandings are to be kept out of dealings between management and workers and their unions. For this purpose, a highly developed form of industrial relations training, for all sides, is an essential requirement of the modern industrial scene.

The mass-media of communications (radio, television and press) inform the public of newsworthy items concerning industrial relations. The treatment given to such reports tends to be coloured according to the political bias of the editorial policy and the level of knowledge the reporter has. The public at large may be influenced by a superficial and biased report but a person trained in industrial relations will be able properly to analyse and appreciate the implications in the report. This is not, of course, even one of the main aims of industrial relations training. The real reason is to provide sound, useful knowledge which will enable everyone concerned in industrial relations to know what they are talking about.

Relationships, by definition, require more than one party; industrial relations training should be sufficiently far reaching to train all current and prospective parties. In the society in which we live there are a number of factors which are constantly affecting industrial relations; legislation, public opinion, economic trends, advancing technology.

These factors further complicate what is already a complex situation. This means, of course, that there is a need to adapt and adjust the training so that it is compatible with the changing situation and that people are prepared when the changes occur.

Approach to training in industrial relations

Prime purpose—relationships

It is legitimate for relationships between employer and employee to be based on both conflict and co-operation. Industrial relations training must deal with this situation by showing how co-operative endeavour (to meet the undertaking's objectives), is affected by conflict which arises on the distribution of benefits—wages, salaries, profits, etc. Training must show that in this situation, the trade unionist has a single purpose; the well-being of his members. Management aims to establish an acceptable balance in the distribution of the benefits; in dividends to shareholders, prices to the customer and earnings for employees, whether union members or not.

The distribution of these benefits, through collective bargaining, is likely to be resolved harmoniously if there is a background of knowledge. This positive aspect is emphasised in industrial relations training.

If training is lacking, poor industrial relations will result which will have an adverse effect on the productivity of an organisation. This situation will be apparent from a number of symptoms: absenteeism; poor time-keeping; high accident rates; high labour turnover. In the end there may be a work to rule or even a strike. This catalogue is indicative of low morale in industry—a solution lies in the improvement of industrial relations via training.

Since the Fawley Bluebook Agreement at Esso, and subsequently the Donovan Commission Report, were published there has been a marked change in collective bargaining with the emphasis moving from a national industry-wide basis to a plant basis. This means that industrial relations training will have to be given to a much larger number of people in management and trade unions.

Level of training

Everyone who is involved in industrial relations needs to be trained in this subject. The level of training is adjusted according to their involvement. The following is a possible outline of training requirements:

1 Board members—a very broad appreciation which will be of value in determining policies which affect industrial relations directly or indirectly

2 Line and staff management—a wide appreciation of all the aspects of industrial relations and the effect they have on planning, organising, directing, controlling and co-ordinating, plus details of current events from 3, 4 and 5

3 Personnel managers or industrial relations officers

4 Trade union representatives

{ Generally, the same as in 2 plus a full knowledge of practical implications as these are the front men—the negotiators

5 Supervisors—broad appreciation of all aspects plus detailed knowledge of current events from 3 and 5

The need to keep up-to-date is, perhaps, obvious: training is a continuous process which takes account of all significant changes in the situation.

Constraints on learning

In many cases the trainee, particularly long-service supervisors and shop stewards, are required to deal with concepts rather than with practical things which they are accustomed to see and handle. This is the major problem facing the trainer and it has to be overcome through effective communication.

Effective communication is the most important tool of any teacher or trainer. Communicating, because it is a two-way system, is hampered by barriers which have to be overcome if the training is to achieve its objective. To be sure that what has been taught has been learned, requires a feedback; the teacher and student act as both transmitter and receiver. Whilst in the transmitting role it is important to anticipate the barriers and if possible avoid them being raised—or at least to prepare to surmount them.

Typical barriers which may be experienced include:

1 Lack of interest

2 Emotional opposition

3 Cynicism
4 Insincerity
5 Lack of motivation
6 Lack of intellectual understanding
7 Semantics—use of jargon
8 Poor physical conditions
9 Loss of earnings

It is unreasonable to expect any but the most highly motivated people to concentrate if their earnings are going to be adversely affected in the learning situation. For this reason care needs to be taken to compensate trainees in a reasonable manner if training is to be taken seriously.

An atmosphere conducive to learning is necessary. Reasonable physical conditions are required such as lighting, ventilation, seating, acoustics and the avoidance of distractions. The possible provision of audio/visual aids should be considered, particularly as a means of stimulating interest and providing variety.

The non-material type barriers (items 1 to 7 above) are much more difficult to overcome or avoid. Avoidance of such attitudes as cynicism, insincerity or emotional opposition is one of the by-products of good industrial relations and really is a pre-requisite of effective training. In a sense it is the chicken and the egg problem and it may well be necessary for senior managers to be trained first to persuade them of the need to put their own house in order and create an atmosphere of trust and confidence within which training might flourish and meet its objectives.

Enquiry into industrial relations training

The inadequacy of training in this subject is implicit in the inquiry which is being made by the Commission on Industrial Relations as a result of a reference from the Secretary of State for Employment. The inquiry is focused upon the questions whether the amount of training in industrial relations is sufficient, whether it is well-founded and directed and whether or not the training given is effective. There is no doubt that this is a most important inquiry and the outcome could play a major part in shaping industrial relations during the era of the 1971 Act. Almost certainly it will renew the jumping on the bandwagon by training consultants—some of whom do a first-class job. The problem will be in finding a criterion by which the charlatans may be recognised before damage is done.

Categories of training

Although managers of all levels are accountable for industrial relations there is clearly a requirement for the training needs to be analysed from several points of view and at various levels. The needs of the senior executive are clearly different from those of the foreman. The results of the analysis of training needs should contain both academic and practical requirements for each group.

One possible breakdown of the categories of employees requiring training is:

1 Personnel or industrial relations officers
2 Line managers
3 Supervisors
4 Specialists, such as accountants and R & D staff
5 Trade union representatives

Personnel or industrial relations specialist

The syllabus laid down by the Institute of Personnel Management provides an excellent basis for the training of the specialist in this field. (This is reproduced in the following section.) The standard of teaching and the approach adopted, however, varies widely according to the calibre of staff employed in the colleges and universities. The IPM attempts to control standards in so far as it grants exemption or recognition in respect of its own professional examination scheme to approved courses. One of the difficulties which it faces in this matter is the natural concern which universities have for maintaining academic freedom. This matter is regularly under review due to close collaboration which the institute enjoys with many of the academics involved.

Further education establishments usually include simulated exercises to enable students to appreciate the application of the theory which has been taught. Although exercises of this type are useful they are a poor substitute for the nitty-gritty atmosphere experienced on the shop floor.

Institute of Personnel Management Industrial Relations Syllabus (Part One)

Objective   Candidates will be expected to obtain a working knowledge of the common practices of the industrial relations function and of the context within which it is carried out.

The structure of industrial relations in Britain

1   The purposes and organisation of employers' organisations at local (district), industry and national (Confederation of British Industry) levels; the purposes and organisation of trade unions at plant, branch (or equivalent), district and national levels, including those of multiple union associations and federations at these levels; particular attention will be given to those aspects of purpose and organisation which are directly related to unilateral and joint regulation of rewards for work and working conditions; the evolution of company and plant bargaining processes and their relationship to those of district and national bargaining.

2   The foundation of formal relationships between employers and trade unions; the types and stages in the development of formal procedural and substantive agreements between these parties, with particular attention to *recognition*, management prerogatives, and union rights, as established by agreement; provision for third party intervention in the relationship between the parties—neutral committees (or equivalent) conciliation, voluntary arbitration by private or public agencies.

Voluntarism and the role of the state in industrial relations

1   The tradition of voluntarism in British industrial relations; its nature and form; the legislative framework within which it developed; the role of the State as facilitator and enabler in respect of voluntary regulation of wages and working conditions; the advisory and conciliation functions of the Department of Employment (Ministry of Labour).

2   Direct intervention by the state:

(*a*)   via regulation of wages (wages councils, fair wages clauses, or incomes policies), hours of work for certain classes of person or employee, and terms and conditions of employment under general and specific legislation; and

(b) via the regulation of the processes and procedures of collective negotiation and the resolution of differences and disputes between the parties (under the Trade Union Acts, the Industrial Courts Act and the Conciliation Act and any new industrial relations legislation which may be introduced); attention will also be given to the changing role of the Department of Employment and of state-created agencies in the industrial relations field (including industrial courts, commissions, committees and tribunals).

The allocation of roles in industrial relations   The roles of officers in the trade union and the employers' association, in both negotiation and disputes settlement; the roles of the shop steward and the personnel manager in relation to both formal and informal systems, and the implications for these of the development of company and plant bargaining; executive and advisory functions in both union and personnel management contexts; the role of the specialist in industrial relations; organisation of industrial relations within the personnel function.

The substance and effectiveness of collective bargaining

1   Analysis of the substance and effects of bargaining processes, including: distributive bargaining over wages and salaries (including local rates and prices and fringe benefits); bargaining over authority in relation to management prerogatives and the union's rule book, the extension of matters recognised as proper subjects for joint regulation, discipline and disciplinary procedures; grievance bargaining including recognised procedures in various industries.

2   Assessment of the effectiveness of industrial relations practice taking into account the objectives of employers, managers, trade unions: with particular attention to the effectiveness of the union as a representative, as a means of securing improvements in wages and working conditions, and as a means of furthering the interests of the trade union and/or its members; and the effectiveness of the industrial relations system in securing the willing contribution of employees to the objectives of the enterprise, whether private or public, and in serving the public interest.

NB Part two level syllabus is available from the Institute. It has special reference to legal aspects of industrial relations.

Line managers

Short appreciation courses are required for middle and senior line managers. The content of the courses should include the following:

The external framework

1 The role of the government and its various agencies
2 The role of employers' federations
3 The role of the trade union officers
4 The extent and limitations of national agreements
5 Statutory legislation

The internal framework

1 Company objectives and policies
2 Organisation structure
3 Staff and line concept
4 Status and authority of various categories of management
5 Agreements, rules and practices
6 Role of the personnel department
7 Role of the manager including the supervisor
8 Role of the shop steward

Industrial relations at plant level

1 Recognition of areas of conflict and co-operation
2 Motivation, discipline and grievances
3 Negotiating, consulting, communicating
4 Procedures
5 Methods of wage payments
6 Precedents and possible consequences
7 Channels of communication
8 Productivity bargains

The minimum amount of time required for this type of course is three days. It is usually more effective and acceptable if it can be on a one-day-per-week basis and held away from the working situation. Academics, trade union officials and consultants are usually willing to assist members of the management team in lecturing or acting as tutors for courses of this nature. Agreement should be reached on fees beforehand: note that a high fee is no guarantee of quality in this field.

Supervisors

Short courses are advocated for this group. They should emphasise the role of the supervisor and the best way of getting work done through other people in an acceptable manner.

The courses should include:

1 Company objectives and policies
2 Organisation structure, staff and line concept
3 Status and authority of the supervisor
4 Works' rules and practices

5 Relationship of the personnel department to the supervisor
6 Relationship of the shop steward and the supervisor
7 Recognition of likely areas of conflict and co-operation and possible attitudes towards them
8 Motivation, discipline and grievance
9 Recognised and acceptable procedures
10 Effects of creating precedents
11 Company wages system and fringe benefits
12 The supervisor's role in communications

Two hours per week over a ten-week period should be adequate for a course of this nature. A discussion group approach, limiting the participants to a minimum of six and a maximum of sixteen, is likely to prove most suitable. Given suitable training in discussing leading techniques, most of the leadership can come from line managers and staff specialists.

Specialists

A brief appreciation is required on similar lines to that for supervisor (see the last section), but with emphasis placed upon the effect of change on the workforce. The importance of consultation and communication, and the dignity of labour, the need for job satisfaction and recognition must be stressed in this particular course. In this way a balance in utilising the resources available to management is optimised.

A single discussion session lasting about two hours and led by an experienced personnel officer should suffice in this often forgotten aspect of industrial relations training.

Trade union representatives

The major problem in this area is the question of where the responsibility lies for training. There are three alternatives:

1   The choice of subject-matter and its treatment is dealt with entirely by the trade unions, with the employer granting paid leave of absence to his shop stewards to enable them to attend.
2   The training of shop stewards is carried out by universities, polytechnics and bodies like the Industrial Society. This type of training may be conducted in the colleges or within the company itself, the representatives, again, being paid whilst they attend.
3   The training is carried out within company premises and the programme is jointly agreed between union and management. Both sides supply speakers for appropriate subjects, the whole affair being run under the tutorship of a member of the TUC Education Department, a WEA tutor, or by an academic.

One of the constraints to be faced is the possibility of stewards regarding training material as a basis for argument. This calls for skill on the part of the trainer if the group is not to be bogged down on individual items.

There is a course run by the Industrial Society which requires three days full-time attendance, and examines the responsibilities and objectives of shop stewards so that they might gain a better understanding of trade union/management relationships and problems. Managers and trade union officials assist the society's training advisers in conducting the sessions which include:

1   The current industrial relations scene
2   The role of the shop stewards
3   Communication in industry
4   The job of the manager

5 Conducting a meeting
6 Grievance interviews
7 Effective negotiating

This type of course tends to be on general lines because the firms represented are so wide and varied. A course held specifically for a single company can be made very much more relevant. Both of these approaches have advantages and disadvantages and companies need to consider which suits their own particular circumstances.

Current sources of training and course content

Government

The Department of Employment has excellent training schemes for its own industrial relations staff. It uses co-operation of employers to enable members of the department to be given experience in an industrial atmosphere. There is no doubt that the calibre of officer in this department is high and this is in no small measure due to the training which is given. The syllabus covers:

1 The nature and significance of strikes
2 Causes of conflict
3 Manpower utilisation
4 Manpower planning
5 Labour turnover and its significance
6 Absenteeism and its significance
7 The historical background to industrial relations
8 The significance of various pay systems
9 Collective bargaining institutions
10 Industrial relations legislation
11 The roles of the state, employers' associations, and the trade union movement
12 The development of white-collar unions
13 Consultation and communication
14 Problems of redundancy
15 Trends in personnel management
16 Agreements at plant level
17 Worker participation in management

The Department of Employment still holds much under-rated basic 'Training Within Industry' courses for supervisors in industry. Its officers collaborate with various organisations in joint sponsorship of conferences and in supplying speakers.

Trade unions

The TUC and some of its more prosperous member unions possess training establishments or hold training courses in industrial relations. They often call upon university and WEA lecturers to supplement their own educational staff. Some employers are unwilling to co-operate and see no value in having their shop stewards trained by the union— possibly fearing indoctrination in subversive activities! The approach of most employers is responsible and constructive. They appreciate that negotiating and communicating is far more effective, and less likely to lead to misunderstanding, if shop stewards have been trained in industrial relations.

Educational establishments

Universities, polytechnics and other educational establishments organise a wide variety of courses which include aspects of industrial relations. These range from postgraduate courses to part-time day release, evening classes or short seminars.

Professional institutes and employers' associations

Professional institutions and associations such as the Institute of Personnel Management, the Industrial Society, and BIM sponsor courses of varying length. Some employers' federations, notably Iron and Steel and the Chemical Industry, together with many individual companies, are aware of the needs and attempt to train and develop their supervisors and managers in the art of industrial relations. Although the list appears impressive at first sight it is really quite haphazard and barely scratches the surface of the problem.

Course content

Most of the courses administered by the aforementioned organisations include some, or all, of the following subjects:

Economic history
Economics
Psychology
Law
Statistics
Sociology

Throughout the years these disciplines have made a contribution to the training in industrial relations. However, as Allan Flanders has noted, the drawback of relying upon several disciplines which have impinged upon the field of industrial relations is that they have failed to offer an integrated view of industrial relations. The shorter courses or seminars often specialise in techniques such as systems of wage payments, job evaluation, productivity agreements, communications and so on.

The Institute of Personal Management arrange, about twice a year, a practical 'Industrial Relations Training Laboratory' which is a five-day residential course. The speakers and tutors include trade unionists, managers, lawyers, academics, government and employer representatives. The training programme is designed to assist delegates to clarify the various influences which are exerting dynamic effects on industrial relations as a result of the change from industry-wide to plant bargaining. An understanding is gained of the social and economic implications of collective bargaining and practice is given in negotiating skills. The laboratory is designed for personnel and line managers who are engaged in collective bargaining or in the preparatory work for negotiations. It is also intended for trade union officials operating at district or area level.

Comparison of training courses

Internal courses

In-company training enables participants to gain an understanding of agreed rules of employment for a particular undertaking. The company's own management style and industrial relations philosophy can be dealt with in depth. A local agreement can be discussed in detail and legislation can be interpreted in highly relevant terms. The organisation structure, channels of communication, wage systems, grievance procedures and disciplinary stages will be able to be dealt with in a manner which is really meaningful.

The examples or case studies used in an internally arranged training programme should draw upon actual situations. They are likely to cause members of courses to reflect on their reactions experienced during the actual incident and to compare their attitudes with what is being advocated in the relatively cool atmosphere of the classroom situation.

The *relatively* cool atmosphere is mentioned because one does not always find calmness in this approach. There is always the possibility of direct or indirect criticism being raised between colleagues if the case is identified. To minimise this problem, care is required in the preparation of the case study to maintain anonymity without losing relevance. Furthermore, all discussion group leaders should be given practice in dealing with incidents of this type. The integration of practical training with theoretical background is likely to be more effective and easier to arrange when training takes place within a company or plant.

Consideration should be given for managers and stewards to train together; at least in some aspects of industrial relations. One problem to be faced in this context is accusations of the course being a device for brain-washing the stewards. Nevertheless, as an approach it can have merit and should not be overlooked. The dangers of controversy can be avoided if the approach is to use a strong, experienced and diplomatic discussion group leader.

Internal courses can lead to boredom if carried on too long without outside participation and the subsequent exchange of broader experiences. The inclusion of well-informed academics or consultants as tutors and guest speakers can help offset this danger and gain some of the better aspects of external courses.

External courses

The advantages of courses being held away from the workplace are that the participants feel much more able to concentrate on the matter in hand without interruption. An environment shared with delegates from other companies and, possibly, different industries may have an exhilarating effect on course members. The likelihood of hearing, and discussing with, experienced professional teachers, and possibly with eminent practitioners or theorists, is far greater with courses and conferences arranged by outside organisations.

Establishments which specialise in training are likely to be much better equipped with training aids than in all but the largest industrial organisations. Such aids will include audio and visual training equipment, the use of well-tried case studies, role-playing exercises and the likelihood of purpose-built training accommodation.

The fees charged for external courses, seminars and conferences vary widely and high fees are by no means necessarily synonymous with quality of courses. Some of the brochures on external courses which appear (in overwhelming numbers) on the desks of managers can be tremendously misleading. Nothing is more annoying than taking valuable time from business to attend a course as a result of reading a glossy brochure, only to find that the subject matter is not in accord with the description, the level of treatment is pitched too low, or that the subject matter is old material with a new label.

Attempts are being made to rate external courses on an independent basis in much the same way as the motoring organisations rate hotels. The two best known avenues from which managers can obtain guidance are the IPCRO Management Courses Index and the British Institute of Management. The latter organisation also publishes a very useful reference book, *A Conspectus of Management Courses*. The Institute claims that it lists most courses available in the British Isles but limits them to programmes of five days or longer.

Other sources of training

Highly motivated individuals who in their own time are anxious to extend their knowledge of industrial relations will find a variety of methods available to them. There are several correspondence courses in personnel management, which includes industrial relations. The BBC and other TV and commercial film companies produce management training films including the management of human resources. These can be used to augment training programmes and enable variety to be introduced in a beneficial manner. Some films are only available for purchase outright, whilst others may be hired.

The subject has not been overlooked by the publishers of programmed learning texts. These are available both in book form and in an approach suitable for use in teaching machines.

No discussion on sources of training would be complete without mention of the written word. There is a tremendous range of information books available in this field. Many, such as this one, are published by commercial houses; and unlike the first two decades after the war it is no longer necessary to look to the United States for all the well-written management text books. Another important publisher for the student of industrial relations is HM Stationery Office.

A publication which is a *must* is the report of the Donovan commission; and since the introduction of the current Industrial Relations Bill there is much more of necessity to be read from HMSO.

Journals with a bias towards the subject are plentiful. The most notable include:

1 *Industrial Relations Journal* published quarterly by Business Publications Limited
2 *Industrial Relations Review and Report* published twice monthly

On a more theoretical level there are occasional articles in the following learned journals:

1 *Occupational Psychology* published quarterly by the National Institute of Psychology, and
2 *The Journal of Management Studies* published three times each year by Basil Blackwell

The Institute of Personnel Management has published with Gower Press the first issue of its learned quarterly journal *Personnel Review* in September 1971. This has proved well worth reading.

Useful up-to-date information is available for reference purposes in the *Department of Employment Gazette* and in *Incomes Data* published by Incomes Data Services Limited.

There is a clear need for training in industrial relations if Britain is to prosper economically and socially. The lead must come from management, but it is desirable that it is in collaboration wherever possible with the trade union movement. Much support will be required from the state, particularly during the difficult period of the introduction of the 1971 Act.

Management must assess the training needs of various categories of employee and decide how best to meet the needs at different levels. In general, a theoretical background in a number of disciplines in the field of the social sciences will be required. Practical experience under the guidance of skilled industrial relations, or personnel specialists is advisable so that practice and theory may be effectively integrated.

I

16

The Conduct of Negotiations – A Viewpoint

Rachel Naylor

Lecturer, Department of Management Sciences, UMIST

In default of the written evidence of negotiating processes, which US government and legal intervention make available to the American writer, the British student of industrial relations must make do with information drawn from personal experience, from published researches, the institutions and the issues of industrial bargaining, and from the relevant work of psychologists and sociologists. Thanks are also due for many of the observations in this chapter, to the managers and personnel officers in the Greater Manchester area who discussed their bargaining experiences. The interpretation of these observations is the responsibility of the writer alone.

Getting the feel of the subject

There are well-researched studies of industrial relations written from a point outside the negotiation room which help students to prepare for entry into it; Turner and his associates throw light on the 'endemic' conflict situation in the motor industry; Marsh has studied the engineering industry in depth; Flanders commented upon the productivity agreements at Fawley after contacts with many of the participants (see references at end of chapter). Reprints by Courts of Inquiry reports and the Commission on Industrial Relations help to give the 'feel' of the subject. The Report of the Royal Commission on Trade Unions and Employers' Associations (1968) gives a useful summary of problems and the Research Papers commissioned for it help to fill previous gaps in knowledge.

Individual studies of strikes are still rare. One of these was *Glasgow Ltd* by T T Paterson (1960). A more recent publication, *Million-Dollar Strike* by J Arnison (1970), covers the dispute at Roberts Arundel in so partisan a fashion that its usefulness is limited. Press, television and radio reports tend to suffer from the defects of their medium and in any case the reporters were not actually inside the negotiating room. The Department of Employment officers, who often are personally involved, are bound to observe confidentiality. A writer 'from inside' is Lord Brown, whose comments on the working of the Glacier system, in spite of its individuality, are interesting to others.[1] His stress on the 'representative' role of the negotiating team member and on the 'unanimity' rule are worth serious consideration, if not acceptance. The Fairfields[2] study was also written by two men closely concerned with the company, one a Board member.

A later chapter deals with the lessons from the behavioural sciences. It is, therefore, sufficient here first to indicate a useful discussion on the *Conduct of Collective Bargaining* and *Internal Adjustment* by Peter Anthony and Anne Crichton[3] which surveys the contributions of Etzioni, Lupton, Woodward and others; and secondly, to draw attention to the article on *Psychological Research and Industrial Relations*[4] in which Williams and Guest discuss the absence of psychologists in the membership of the Donovan Commission and the little impact which psychological research has made on industrial relations, partly because this has commonly been conceived as limited to regulated relationships. Nevertheless, psychological texts such as *A Behavioural Theory of Industrial Relations*[5] (Walton and McKersie); *The Behaviour of Industrial Work Groups*[6] (L R Sayles); *Managerial Psychology*[7] (H R Leavitt) are useful preparatory reading.

Fortunate students of negotiation will have the opportunity to test the relevance of their reading by being allowed to sit in on bargaining sessions during training programmes arranged by their company. Fo the full-time school of management student such a learning experience is difficult to arrange. At UMIST, it has been found that trade union officials may be willing to arrange the attendance of students at some of the less sensitive meetings. Managements have seldom responded to a direct request for such facilities. The question is raised again for their consideration.

With the limitations of the evidence fully in mind, an attempt is made below to codify the main stages of the negotiation process from management's point of view. No golden rule emerges nor appears likely to emerge, but it seems that Anthony and Crichton are right to divide the process into three main stages, each of which is considered in the following sections:

1 The preparation for negotiation, including the determination of management's general objectives
2 The negotiation/confrontation situation
3 The outcome of the negotiations

Preparation for negotiations

Negotiations occur at various levels according to the structure and policy of the organisation and the issues under debate. Hospital service negotiations on wages and salaries illustrate a highly centralised bargaining pattern—though there is a slight break away to local negotiations even here. Large organisations such as ICI or the nationalised industries have different bargaining patterns from those of unit firms. The writer's attempt to identify the general variables governing the locale of bargaining was in the end unsatisfactory and is left for later research.

Negotiations can begin because of trade union pressure, because of individual employees' grievances or comments, or because, as must increasingly be the case, managements' wish to initiate changes leading to greater efficiency/profitability. (The rights of managements to do this are not argued here. The likelihood of trade union resistance is discussed.)

Levels of negotiations

Negotiations are unlikely to be successful unless management's overall objectives (corporate plan and strategy) have been determined and made known to those handling the negotiations at any level. Levels are categorised below according to extent of impact and time constraints on response:

Minor disagreements   For example on work instructions or on interpretation of agreements. These are often settled on the organisation floor and as Lord Brown points out may be resolved without undue difficulty if line executive authority is clear (often at the bottom it is not), if policies and agreements are known, accepted and do not clash. It also assumed that staff are adequately trained and that the structure within which they work does not produce difficulties in making operational the ideas generated at management/supervisory development courses.

Disagreements with wider implications but not necessarily demanding an immediate answer   For example differences of interpretation of agreements or practices, requests for concessions on finishing time, manning schedules, and so on. Delays in answers may be necessary; long delays may be inadvisable yet tolerated if past experience is that an answer will be given eventually. As with minor disagreements managements must check the implications and the existing practices and agreements. It is unfortunate if a shop steward is able to write about a 'manning' disagreement: 'They didn't know what the agreements were, so I was able to play merry Hell with them—*and* get something on the rate, which I didn't expect when I went in.'[8]

These problems also are likely to be settled locally unless they escalate.

Far-reaching changes proposed by management; claims made or changes resisted by unions   These will include (*a*) formal procedures such as an annual re-negotiation of rates/salaries, and (*b*) the problem-solving type of joint group formed, for example, to work on an *efficiency type* bargain. They also include resistance by trade unions to impending alterations of method, venue, staffing, etc., or to a declaration of redundancy. The setting and *modus operandi* of procedures (*a*) and (*b*) differ, though each may, during the same negotiation, shade into or move away from the other.

Where bargaining occurs will depend upon the circumstances. The points made in this chapter largely relate to local bargaining situations, though some are applicable to central negotiations.

A balancing of internal and often conflicting objectives is likely to occur in each 'pluralist' group prior to and during the negotiations, when additionally each group will seek to achieve with the other group a balance which is at best favourable, at worst just acceptable. This is a fine balancing feat and, as Drucker says, sharply separates the competent from the incompetent. But there is no formula.

Information

The Information Exercise is an important preparatory step. Firms (and nowadays unions through their headquarters research staff and academic friends) may assemble all possible marketing, financial and production information, current and future, together with published and internal data on earnings, conditions and trends. They may consult the *Department of Employment Gazette*, Incomes Data publications, Office Management Association's and consultants' published surveys, for example AIC's survey on management salaries; associated companies, employers' associations, and any other professional or personal contacts may be tapped. Increasingly the Institute of Personnel Management is instituting local wages and salary surveys sold at about £5 per survey (normally, though not exclusively to participants) and supplementing information obtained through the grapevine, from employees leaving or entering (this information to be treated with care). Such surveys may cover other benefits, for example holidays, sick pay, subsidised travel, staff sales, catering and further welfare benefits.

Assessment of predicted demands of the union, and whether these are in fact their real demands, with some order of priorities, is often the next step. The tactics they may use are discussed, together with what is known of their current temper and that of the employees. With a new union official an assessment may be difficult as professional relationships need time to develop. The four staff changes, through promotion and retirement, experienced in the past four years in the Manchester Divisional Office of the AUEFW have probably caused more problems than they have given opportunities for a fresh start.

At least some of the necessary information inputs are available to managers. It is suggested in Chapter 6 that they know the union structure and the general conditions under which the officers work as well as keeping themselves abreast of public pronouncements—on, for example, the democratic rights of members, which will probably mean the presence of shop stewards and perhaps some ordinary members at the negotiating table. It is well, too, to remember Etzioni's classifications of unions as mixed remunerative-normative organisations, to whom the factors surrounding an offer, as well as the offer itself are important.

An understanding of the employees' motivation, in the particular setting in which the negotiation takes place, is naturally important. The skill lies in determining whether a particular group of stewards or employees wants high earning opportunity and if so at what price in terms of reduced leisure, higher work speed, different methods and so on. Obtaining such information from stewards through reasonable working relationships which yet do not subject them to the accusation of being 'bosses' men' is not easy. The steward's foremost role is to represent not to give helpful information to management, nor can he be held accountable, as can a member of management, if that information is faulty.

Members of management also, particularly junior members, are unlikely to pass up unpalatable information if it is not in their interests to do so. They may mislead the negotiating team because of their efforts to conform to the stereotype of the optimistic, confident extrovert they think they are supposed to resemble.

Preparation for all possibilities

Adequate preparation for all conceivable demands and eventualities, with the appropriate calculations in as nearly qualified terms as possible, is the next step.

The establishment of parameters—the upper point to which the negotiators are prepared to go and the 'sticking point' below which they are not prepared to concede need to be established, for purposes of preparation, possibly to be reviewed during the negotiations. Bargaining is *not* an all-or-nothing exercise, it in fact ceases to be bargaining unless views can change during the process.

Tactics are usually considered not as a formulation of a rigid schedule but as determining the chairman, the role of other members, and the opening points.

Job progress sheets, with timings, or critical path analyses are used by some managers to aid in planning and progressing negotiations. Timing may be decided by the company—say an annual review or an efficiency exercise—or by union pressure. Practice varies on whether wage and salary reviews take place at approximately the same time. In companies belonging to a group, salaries may or may not be fixed centrally away from the group. At some of the firms recently contacted efforts were being made to group negotiations with the various unions concerned so that they could be held at the same or similar times thus cutting down the risk of 'leap-frogging' claims. Naturally, this had provoked union resistance and was incomplete in some firms visited. These firms hoped that at least the craftsmen, the general workers and the administrative and clerical workers could be dealt with as three groups at the same or similar times. At one firm, DATA, was vigorously opposed to such a move.

The analysis and discussion of information may take place away from the company so that concentration may be maintained without interruption or at the plant where there may be readier access to extra information required. A deadline for completion often ensures a highly pressured working situation.

Negotiating team

The selection of the negotiating team may take place during this period, usually keeping the numbers as low as possible, but including:

1 A senior member of management with responsibility for the outcome—and in most cases power to decide.
2 The relevant expertise, for example the personnel officer, perhaps the work study officer, plus the Engineering Manager in engineering cases, the Production Manager in production cases, and so on.

No examples were found of management trying to balance the predicted number of union representatives. An example of union officials' likely reaction to being outnumbered by the manager and his (silent) specialists at an employers' association office is known to the writer. The comment 'we wish we'd brought our troops, too' was only half in jest and followed by a longish pause of apparently uncertain outcome.

The negotiation/confrontation situation

Here one is on even less certain ground, but there is evidence that the following points relate sufficiently to experience to be produced for consideration.

The formal negotiating meeting

The negotiating meeting is led by a manager whose degree of seniority appears to vary with his interest and skill and the situation in hand. (The Personnel Director, if he exists, may not take part in local level negotiations.) The management team is likely to form a 'unitary' group as long as it remains in the negotiating room, though not either before or after the meeting.

The trade union team may vary from that led by a paid official to that led by a shop steward or convenor. In many unions nowadays, particularly in general unions, the official will be accompanied by stewards and/or members. The behaviour of this group is likely to be much more 'pluralistic,' a factor which may on the face of it appear to hold up otherwise speedy progress. But the union group may have less opportunity for the pre-resolution of differences (some managements give time and facilities for this), or there may be personality clashes. The group may be demonstrating members' rights to be heard as much to their own men as to management; they may be playing for time until they can get their bearings on the situation; or being encouraged by a wily union official who feels that they may provoke an unguarded response from one of the management team who can less easily extricate himself from any false situation than the union members who may plead that anything they say is 'subject to ratification by our members.'

Initial briefings

The management role in the initial stages is to state clearly what, in their view, the purpose of the meeting is, for example to discuss certain topics, to resume an adjourned meeting, etc.—and to obtain agreement that this is in fact so, or that the meeting is indeed about other defined matters. The briskness with which a meeting gets past a ritual 'exchange of the usual pleasantries' seems to vary according to company and union style and the initial period may in reality be an important part of the 'sizing-up' process. The line between avoiding time-wasting and avoid unnecessary tension is a difficult one to draw. It is obviously important that hard-pressed staff on either side of the table should not feel themselves asked to make undue time available. But the union official particularly may have to 'recover his breath' and switch his thoughts from his last meeting; particularly, though not exclusively, if he is a local official.

Briefings of union representatives is a delicate area which if directed to shop stewards may be rejected as brain-washing even it it is normally part of the organisation's policy to inform them on matters concerning them. There are indeed apparently unresolved problems on the transference to stewards of financial or other information for bargaining purposes, both in terms of their understanding and trust and because of possible advantage to competitors.

The briefing of a union official may require even greater delicacy. Tremendous pressures on his time and insufficient office help may mean, according to management complaints, that he arrives hot foot from another meeting and badly briefed. It will not help negotiations if the union official because of gaps in his information gets himself into a difficult position, and even to practised negotiators this may happen. In another case the official may be newly appointed and the beads of perspiration on his brow when facing his first official negotiation may show the strain he is feeling.

This may be an infrequent occurrence, but in such circumstances the experienced manager does what he can, by going over material again for the further benefit of stewards and employees, and the official. Visual aids or documents which can be taken away may help if there is time to read them. An unofficial practice, not necessarily to the liking of the stewards, is that the manager or the personnel officer 'happens to meet' the union official, either because they are 'passing his office door' or attending the same outside meeting, or the official is at the plant on another matter. Sundry convivial occasions to which union officials are invited also serve this purpose. Sometimes the official may in fact call in the Personnel Office for a coffee and short discussion before a meeting starts.

At national level union officers are increasingly likely to be very well briefed. The efforts of their research officers and their academic friends has already been noted. These situations present a clear challenge to management's negotiating skill.

Negotiation, not communication

Amongst the policy decisions discussed earlier which need to be made is that concerning the attitude of the firm to the exercise of managerial prerogative. Negotiation is essentially a two-way exercise if it is to lead to more than a short-term truce. The likely reaction to a one-way imposition of change is illustrated by the union's fear that the Fawley Blue Book was an 'all or nothing,' 'take it or leave it' exercise which they would be unwise to accept at that stage.[9] Past experience with some managements may have taught this and psychologists know that unlearning is a difficult and long-term exercise, particularly for older employees. Even a generous offer, if unexpected, may be treated with suspicion. It is said that when Ernest Bevin, then General Secretary of the TGWU, heard that Lloyd Roberts, the ICI Chief Labour Officer, was considering sick-pay schemes, his reaction was that this was a real stab in the back: how could the union increase its membership if benefits need not be earned by their efforts? The 'achievement' factor, in Herzberg's terms, in obtaining, say, five-eighths of an old penny in a hard day's bargaining is considerable. (See *The Motivation to Work*, F Herzberg, *et al.*, 1959.) Perhaps another aspect of this factor should be remembered: the satisfaction derived from 'achievement' was one of the shortest in duration.

Group behaviour

Anthony and Crichton, as previously noted, review some of the more important findings which may be relevant, and show groups struggling to establish some control at least over factors which affect them closely, and resenting managerial attempts to impose. Leavitt's (*op. cit*) comments on group behaviour show that the 'untidy' 'disorderly' group which such reactions produce may yet be an effective group. He believes that one of the central problems is that of communication and perception, that is people viewing the situation from particular standpoints tending consciously or unconsciously to refuse to understand another point of view (the concept of cognitive dissonance).

Exercises on negotiation skills run by ICI amongst others, and using closed circuit television, demonstrated to course members that one of the problems in the early stages of negotiation is that people do not listen to each other. Their attention is concentrated solely on their own presentation so that no communication in fact occurs, though each side is convinced that if they could get the other side to listen the superiority of their own case would be accepted. As the ICI exercise continued—as in the real-life situation—people started to listen and the breakthrough came when they began seriously to consider points made by opponents or even their own side.

A problem-solving type group, working together over a period, may more easily experience this kind of breakthrough, since their efforts are inevitably directed more towards securing a balance between objectives than to the domination of one party. This bears less relation to the 'fixed-sum' theory—what one wins the other loses—and more resemblance to an outcome in which both can win or lose. Willingness to consider or reject solutions may cut right across normal employee *v.* employer groupings. The likelihood of joint solutions is greater. At the Shell Carrington plant it seemed impossible finally to attribute ideas and suggestions for productivity deals to either side, even allowing for the skill probably possessed by both in implanting ideas into others' heads. As in a number of such situations, formality was abandoned in the long and late sessions, first names freely used, and in spite of the strain, apparently a fair amount of psychological satisfaction experienced from the joint endeavour in seeking not a 'perfect' but a 'satisfactory' solution. This does not mean, of course, that in the straight negotiating sessions during this exercise hard bargaining did not take place with some re-emergence of traditional attitudes. It is unwise to assume that a state of balance in relationships between unions and management is other than a delicate, vulnerable and probably short-term phenomenon needing constant attention.

Communications

The psychologists' researches are very relevant here. Mention of a negotiating party's difficulty in receiving communications was made above. Some repetition and recapitulation is necessary at a later stage in the negotiation process if misunderstandings are not to occur. Noisy and disorderly queries also need to be accepted in order to establish a two-way flow of effective communication. Experiments show that one-way communication is more rapid and orderly, but that a two-way flow is more accurate. The receiver is able more easily to ensure his understanding of what is being said and the communication sender, though perhaps feeling much more psychologically exposed to critical cross-questioning, can check the receipt of the communication.

The difficulty the manager has in revoking any communication has already been mentioned. It is essential, though difficult, not to make irrevocable statements under pressure to 'come clean,' since often these must be revoked, making the negotiations more difficult because of damage to the credibility of an important party in the negotiations.

Outcome

Sociologists have written much on conflict situations and it would be foolish to deny their existence in industrial relations. There are conflicts of interests and of interpretation. On occasions there are indeed ideological conflicts which no amount of painstaking care lavished on industrial relations can touch. Shop steward groups will usually have at least one member who believes that neither justice nor dignity is possible in a capitalist society. Interestingly enough, these same men may be highly pragmatic in their approach to union affairs and 'good to deal with' from management's viewpoint, since their known opposition to the management class makes it likely that their members will more readily accept bargains negotiated by them.

Thus the outcome, even of hard bargaining with difficult opponents, may be an agreement. It is important, of course, that this is in line with management's objectives and that important concessions are not inadvertently made to get an agreement which is just beginning to appear possible. The agreement when reached must be put into operation and monitored with as much care and attention as has gone into the negotiating process, if it is to work.

If an agreement apparently cannot be reached, it may be possible to get both sides to agree to an adjournment. This is particularly wise if new queries come up.

If at the end of the road, there is no agreement, then the firm risks either a strike or a lockout. There are contradictory views on the actual result of strikes for the company. Paterson (*op. cit*) states that productivity increased after the strike and H A Turner (*Is Britain Really Strike Prone?* 1970) thinks the economic effects have been much exaggerated. The decision to 'take a strike,' however, is a very serious one. Not only does it disrupt production, it disrupts relationships in a way which may take years to repair. The answer to the union's frequent query: 'Is that your final offer?' is always a difficult one, and is likely to change with circumstances in the negotiating field, such as a genuine strike threat which seems unlikely to be called off at the last moment. The answer may also depend on commercial circumstances. If a large contract is signed while negotiations are proceeding, the original data on which an answer might have been based will be out of date. If the firm is told by a customer to hold deliveries for a while, it may be 'to their advantage' to do little to prevent a strike.

There are no figures giving the number of strike threats which are made and then withdrawn, but in British Rail alone there are, obviously, many. Managements may decide to risk strike action by standing firm, in order to regain control over their operations. If strike action does occur, one of the main problems will be the loss of contact with the strikers and thus the loss of opportunity to restart negotiations. This is particularly the case in unofficial strikes where managements refuse to negotiate 'under duress' although the history of industrial relations is strewn with cases of negotiations restarted under such conditions. The approach may, of course, be indirect. Although the principals preserve a splendid isolation, staff from other levels or associated but not directly concerned posts may in fact carry messages between the parties bringing nearer the time of work resumption. If communication remains severed then in most cases there is little hope of a resumption of work.

This chapter has attempted to identify the various stages in the conduct of negotiations at various levels and comment upon them. One of the main factors emerging is that negotiations in industrial relations cannot be separated usefully from any other aspect of an organisation's life. Furthermore, they belong to an on-going process in which there are problems of balancing different term objectives. The more examples we have of what actually happens in the negotiating room the nearer we may come to understanding it and applying the knowledge already available, some of which is indicated by this chapter.

References

1 *Explorations in Management* by W G BROWN, Heinemann, 1960
2 *Fairfields: a study of industrial change* by K J W ALEXANDER and C L JENKINS, Allen Lane the Penguin Press, 1970
3 *Industrial Relations and the Personnel Specialist* by P ANTHONY and A CRICHTON, Chapters 6 and 7, Batsford, 1969
4 'Psychological Research and Industrial Relations' by R WILLIAMS and D GUEST, *Occupational Psychology*, Vol. 43, Nos. 3 & 4, 1969
5 *A Behavioural Theory of Industrial Relations* by R E WALTON and R B MCKERSIE, McGraw Hill, 1965
6 *The Behaviour of Industrial Work Groups* by L R SAYLES, Wiley, 1958
7 *Managerial Psychology* by H J LEAVITT, Chicago University Press, 1964
8 *British Workers' View of Industrial Relations* by S R CHOUDHRI, unpublished MSc thesis, UMIST
9 *The Fawley Productivity Agreements* by A FLANDERS, Faber & Faber, 1964

Part Three _____

THE UNION
VIEWPOINT

_____

17

Working with the Union

Roger Lyons

National Officer, Association of Scientific, Technical and Managerial Staffs

Intimately linked with any endeavour to build constructive industrial relations with a trade union must be an understanding of the trade union movement itself. The single most important feature of British trade unions is their diversity. There is no neat post-war rationalisation into a dozen or so industrial unions as in West Germany, nor a straight-forward political and/or religious delineation as in France or Italy. British trade unions come in all shapes and sizes. Some have inclinations towards a vertical industrial sphere of interest, while others have developed into horizontally organised general unions. In order to work effectively with trade unions in this country it is fundamentally necessary to understand this basic diversity; for every single union is different from the next one.

Images of 'the unions' gleaned from the press or television will not assist those whose concern is the improvement of industrial relations and who wish to co-operate as harmoniously as possible with full-time trade union officials.

Individuality of unions

It is important, therefore, to examine and to understand the distinguishing factors contributing to the make-up of each union with which one may have to deal. Each union should be judged by its own individuality, rather than being viewed as a replica of any other union. The same applies to the union's officials and to the union's rules and practices.

Not only is each union rule book unique to the union concerned, but the interpretations, customs and practices built up over the years have further served to produce a particular and distinctive corporate image. Historical experience and time-served traditions cast many webs across contemporary trade unionism. More recent technological and organisational changes in industry, combined with developing socio-economic trends within the membership of the unions are ever-increasingly re-shaping the trade union movement itself.

Today almost every traditional 'craft' union includes semi-skilled workers in its membership. The rapid development of white-collar unionism in the private sector of industry and commerce has led many unions, with a previous antipathy towards organising staff employees, to completely rethink their policies. In particular, the growth of a number of specifically white-collar unions, unencumbered with the organisational impediments or mental straitjackets endowed by past generations, has led to a new dynamic force in the trade union world.

Those concerned with industrial relations are well advised to concentrate on the contemporary realities of the unions with which they might have to deal. Simultaneously, trade unions and their officials are having to revise traditional practices as industry changes its methods and structures. The increase in mergers and the rise of the multinational company induces significant changes among the trade unions. Industrial relations practitioners must equally come to terms not only with the diversity of British trade unions, but more especially with the major alterations that have occurred and are occurring in the trade union community. Constructive industrial relations requires a full comprehension of each party by the other.

This point is emphasised because many trade union officials either fail to understand or actively resent the ill-informed opinions often found on first contact with management representatives who handle the industrial relations of a company. Trade union officials may sometimes be rightly accused of failing to understand the role of the management. However the reverse is also true in many cases.

Contact

It is advisable that any official relationship with a trade union is preceded by a frank exchange of views. Rather than hoarding misconceptions that could cause difficulties at a later, and perhaps more delicate, stage in the relationship, it is preferable that all relevant questions are posed at the earliest possible stage. No company should avoid informal exchanges well prior to a more formal relationship. To treat the official of a bona fide trade union with what may be regarded as discourtesy by avoiding a frank exchange of views, will help to build up resentments that will impede good industrial relations.

Meeting union representatives

Even if the company has no short-term wish to recognise the union it could be taking considerable risks in resisting an informal meeting. After all, the company would show some courtesy to an individual employee's solicitor or minister of religion. The company's rejection of informal approaches by the union automatically hardens attitudes. With public opinion firmly in favour of collective bargaining such an attitude may stimulate antagonism from the trade union movement.

Initial contacts on an informal basis should allow each party to build up the fullest picture of the other. Each management has its own individual features; so does each trade union. The trade union official is keen to know the attitudes and organisational pattern of the management while no doubt the company desires to know the union with whom it will deal. Just as management would dislike having its distinctive features ignored, in being classed as 'just another employer,' so the trade union official would expect individual attention and understanding. Potential industrial relations problems arise for a company in industry A, when their new industrial relations manager tells the union official that he has already learnt all he needs to know about unions in industry B.

Some of the very *worst industrial relations situations* have arisen when the management representative has attempted to apply an inappropriate practice from another organisation to an approach by a trade union.

Occasionally attempts have been made to supplant the union initially involved with another of the employer's own choice. This kind of stratagem is increasingly coming to grief, and in any case is outlawed by public policy. If it is attempted however, and the original organising union remains involved, there is usually no easy road to 'working with the union.' In a number of cases the industrial relations manager responsible for such a confrontation has been dismissed in order to allow normal industrial relations to develop.

Recognition of the union

Whether in making the first contacts with a newly organised union, or in dealing with a formal recognition claim, the best place for contact is over the green baize table. The trade union official readily recognises that the pace of development in collective bargaining will vary from company to company and will be able to advise the membership of his union in accordance with his assessment of the situation. A full assessment can only be made after full and frank discussions with the company concerned; a refusal to meet the union even on an informal basis, is the start of industrial relations problems.

Procedural agreements

A very common feature in contemporary industrial relations is the establishment of more formal procedural machinery, or the improvement of any procedures that may exist. Such an exercise can only be brought to a mutually agreed conclusion when the original draft submitted is treated as fully negotiable. Trade union officials are sometimes forced to sign unsatisfactory procedural agreements as an expediency and the company's unilateral attitude may well undo much of the presumed advantages of the procedural agreement. The policy adopted by the employer in relation to the agreement on the procedures to be followed is treated by the union as a major indication of the company's genuine acceptance of the principles of collective bargaining or otherwise.

It can be very useful to precede formal discussions on a procedural agreement with a round table discussion, to examine the various possibilities and suggestions in great detail on an informal basis. All those who will have to use the procedures at the end of the day should take part in these discussions; line management and lay representatives. This close examination, preferably combined with fairly regular follow-up meetings can create a procedural relationship that obviates the necessity for sudden clashes following accusations of bad faith or misunderstandings in the workings of the procedure. Trade union officials would far prefer that the overwhelming bulk of, if not all, plant grievances or problems were to be resolved at domestic level, without having to involve the official. To secure this goal, the procedures should be kept as up-to-date and as relevant as possible.

Grievances

If the full-time official does, however, become involved in a relatively minor grievance situation at plant level, it is most conducive to settlement if neither party has taken too hard a position on the question. The most intangible obstacle to resolution of industrial conflict situations is the 'loss-of-face-factor.'

If the involvement of the full-time official is not to become a time-wasting farce, the company must be able to provide a senior representative with the capacity to jointly examine the grievance in an open-minded manner. Where experience shows that company representatives at all levels reiterate the identical attitude on relatively minor grievance situations in order to avoid loss-of-face, the official becomes increasingly inclined to abstain from participation. With the procedural arrangements falling into disrepute he might indicate to the membership that the only way to resolve the problem appears to be by direct action, in place of pursuing the problem fruitlessly through procedure. It may be valuable for the company to agree to the full-time official becoming involved, at domestic level on a more informal basis, in seemingly intractable but minor grievance situations since, usually, the further through the formal procedure, the harder the respective positions may be drawn.

Negotiations

The trade union official will probably be involved in the major wages and conditions claims. A variety of procedures determines the stage at which the full-time official enters the negotiations. In some cases the official presents substantive claims in the first instance, while in others he only participates, if necessary, following the breakdown of domestic talks. The forward-looking company will wish to base collective negotiations on wages, salaries or conditions on factual and up-to-date information.

Providing facilities

To facilitate such developments, the official should have the fullest possible access to company information such as wage-rate comparisons, differentials, grading schemes, costings, etc. The official must be able to consult as extensively as necessary with the membership and the lay representatives. For this purpose, facilities should be provided during working hours, well in advance of the negotiations themselves. The official and the union lay representatives will consult to prepare their claims and to consider all relevant information that might have been requested from the company. In the absence of facilities of this nature, the company might well have itself partially to blame if it considers itself faced with 'half-baked,' 'ill-informed,' or 'intemperate,' demands.

The full-time official must have all reasonable facilities during the course of the negotiations to communicate and consult with his constituents. The fullest participation takes place at meetings on company premises, held during normal working hours. A hardening of attitudes by the company against the provision of facilities during negotiations must be expected to result in a hardening of attitudes by the union against the employer. Companies differ widely in the extent to which they provide facilities to the full-time official for communication with the union membership. It is clear to many officials that those employers currently refusing reasonable facilities are merely displaying their prejudices in public. Progressive companies have lost nothing and possibly gained a great deal through provision of the reasonable facilities that are necessary for the maintenance of good communications in modern industry and commerce.

Effective co-operation

If the manager desires effective co-operation from the trade union and its officials the union must be treated as an equal in all dealings with the company. To many within the ranks of management this might sound like a subversive, or even revolutionary idea. To others it may appear irrelevant. If an employer insists on dealing with a union, and its full-time officials, as a supplicant, the day will surely come when the roles will be reversed with a vengeance. Most trade union officials consider that the employer enjoys predominant economic strength at the bargaining table. Conversely, some employers might argue that they were, in fact, the 'underdog.' Either way, the surest route to good industrial relations is for the full-time official and his colleagues to be given completely equal treatment. This applies not only at the negotiating table but also at all other levels of contact.

Union representatives

Different unions have varying policies on the degree of involvement of lay representatives. The Association of Scientific, Technical and Managerial Staffs and most other white-collar trade unions as well as the Transport and General Workers Union and a growing number of blue-collar unions), believe in full lay representative participation at the negotiating table. Wherever this policy is applied, the full-time official performs the role of adviser and spokesman, rather than representative, since the lay representatives are present at the table. At the moment there is a very determined trend towards further strengthening the lay element at all levels of the negotiating machinery. The experiences at Pilkington Glass, St Helen's has shown clearly the hazards of allowing full-time officials to monopolise the employee side of the machinery. Full-time officials are having to come to terms with the trend towards increased lay participation; willingly or reluctantly?

This development affects past negotiating practices and some managements tend to seek semi-clandestine meetings with the full-time officials in advance of, or during, formal negotiations. Any form of secret meetings presents potential dangers to both parties involved. The supposed need for such happenings shows an absence of mutual trust in the negotiating machinery. 'Off-the-record' discussions may become necessary in time of dispute and may be useful in particularly sensitive individual cases. However, if they became a regular practice during regular negotiations they would completely undermine the confidence representatives in their full-time officials and in the negotiating of the machinery itself. Thus, while informal relationships may justifiably exist at other times, it is inappropriate to pursue them at times of major negotiations.

Should the negotiations break down, or the procedural arrangements become exhausted, there is nothing to prevent the re-establishment of contacts between the full-time official and management with the full knowledge of the lay representatives. The trade union official should be an integral part of the union, and managements often have to pay the price for having over-fostered their relationship with the full-time official. In the face of what is widely considered an unnatural arrangement the membership may react by rejecting all advice and leadership from their official. Hence it is important that relationships, perhaps established in the best interests of good industrial relations, do not become too familiar.

Regular consultation

Contacts between the management and the full-time trade union official are best built up by regular consultation. If the official is involved only when there is a crisis situation both parties run the risk of mutual misunderstandings further escalating the immediate crisis. On the other hand, regular contact through consultative meetings can help to broaden the outlook of both union and management representatives. This is particularly true when industry and commerce are undergoing rapid change. These include the growing application of the computer and advanced automated techniques of many kinds, the introduction of consultants, new working methods, the expansion of the white-collar work force and the diminution of the unskilled workers. Regular consultations between the management and the full-time official will not avoid employee resistance to changes unless adequate safeguards are attached. Nonetheless, it will provide for the maximum areas of co-operation to be formulated as well as obviating unfounded suspicions which could otherwise act as a powerful force against change.

Redundancy problems

At a time of relatively high unemployment close consultation with the full-time official may provide for schemes of work-sharing, revised shift arrangements or agreed voluntary severance terms linked with availability of alternative employment. Years of patient work in building up good industrial relations may be shattered in hours by a unilateral declaration of involuntary redundancies. While many companies have been willing to put their industrial relations, their employees' career security and general morale and efficiency at jeopardy, by executing involuntary sackings in the guise of redundancy, others acting in close consultation with the trade union officials have chosen more humane alternatives. Trade union officials will confirm that the issue of 'surplus labour,' and how it is dealt with, constitutes the fulcrum point of industrial relations and if any action is taken by a company prior to full consultation with the full-time official, the management can expect a serious breakdown in co-operation.

Management may not realise that the full-time trade union official has a very deep commitment to the maintenance of the fullest possible employment in the area within which he has responsibilities. Long-term benefits in the field of co-operation with the union officials may be won by the company that takes a permanent and public interest in the local employment situation. While the official expects the company to give first priority to its own needs, a more altruistic involvement will create a more co-operative climate for the employer. The company could fully participate on a joint basis with the unions and other employers in schemes to retrain and redeploy the unemployed, satisfactorily to place school-leavers and to maintain constant contact with the union officials over all employment questions. At present there are too many instances where merely lip service is paid to these questions by the employer.

Local community issues

The trade union full-time official will welcome the keen interest of management in employment questions but co-operation can also extend to other matters of concern to the community. Managements and full-time officials may deal with issues of industrial expansion, public transport, provision of housing and recreational facilities, school building, further education and any other local problems or developments. In some areas this co-operation already takes place but, too often, joint action is not undertaken until a local crisis situation has arisen. The manager would do well to discuss with the trade union official any possibilities for local initiatives. Whatever suggested areas of co-operation actually come to fruition, the manager should certainly set his horizons for co-operation with the full-time official a great deal wider than an annual invitation to the company's Christmas Party.

Training

Management can also co-operate with the local full-time trade union official in the training programmes of both the union and the company. In recent years there has been a rapid increase in the number of training sessions run for the trade union lay representatives. These courses have been organised by trade unions, by the unions and company together, or by acceptable outside third-parties. The TUC insists that any training courses in industrial relations for lay representatives must be acceptable to the trade union movement. However this does not prevent useful co-operation between managements and full-time officials in arranging for management representatives to participate in certain sessions within a course. Equally, management can provide full facilities for the trade union official to hold courses during working hours on company premises. Under no circumstances should management contemplate running industrial relations training courses without the agreement of the full-time official, for any such action can invite instant boycott.

Certain companies involve the trade union official in their in-company training. In particular, it is considered beneficial for all sections of management to be able to meet the official. Question and answer sessions often turn into very stimulating dialogues, with long-term advantages for all concerned. A company's industrial relations practices should never be kept a private reserve of the industrial relations manager alone leaving other sections of management to fend for themselves and, perhaps, inadvertently one day help to cause a major breakdown in industrial relations. Management at all levels should be able to understand the role of the trade union in their company, and this can be accomplished in large measure by the involvement of the official from time to time.

Contact with senior management

The management should take every reasonable opportunity to bring the local trade union official into contact with senior decision-makers in the company heirarchy. Industrial relations will suffer if the official is seemingly fobbed-off with a junior management representative on every approach. Access to the highest decision-making levels should at all times be possible, though, of course, the full-time official would normally reserve this channel for special occasions. It is also useful to introduce the official to newly appointed senior company personnel. Similarly, when a new local trade union official arrives on the scene, appropriate introductions should be arranged.

Establishing sound industrial relations

The above suggestions may seem rather mundane, but they are part of an infrastructure necessary for the construction and maintenance of good industrial relations. At a time when the stage of much major collective bargaining is at the level of the national industry and nation-wide company grouping, it is all the more important that relationships are maintained at local level. All too often, when major questions are dealt with at a higher level, relations at the grass-roots between the local management and full-time trade union official may be allowed progressively to wither away. In the event of a sudden localised industrial relations crisis, the lack of meaningful relations will be sorely felt. Thus the maintenance of relationships at local level, even in the absence of major bargaining, is a form of insurance policy.

When a dispute situation does occur tempers may rise on both sides with many angry words spoken, perhaps in haste. Whilst both sides may take up hard positions it is important for both the management and the full-time official to remember that at the end of the day the overwhelming majority of disputes are settled by a mutually acceptable compromise formula. Such a formula can more easily be obtained if both management and the official are able easily to resume contacts; they will have to re-establish relationships when the dispute is resolved. It may be the case that, as a result of one severe clash (during which, say, the official was expressing the mandate of the membership), the manager concerned feels unable to co-operate in future with the local official. This is a recipe for further industrial relations problems.

Differences in policies and attitudes

Both the manager and the local full-time trade union official are, in effect, spokesmen for their respective constituencies. Differences in policies and attitudes need not necessarily be an obstacle to dialogue and the maintenance of reasonable relationships. After all, in international relations, diplomacy is conducted between states with often very conflicting ideologies and outlooks. As long as most of industry and commerce is organised in the present way, with the owners and managers of capital employing labour in order to produce private profit, there will continue to be a basic difference between the interests of the owners of capital and those who provide their labour, in whatever capacity. Every meaningful attempt to understand industrial relations has to recognise this fact. The overwhelming majority of trade union officials far prefer to meet and negotiate with management representatives who are ready and willing to accept the premise of fundamental conflict of interest in industrial relations. Full-time officials refuse to believe it is possible to have a genuine alternative economic system operating in one factory in the midst of a capitalist society.

This does not, of course, exclude the acknowledgement of varying forms of company or enterprise structure within the society. Nevertheless all managements, whether representing a consumers' co-operative society, a public corporation or a private company, must expect the trade union official to at least seek to maximise the return to the employee of the labour value accruing to the enterprise through his or her labour. In a capitalistic economic structure, such an aim is an integral part of the market forces. To the trade union official, the practices of industrial relations relate to this aim and consequently, while the present economic system continues, potential industrial relations problems will remain with us.

Avoiding conflict

Many of the potential problems may be avoided by the company, through the development and maintenance of good industrial relations practices in dealings between the management and the union. The features outlined in this chapter represent some of the ways in which co-operation between the management and the full-time official can be furthered.

The effect of the Act

The Industrial Relations Act, currently taking effect, holds many possible dangers for good industrial relations. This is why so many companies have already agreed to non-legally binding clauses in existing and future agreements. Trade union officials have experienced no great difficulty in gaining management's assent to keeping as much of industrial relations as possible out of the hands of the courts thereby negating a major intention of the Act. Managements should take note of this development, which is in the best interests of good industrial relations. At the end of the day relationships are better conducted over the green baize table than through prison bars.

18

The Role of the Shop Steward in Industry

J Murray

Chairman and Works Convenor, Vickers Shop Stewards

Contrary to popular opinion, the shop steward is neither the satirical creation of Peter Sellers (in the film *I'm all right, Jack*), nor a recent phenomenon in British industry. The shop stewards' movement has been established for the last fifty years and shop stewards were active in industry long before that. Since the Industrial Revolution when man left the land for the factories there has been a struggle by the workers to 'humanise' the workshops in the harsh world of industry subject to the iron laws of economics. The shop steward is the expression of man's desire to influence and control that industrial environment. To appreciate the function of the shop steward it is necessary to know of his historical development—to know why he is there.

Conception of shop stewards

In 1878 a delegate conference of the Amalgamated Society of Engineers authorised their District Committees to appoint shop stewards. The Conference set the seal of approval on a development in industrial relations that was already growing, i.e. representation of the workers

K 269

in negotiations with management by the men from the shop floor. The employers and their associations refused official recognition to shop stewards, preferring to deal with full-time officials of the unions when any problems arose in their establishments.

Forty years later, in 1918, the issue came to a head when the whole of the engineering industry in Britain came out on strike. The strike began in Rochdale when a local employer broke the dilution agreement (this allowed unskilled workers to carry out skilled work on armaments and munitions but not on commercial products) by putting women workers on to grinding spindles for cotton machinery. When the men elected representatives to negotiate with the management these were promptly sacked. The strike ensued and within two days the whole of Lancashire had stopped work in support and within a week the British engineering industry had ground to a halt. The strikers' original demands included an end to the war and the establishment of a Socialist Commonwealth, but gradually their demands came to centre around the recognition by the employers of workshop representatives—shop stewards.

Prominent, in both the strike and the unions at that time, were members of the Socialist Labour Party and the Syndicalist League, one of their leaders being Tom Mann, who was to become the first general secretary of the Amalgamated Engineering Union. The Syndicalists believed that political power should be vested in the workers in industry who had created the nation's wealth, and that Parliament, representing the interests of the ruling class, should be abolished. They saw the shop steward as being the base of their Industrial Parliament and the leaders of the workers' control movement. The discussions and negotiations held at the time of the strike revealed that the employers too believed that the recognition of shop stewards would undermine their authority in the factories.

Taking part in these discussions was Jack Bowman, at that time a founder member of the Armstrong Whitworth's Shop Stewards' Committee, and a lay member of the National Executive of the Steam Engine Makers' Society. At the age of 80, still alive today, he recalls that at one meeting the union spokesman, putting the case for recognition, frequently mentioned the terms shop steward and works convenor. The chairman of the employers' side, in reply, protested that the terms 'shop steward' and 'works convenor' did not exist in the English language and that he had never heard of them. Furthermore, the shop steward being of equal standing to the foreman would undermine authority and, having a works convenor above the shop stewards equal to managers, would create anarchy. He ended by declaring that he would not have shop stewards and convenors in industry. The delegate of the Boilermakers' Society, at the meeting, intervened to ask, 'Would it help the Chairman of the employers' side to recognise them if we called them Bishops and Archbishops instead.' This novel suggestion was not accepted, and shop stewards and convenors they became.

Birth of shop stewards

It was not until two years later that the agreement on the recognition of shop stewards was signed by all the unions except the Engineers. They considered that the agreement gave too much power to the employers. That union (now the Amalgamated Engineering Union) signed it in 1922 after their defeat at the hands of the engineering employers, who locked them out of the factories, and the signing of it has rankled with them ever since.

At last the shop steward, who had been born some time before, was declared legitimate. His legitimacy had been achieved against opposition from the employers, from some of the officials of the unions, and with the participation in the struggle of political groups—factors which are still considered an active part of the shop stewards' movement today.

Shop stewards and works committee agreement

The text of the agreement signed in 1922 is as follows:

Shop stewards and works committee agreement

With a view to amplifying the provisions to avoiding disputes by a recognition of shop stewards and the institution of works committees. It is agreed as follows:

Appointment of shop stewards

1 Workers, members of the trade unions employed in a federated establishment may have representatives appointed from the members

of the unions employed in the establishment to act on their behalf in accordance with the terms of this agreement.

2   The representatives shall be known as shop stewards.

3   The appointment of such shop stewards shall be determined by the trade unions concerned and each trade union party to this agreement may have such shop stewards.

4   The names of the shop stewards and the shop or portion of the shop in which they are employed and the trade union to which they belong shall be intimated officially by the trade union concerned to the management on election.

Appointment of works committees

5   A works committee may be set up in each establishment consisting of not more than seven representatives of the management and not more than seven shop stewards who should be representatives of the various classes of work people employed in the establishment.

The shop stewards elected to the works committee shall, subject to re-election, hold office for not more than twelve months.

The shop stewards for this purpose shall be nominated and elected by ballot of the workpeople, members of the trade unions parties to this agreement employed in the establishment.

6   If a question failing to be dealt with by the works committee in accordance with the procedure hereinafter laid down arises in a department which has not a shop steward on the works committee, the works committee may, as regards that question, co-opt a shop steward from the department concerned. An agenda of the points to be discussed by the works committee shall be issued at least three days before the date of the meeting if possible.

Functions and procedure

7   The functions of shop stewards and works committees, so far as they are concerned with the avoidance of disputes, shall be exercised in accordance with the following procedure:

(a)   A worker or workers desiring to raise any question in which they are directly concerned shall, in the first instance, discuss the same with their foreman.

(b)   Failing settlement, the question shall be taken up with the shop manager and/or head shop foreman by the appropriate shop steward and one of the workers directly concerned.

(c) If no settlement is arrived at the question may, at the request of either party, be further considered at a meeting of the works committee. At this meeting the ODD (now the DO) may be present, in which event a representative of the employers' association shall also be present.

(d) Any question arising which affects more than one branch of trade or more than one department of the works may be referred to the works committee.

(e) The question may thereafter be referred for further consideration in terms of the 'Provisions for Avoiding Disputes.'

Provisions for avoiding disputes

1 When a question arises, an endeavour shall be made by the management and the workman directly concerned to settle the same in the works or at the place where the question has arisen. Failing settlement deputations of workmen who may be accompanied by their organiser (in which event a representative of the employers' association shall also be present) shall be received by the employers by appointment without unreasonable delay for the mutual discussion of any question in the settlement of which both parties are directly concerned. In the event of no settlement being arrived at, it shall be competent for either party to bring the question before a local conference to be held between the local association and the local representatives of the society.

2 In the event of either party desiring to raise any question a local conference for this purpose may be arranged by application to the secretary of the local association or to the local representative of the society.

3 Local conferences shall be held within seven working days unless otherwise mutually agreed upon, from the receipt of the application by the secretary of the local association or the local representative of the society.

4 Failing settlement at a local conference of any question brought before it, it shall be competent for either party to refer the matter to a central conference which, if thought desirable, may make a joint recommendation to the constituent bodies.

5 Central conference shall be held on the second Friday of each

month at which questions referred to central conference prior to fourteen days of that date shall be taken.

6   Until the procedure provided above has been carried through, there shall be no stoppage of work either of a partial or a general character.

General

8   Shop stewards shall be subject to the control of the trade unions and shall act in accordance with the rules and regulations of the trade unions and agreements with employers so far as these affect the relation between employers and workpeople.

9   In connection with this agreement, shop stewards shall be afforded facilities to deal with questions raised in the shop or portion of a shop in which they are employed. Shop stewards elected to the works committee shall be afforded similar facilities in connection with their duties, and in the course of dealing with these questions they may, with the previous consent of the management (such consent not to be unreasonably withheld), visit any shop or portion of a shop in the establishment. In all other respects shop stewards shall conform to the same working conditions as their fellow workers.

10   Negotiations under this agreement may be instituted either by the management or by the workers concerned.

11   Employers and shop stewards and works committee shall not be entitled to enter into any agreement inconsistent with agreements between the federation or local association and the trade unions.

12   For the purpose of this agreement the expression 'establishment' shall mean the whole establishment or sections thereof according to whether the management is unified or sub-divided.

13   Any question which may arise out of the operation of this agreement shall be brought before the executive of the trade union concerned or the federation as the case may be.

2 June 1922 (Amended 10 August 1955)

The above agreement, which recognised the shop stewards, also set out the procedure to be used when any claim for improved wages and conditions was progressed from the factory floor. Making provision for a panel of employers at district level to examine claims and at national level 'an employers' court'; the agreement suggests some judicial quality to the decisions that are reached. In fact, all they invariably do is support what the employer has stated or offered to the shop stewards at factory level. This atmosphere of the court room is apparent in the Victorian conference rooms of local employers' associations with their conference tables the size of football fields, designed to impress the unions' representatives (today's shop stewards are not so impressionable).

Central Conference

The agreement also makes provision for the monthly farce known as the Central Conference. At the Central Conference some hundreds of union officials and shop stewards, personnel managers, and representatives of local employers' associations, sit in the lobby of the Station Hotel at York. All day they gaze up the grand central staircase waiting for their national officers to descend and hand out the decisions of the employers' court on the claims they have been progressing for several months. The local representatives are not allowed into the discussions, presumably, because their knowledge of what the issue is all about might disturb the cloistered calm in which the court reaches its decisions. The almost total lack of success of the Central Conference procedure is illustrated by this report of part of the proceedings at the Engineering Employers' Central Conference, held in York on Friday, 13 August 1971, dealing with claims progressed by the AEU Central Conference

Report (part) of proceedings at Central Conference

Representatives of the Executive Council met the Engineering Employers' Federation at York on Friday, 13 August 1971, when the following questions were discussed: Coventry (Employers') Reference

To replace the existing methods of payment for all hourly paid male and female employees carrying out direct or indirect work at the Parkside and Quinton Road Works of Rolls-Royce (1971) Ltd, Bristol Engine Div., Coventry, who are currently in receipt of the Indirect Bonus and Productivity Deals by an Interim Agreement—Rolls-Royce Ltd, Bristol Engine Division. After discussion the parties were unable to arrive at a mutual recommendation.

Coventry (Employers') Reference

To implement a trial agreement for all direct hourly paid employees in the middle and lower machine shops at the Parkside Works of Rolls-Royce Ltd, Bristol Engine Division, Coventry—Rolls-Royce (1971) Ltd.

After discussion it was agreed that the question be referred back for final settlement at works level.

Coventry (Employers') Reference

To replace the existing piecework system in the Heavy Machine Shop by a new incentive scheme as outlined in the Company's proposals of 9 November 1970—Wickham Machine Tool Manufacturing Co Ltd.

After discussion the parties were unable to arrive at a mutual recommendation.

Coventry Reference

To consider the rate paid to a named inspector member transferred from the Toolroom to production during the recent redundancy negotiations—Herbert BSA Ltd.

After discussion the parties were unable to arrive at a mutual recommendation.

Coventry Reference

To consider the duties of a named foreman employed by Coventry Motor Fittings Ltd.

After discussion the parties were unable to arrive at a mutual recommendation.

Sunderland Reference

Interim Payment—Hepworth and Grandage Ltd.

After discussion the parties were unable to arrive at a mutual recommendation.

Bradford Reference

1   Setters—Claim that auto and semi-auto set up operators have been wrongly graded.

2   Tool and Cutter Grinders—Claim that tool and cutter grinders currently on F grade should be re-classified as G Group.

3   Craftsmen's Grade Inspector—Claim to be placed in Craftsmen's Grade—International Harvester Co (of Great Britain) Ltd.

After discussion the parties were unable to arrive at a mutual recommendation.

Halifax Reference

100 per cent Trade Union Organisation—Nu-Swift International Ltd.

After discussion the parties were unable to arrive at a mutual recommendation.

Leeds Reference

Substantial increase to all hourly paid maintenance workers—West Yorkshire Foundries Ltd.

After discussion the parties were unable to arrive at a mutual recommendation.

'The parties being unable to arrive at a mutual recommendation' means they could not find a solution to the matter under discussion and this applies to the vast majority of claims. The lack of success of the procedure machinery in solving disputes and the length of time taken in dealing with them has meant the growth of what the Donovan Report (The Royal Commission on Trade Unions and Employers' Associations) called the 'informal system' of bargaining. This informal system of bargaining, which takes place on the factory floor, has meant the increased importance of the shop steward. It has been suggested that the failure of the procedure machinery has also meant the growth of unofficial industrial action. Trade unionists see more advantage in putting pressure on management at domestic level than taking a claim through procedure, which is generally a lengthy business.

Duties of shop stewards

Union rule books tend to be rather short on information which defines the duties and functions of the shop steward. For example, the AEU rule book lays down four basic duties for shop stewards and convenors. These are:

1   To examine and sign the contribution cards of all members at least once a quarter

2   To use every endeavour to see that all men starting work are duly qualified trade unionists

3   To see that all persons are receiving the approved rates
     and complying with shop and district practices and to
     examine pay notes for that purpose
4   To report to the District Committee any position which
     is not satisfactory and which cannot be adjusted in the
     shop

It is clear from these rules that the unions saw the shop steward in
the role of a policeman, ensuring that the conditions negotiated by the
officials were being carried out in the factory. What the shop steward
has now become is the initiator of claims for improved wages and
conditions and in many cases agreements are concluded inside the
factory. While it is true to say that most union rules state that the
shop steward has no authority to call a strike, in practice he will
generally receive the support of his union in taking industrial action
if this should be against a management decision altering the *status quo*.
When the steward is seeking an improvement in conditions the union
normally insists that procedure must be carried out and Executive
Council approval given before industrial action commences.

Shop stewards' relationships

With his work group

The role of the shop steward in the work situation is like that of the
street gang leader. The work group, seeing the management as the
enemy and recognising that a correcting balance is needed to the
powers at the disposal of the management, act together—the union.
The union of the work group needs a leader who can act as their
spokesman and negotiator—the shop steward. As an official of the
union under the control of the District Committee the shop steward,
in carrying out the union policies, occasionally finds himself in conflict
with his work group. The most consistent example of this is the
restriction of overtime which is unpopular with the men he represents.
It is sometimes necessary, in exercising his authority, for the shop
steward to discipline individual members of the group. He cannot do
this himself but must report these cases to the District Committee
who have the power to fine or expel members. It is unusual for these
powers to be used as the shop steward generally relies on the power

of persuasion to carry his members with him. He is, of course, always subject to removal from his position by his members by a vote in the shop at any time.

With his union

Shop stewards, after election by the work group, cannot function unless their election has been endorsed by the union generally at district level. He must also carry out the policies and decisions of the union even when these appear to conflict with the interests of the members he represents. In representing his members' wishes he may find himself in conflict with the full-time officials of the union or the District Committee. His members, in return for money offered, may be prepared to agree productivity concessions (for example the use of a stop watch) to which the union is opposed, and invariably he must retreat in the face of union opposition.

Shop stewards generally receive a nominal payment from their union to underline that the union controls them. For instance, an AEU shop steward receives £0.80 per quarter year. If he also collects union dues he receives a percentage.

With the management

The shop floor attitude to management is perhaps best epitomised in the Tyneside story:

'Joe, an old labourer, is trudging through the shipyard carrying a heavy load on his shoulders. It is a filthy, wet day and the sole of his shoe is flapping open. The shipyard manager, passing at the time, stops him, saying 'Hey, Joe, you can't go around with your shoe in that state on a wet day like this' and reaching into his back pocket takes out a bundle of bank notes. Joe beams in anticipation. 'Here,' says the manager, slipping the elastic band off the bundle of notes, 'put this round your shoe, it will help keep the wet out'

This attitude is a help to the shop steward when he appeals for solidarity but it can work against him when he is convinced by the management's case on an issue but cannot carry his men along with him. The sharp distinctions made by most companies in dealing with the shop floor worker as opposed to the staff worker reinforces this suspicion. In pensions, sickness payment, job security, even the canteen and lavatory facilities, the shop floor worker is aware that the management regard him as a different animal from the staff worker. When we realise that the primary function of management is the maximisation of profits for the company, and the function of the shop steward is to get the best possible wages and conditions for his members in the company, the wonder is how these two diametrically opposed forces can be reconciled.

What they do both share is a joint interest in keeping the company a going concern to provide them with jobs. Working together in this state of *antagonistic co-operation* the shop steward and the manager can sometimes come to see the other as:

1   Someone who is working for the downfall of the company; someone who can be used as a management tool to police the workers; someone (if he is being awkward) who can be got round by making a direct appeal to the men he represents. *This is the manager seeing the shop steward.*
2   Someone who is trying to rob the workers; someone who is trying to undermine your position and that of the union; someone you can get round by going to see the personnel manager. *This is the shop steward seeing the manager.*

They can treat each other as equals; sensibly acting as they should and recognising that they both have authority and responsibility, both have a job to do. With their first-hand knowledge they can work out the best solutions to problems arising in their work unit.

Turnover of shop stewards

The evidence of the high turnover of the shop steward in industry suggests that the position has its difficulties. If this is the case, what are the motives of anyone accepting the job?

The desire to lead or serve? A power complex? A career ladder to a job in union or management? The fact that trade unionists recognise that someone has to do the job?

It can be any one of these motives or a composite of them but the reasons why he is a shop steward are seldom a guide to his performance in the job. When the shop steward takes off his overalls and enters the office to discuss matters on an equal footing with the manager the job has its compensations. Being at the centre of communications he is the best informed man in the shop as to what is happening in the executive suite and the union's district offices, and this gives him standing. Recent agreements on the payment of average earnings to shop stewards while negotiating means that he no longer loses money on the job as he did in the past.

Politics and shop stewards

During the Seamans' Strike in 1967, the then Prime Minister, Harold Wilson, described the National Union of Seamens' Executive Committee, in the now well-known phrase as a 'tightly knit, politically motivated group.' The description has become a favourite of newspaper leader writers when writing about shop stewards. Is this true? The truth is that the vast majority of shop stewards vote Labour, are conservative in their outlook and are unaware of the revolutionary traditions which played a part in the building of their movement.

The influence of the Communist Party is also suggested as a cause of industrial unrest. If we look at the 25 000 or so members of the Communist Party (of whom only a part work in industry) in relation to the estimated number of shop stewards of around 200 000 (TUC Annual Reports) it is seen that numerically their influence is small. While it is true the average party member is almost always prepared to accept the shop steward's job, and that they occupy prominent positions in the movement, the opportunities and the desire to use their position for political ends is proscribed. Revolutionary political grouping's influence in the movement is virtually non-existent because of class differences, and the resistance of the average shop steward to accepting leadership from outside the movement.

The size of the shop stewards' movement indicates that it is more representative of the attitudes of the British working class than it is representative of any political ideology. It is an illusion to seek these motivations to explain industrial troubles.

Working with the shop stewards means recognising that he is subject to pressures and controls from outside; in the same way as a manager is. It means recognising that in many cases he has the same qualities of leadership that has made the manager a captain of industry. The manager who recognises these facts is well on the way to ensuring that industrial relations in his department will be conducted realistically.

Part Four

THE SOCIAL FRAMEWORK

19

Lessons from the Behavioural Sciences

A W Gottschalk

Staff Tutor in Social Psychology, Department of Adult Education, University of Nottingham

---

In recent years the term *behavioural sciences* has gradually come to have a greater significance for managers concerned with problems of change. This has been facilitated by the intensive growth of plant productivity bargaining during the last decade which increasingly sought and utilised the concepts, methods and language of the behavioural scientist. One can now predict with some confidence that the introduction of change in industrial relations within the context of the organisation, be it large or small, will continue to draw upon the behavioural sciences. Only one factor will rival this approach in importance and that is the move towards legal regulation contained in the Industrial Relations Act.

This chapter has two separate but related tasks. The first is to report briefly on some of the most important findings of the behavioural sciences for managers. The second is to show how this knowledge may be utilised by managers to help deal with the industrial relations problems which they encounter within their organisations. The pattern of this chapter will therefore reflect the twin purposes. After a statement of what is meant by the behavioural sciences the research findings will be assessed under three headings; namely our knowledge about individuals, groups and organisations. The second part of each section will deal with the application of these researches to contemporary problems of change within industrial relations at the work place.

The term behavioural sciences has an elasticity which is both a benefit and a hindrance. Within this chapter it is taken to refer primarily to a collection of overlapping theories and concepts. These have arisen in response to the failure of conventional wisdom and practice to cope with the problems and consequences associated with social and organisational changes. From all this there has emerged a new concept of man, of power and of organisations. The implications for the managers are profound. The traditional view of industrial relations as being concerned primarily with job regulation has been broadened out. A new dimension is offered which aims to place industrial relations in a more relevant and truer framework, that of the organisation undergoing different degrees of change, whilst not forgetting that the employment relationship is basically an economic one. This approach can also aid in the analysis of variations in industrial relations behaviour and help to overcome some of the difficulties of forecasting in this field.

Before embarking upon the report of the most important research findings one problem of clarification needs to be dealt with. What is meant by the term *management?* A clear answer to this question has been given by John Child who writes 'Management may be regarded from at least three different perspectives; first as an economic resource performing a series of technical functions which comprise the organising and administering of other resources; secondly as a system of authority through which policy is translated into execution of tasks; and thirdly as an *élite* social grouping which acts as an economic resource and maintains the associated system of authority.'[1] The distinction between the technical *activity*, the system of *authority* will be referred to throughout this chapter when we assess the implications of the behavioural sciences for managers concerned with industrial relations problems.

People in organisations

The focus of much early research by behavioural scientists has been upon aspects of individual behaviour within the context of work organisations. They have been particularly concerned with the problems of perception and motivation. Our understanding of the physical and mental world about us depends upon information obtained via our sensory functions. Each of us comes to know the properties of objects and people by the sensory experience we derive from contact with them. This perception does not however give us *reality*, only an image which differs substantially from one person to another. We behave in accordance with our own image of reality. Thus the work organisation is seen quite differently by people who occupy different roles. The departmental manager, the foreman and the shop steward may all work for the same company but each sees it differently. The manager sees it as dynamic, the foreman as badly organised and the shop steward sees it as being anti-trade union.

Perception becomes more uniform among people as they share common experiences, whereas differences arise as a result of different experiences. The assembly line worker and the salesman both have a biased perceptual sample as a result of different occupational 1oles. Each probably perceived the recent *Quality and Reliability Year* very differently. One saw it as another pressure to be coped with, the other as a new selling point. This problem of biased sampling becomes particularly marked when little or no contact exists with the phenomena in question. Many managers have relatively little or no contact with the trade unions; their image comes from the mass media or from other individuals. Hence the manager in frequent contact with trade unions through negotiations and consultations will perceive the shop steward (or the Industrial Relations Act) quite differently from his management colleague in the research department of the same company. Their perception is further distorted by their occupational role. The job description which so clearly defines this role within the work organisation more or less automatically determines the perceptual field. The personnel manager and the financial controller are alert to any signs or cues that indicate interference with the smooth functioning of the organisation. One becomes sensitive to labour turnover figures, the other to the volume of work in progress. Differences in perception may also be influenced by the socio-economic status of the individual. The current debate about the value of payment-by-results system is a good example of how socio-economic status influences perception. Many production workers see the system as *fair* and many managers see it as *disorganised*.

Earlier work on perception was followed by detailed studies of motivation. These have shown that the assumptions which are made about motivation by many managers have not always been fully supported by the findings of the behavioural scientist. It is possible to identify four sets of assumptions about people in organisations which have all reflected particular social philosophies and which in turn have served as a justification for particular organisational systems and procedures. These are discussed in their order of historical appearance.

Rational economic man

Employees are primarily motivated by economic incentive and will do that which yields the greatest economic gain. As the organisation controls the functioning of economic incentives employees are essentially passive and can be manipulated or controlled in order to realise certain identifiable goals. Man's feelings are, however, essentially irrational and these interfere with his rational calculation of self interest. Therefore, the organisation must be designed to neutralise and control these unpredictable traits.

Social man

Employees are primarily motivated by their social needs and obtain identity through their relationships with others. The consequences of industrialisation and continuing technological change is that work no longer holds its former meaning with the result that relationships at work become all important. Employees thus are more responsive to work-group pressures than the incentives and controls of management.

Self-actualising man

There exists for each person a hierarchy of motives and as lower level ones are satisfied they are replaced by more sophisticated higher level motives. At the lower end of the hierarchy are simple needs for survival, safety and security and then for affiliative needs. These two categories are followed by ego-satisfaction and self-esteem needs, needs for autonomy and independence and finally self-actualisation needs in the sense of the fullest use of all the individual resources. Employees seek to be mature individuals and are capable of achieving this. In this situation externally improved incentives and controls threaten self-motivations and self-control.

Complex man

Employees are infinitely more complex than either rational-economic man, social man or self-actualising man suggests. They are also highly variable, capable of learning new motives and of finding fulfilment of social and self-actualising needs in different aspects of the company's life. Equally they can become productively involved with the work organisation.

Changes within industrial relations

The industrial relations implications of these four assumptions about employee motivations are very great.

Rational economic man The manager who wholeheartedly accepts the *rational economic* view oversimplifies a highly complex situation. Employees are more characterised by their heterogeneity than their homogeneity. To assume only a calculative involvement encourages an almost mechanical approach to the organisation and the placement of the burden for organisational performance entirely on management. Experience of informal output restrictions amongst operatives under piece-work payment system shows that this simple view is inadequate. It cannot explain differences in patterns of industrial relations behaviour in the same company, nor can it explain differences between companies in the same industry.

Social man The social man concept, which is associated with the human relations school, draws upon researches dating back to before the Second World War. The behaviour of the individual is modified through his membership of a work group. The Hawthorne studies drew attention to the fact that acceptance and the need to be liked by one's fellow workers was at least as important, if not more, than the economic incentives offered by management. Managers were therefore encouraged to view all problems dealing with the use of human resources primarily in terms of the group. Democratic leadership and a problem solving approach could foster participation and the acceptance of organisational goals. In industrial relations this resulted in the development of institutions aiming to facilitate joint consultation which were designed to improve communications between managements and the employees. The degeneration and ultimate collapse of consultative procedures can be traced back to their failure to cope with certain forms of conflict within the organisation. The distinction between communication and negotiation was never completely feasible. Effective communication is only part of the solution to organisational conflict.

Self-actualising man The last decade has seen the development of the concept of self-actualising man. It has received support from both research findings and propagandist writings. The division between these two has often been blurred and this has resulted in some problems of application. Meaning may have been removed from work but this is not related so much to the employee's social needs as to his need to use all his capacities and skills in a mature and productive way. McGregor has characterised the organisational response to this situation as Theory X and Theory Y. The former assumes that most employees dislike work and avoid it whenever possible. Accordingly they have to be coerced, directed and pressurised if they are to make the required effort in their jobs. Theory X also suggests that most employees prefer to be directed, to avoid responsibility and search above all else for security. Theory Y is the exact reverse of the propositions contained in Theory X, i.e. the ordinary person does not inherently dislike work; he will exercise both self direction and self control to realise objectives to which he is committed; under proper conditions he will not only accept but actively seek responsibility; and that by implication the potential of the employee is not being fully used. Argyris', complementary approach to motivation suggests that there are three aspects to this problem of people in organisations. Firstly the development of the individual towards *maturity*, secondly the growth of interpersonal skills and competence in dealing with other workers, and finally the nature of the work organisation itself.

It is with the results of Herzberg's two factor theory of job attitudes (alternatively known as the motivation-hygiene theory) that the concept of self-actualising man has made most impact in British industrial relations. Herzberg draws a clear distinction between motivation and hygiene factors. The former are responsibility advancement, achievement and recognition which are intrinsic to work; they arise out of the performance of work itself. Hygiene factors are extrinsic and include such items as working conditions, pay and supervision. In a recent review of productivity bargaining Daniel has suggested that, although there were limitations to the general theory, it was very useful in helping to understand why changes that had been strongly resisted (and accepted only after hard bargaining) were later viewed favourably largely in terms of job satisfaction.

Complex man The difficulties of trying to generalise about man are becoming greater as society and the organisations within society are themselves becoming more complex and differentiated. Man is much more complex than any of the three approaches mentioned suggest. Previous empirical research has given only limited support for the simple generalisation. Hence the most recently advanced concept stresses the need to develop a notion of *complex man* which also takes into account factors like technology and community. Gellerman has also cautioned us from adopting a simpliste explanation of economic rewards which can and do have very different meanings to different people. In practice this will create a need for the company to re-examine its approach to various payments systems and fringe benefits, not only at different levels within a particular organisation but also between different plants in the same organisation. Again the acceptance of measured daywork by employees will be influenced by a whole range of factors; the size and age of the plant, technology and product demand, level of trade union organisation and the acceptance of particular values etc. The manager who is confronted with a particular problem of motivation may feel exasperated by its complexity. The recognition that he is dealing with a complex situation is the first essential step towards finding a viable solution.

In this section emphasis has been given to the problem of individual perception and motivation because it is an area in which myths and misconceptions abound. These assumptions have a direct bearing upon the relationship between people working at different levels within the organisation particularly in the field of industrial relations. These will now be examined in terms of group behaviour.

Groups in organisations

For many years the study of group behaviour has formed a focus for the research interest of both social psychologists and industrial sociologists. In the last decade a shift in the emphasis of research can be identified which itself parallels the growth in the use of the term *behavioural scientist*. Earlier research, both in the social laboratory and the field situation, was concerned with the study of one or two specific variables, for example leadership, communications patterns or group productivity. More recently the behavioural scientist has been concerned with relating his earlier research findings to the more specific problem of change. The focus on a dynamic situation has resulted in three important consequences:

1 A recognition of the limitations of many of the previously held ideas; in particular those associated with the human relations school
2 The development of a more sophisticated analysis of group behaviour within the context of the organisation
3 It has stimulated the growth of methods of improving the social skills required in working with people in a change situation

This section will therefore begin with a brief review of the earlier research and this will be followed by an analysis of current trends.

Formal and informal groups

The definition of a group which will be used in this chapter is that it comprises any number of people who interact with one another, are psychologically aware of one another and regard themselves to be a group. Within the company there exist two types of group; the formal group which is created to fulfil certain organisationally determined goals or tasks and the informal group which develops to meet the psychological requirements of the individual. These needs can be listed under four headings:

1   The need for affiliation
2   The need for developing, enhancing, or confirming a sense
       of identity and maintaining self esteem
3   A method of establishing and testing reality
4   A means of increasing security and a sense of power

All organisations are full of informal face to face groups that offer satisfying interpersonal relations and support to their members. These groups invariably cut across the formal structure although they can occasionally complement it. The earliest recognition of the influence of the informal group upon the behaviour of its members in the work situation can be found in the classic Hawthorne studies dating back to the late 1920s and the early 1930s. These researches resulted in the first shift from 'rational economic man' to 'social man.'

Human relations school

The human relations school began to emerge in the mid 1930s and continued to be influential until the late 1950s. From studies of this period it was realised that a democratic leadership style was most effective in small groups. The supervisor as a formal leader should aim to establish what Likert called the principle of supportive relationships. Few readers would wish to argue with Likert's principle but in practice it presents problems. For supervisors and managers alike the conflicting demands of the job and the employee have somehow to be resolved. Further contemporary studies concerned with examining the consequences of participation by the work group stressed its importance in contributing to increased productivity, high morale and the acceptance of change at work. These results could only be achieved through the development of two-way communication and the growth of a supportive relationship between superior and subordinate. Thus the human relations school appeared to indicate how managers ought to behave in order to avoid industrial relations problems. The prescription was however based upon only a partial explanation since the distribution of power and the nature of conflict were to a great extent ignored.

Modifications to human relations school approach

The earlier human relations approach was modified in the late 1950s by a British study (by Trist and his colleagues from the Tavistock Institute) of miners' coping with technological change. This represented a major advance in conceptual terms on the earlier work. The interaction between the technological requirements of a production system (which determined equipment and process layout) and the work organisation was clearly identified. For the manager the lesson to be drawn was that technological change dictated by rational engineering considerations could so seriously disrupt the social organisation of the work group that the anticipated production benefits of the new system could not be realised. In addition the supervisor's role as outlined by Likert needed redefining in this change situation. This was necessary if conflict was to be avoided between the two aspects of the supervisor's leadership, namely task leadership and socio-emotional or maintenance leadership. The former is self-explanatory, the latter refers to the need of a leader to fulfil the members' psychological needs within the group.

Technology and work groups

The more complex relationship between technology, the system of work arrangement and the pattern of industrial relations has been examined by Sayles.[2] He studied a wide variety of work groups, drawn mainly from mass-production industries, to see whether those who had common industrial relations behaviour patterns shared any other characteristics. His research suggested that four distinct types of work group could be identified in terms of work organisation and industrial relations. Each behaved differently and in doing so would demand different leadership styles which could not be explained in the terms of the earlier human relations school. The four categories of groups which were identified were 'apathetic,' 'erratic,' 'strategic' and 'conservative' and differed considerably in terms of status, skill and interaction. The diagram below illustrates Sayles findings.

TYPE OF GROUP	SKILL	INTERDEPENDENCE AND INTERACTION	STATUS	EXAMPLE
Apathetic	Low	Low	Low	Labourers
Erratic	Low	High	Low	Packaging crews, polishers on assembly lines
Strategic	High	High	High	Skilled metal finishers and grinders
Conservative	High	Low	High	Maintenance craftsmen

The practical implications of this and similar researches are considerable. They show how in seeking an explanation of particular forms of industrial relations behaviour the manager must be prepared to take into account a much wider range of variables. Explanations based only on personality, political affiliation, the method of wage payment and the presence or absence of disputes procedures may be only partial ones and thus be of limited value. In the last decade there has gradually grown an acceptance of the need for a sophisticated analysis of work-group behaviour. This has encouraged the behavioural scientist to focus his attention on other problems, in particular that of the analysis and development of training in social skills which can be utilised to facilitate the introduction of change in organisations.

T-group training

It has long been recognised that the major determinant of group effectiveness is the sensitivity of the group members and their leaders to the problems which the group itself generates. *T-group training* methods, which are alternatively known as *sensitivity training* or *group dynamics*, focus their attention on the relationships within groups. The methods used contrast quite markedly from those previously employed like case studies, role playing exercises and discussion groups, which possess certain limitations. They tended to be prescriptive, abstractive and emphasised the benefits of participative management without acknowledging its limitations. The goals of T-group training are:

1   To increase the participant's sensitivity and in particular his ability to perceive accurately how others react to his own behaviour

2   To develop a diagnostic ability, that is the ability to perceive accurately the state of relationships between others

3   To increase action skills, that is the ability of the participant to select and carry out the appropriate behaviour

At first sight such goals may seem to have little relevance to industrial relations policies and practices but in a recent review of experience with T-groups, Smith has drawn attention to the use of such groups within companies. He suggests that appropriate goals might be the establishment of new norms or values and the development of new working procedures. Inappropriate goals would include the attempt to secure short-range improvements, an attempt to bring pressure on senior levels by training the lower level or attempting to transform the organisation without regard to technical or economic factors. The legitimate goals are certainly relevant to industrial relations. For example, all levels of management need to be given an opportunity to re-examine the existing organisational values which they have internalised to see how they affect personnel and industrial relations policies. ICI Ltd used T-groups to allow some managers an opportunity to explore the implications of productivity bargaining upon their organisation. The attempt to negotiate comprehensive plant agreements may be equally facilitated by the application of such methods.

Modifications to T-group training methods

A significant modification of T-group methods has been suggested by two American behavioural scientists, Blake and Mouton.[3] The authors start from the assumption that it is the manager's task to develop the attitudes and behaviour which promote efficient performance, that encourage creativity and a receptiveness to change and innovation. The managerial grid which they have developed provides a simple diagnostic framework which seeks to help members of a T-group describe the behaviour of others more accurately. The grid itself results from combining the two basic elements of management behaviour, namely the concern for people and the concern for production. What emerges is a grid which reveals very simply not only many typical combinations seen in management behaviour but also some indications of the desirable combination; team management where production has successfully integrated task and social requirements.

The approach of Blake and Mouton to conflict is particularly useful. They accept that inter-group conflict will occur and that it can only be resolved through the development of a problem solving approach. They have described the sequence and time that should be devoted to the eight phases of a two-day union-management inter-group laboratory that aims at enabling the parties to analyse the conflict that exists between them. One note of caution is however sounded by Blake and Mouton; up to five years may be needed before the causes of the old conflicts have been completely replaced.

The behavioural scientist's study of group behaviour has not resulted in development of a brief check list for action which can be applied universally by the manager in an industrial relations situation. Earlier views have been qualified. The group equivalent of social man has been replaced by complex man. The recognition of this complexity may be cold comfort but it is the only basis upon which the managers can develop realistic long-term industrial relations policies within the context of the organisation. The organisational factors which must be taken into account will now be analysed.

The organisation

We shall briefly review the findings of the research on organisations conducted by behavioural scientists from a number of standpoints:

1   Examination of some of the major developments in our knowledge of organisations
2   Assessment of the impact of this new knowledge on management's conduct of industrial relations
3   Assessment of the problem of conflict in organisations and recurring difficulties of conflict resolution through collective bargaining

In order to avoid subsequent confusion one must however define what is meant by the term *organisation*. It is taken to mean the rational co-ordination of activities for the achievement of specified purposes through the division of labour and a hierarchy of authority.

The most important single feature which emerges from all the recent studies of organisational behaviour is its complexity and variety. Behavioural scientists have therefore not followed their professional forefathers and attempted to enunciate general principles as such. The earlier concern with such statements have been recognised to be over-generalisations based often on anecdotal evidence and which therefore ignored both the dynamic and complex nature of organisational behaviour. Classical writers like Weber, Fayol, Taylor and Mary Parker Follett were concerned with structure and administration. They assumed that the ability of the manager to influence behaviour was much greater than it was in reality. Writing before the advent of the human relations school, they ignored the impact of group behaviour, technology and the community context on the organisation. The importance which they gave to procedures, system and charts, however, still lingers on in some public service agencies.

The view of the organisation as a system gradually replaced the earlier structuralist approach. The most telling argument for a systems concept of the organisation is the recognition that the environment within which the organisation exists is becoming increasingly unstable. The early attempts to develop a systems approach are associated with the Tavistock Institute whose work on the mining industry has already been referred to in this chapter. Work conducted in the textile industry by Rice linked the notion of a socio-technical system to that of a more general open system concept of the organisation. Rice suggested an organisation *imports* from its environment, undertakes a *conversion process* and then *exports* its products and services back into the environment. The function of an industrial relations policy is therefore one of facilitating the conversion process, not one of simply achieving control for control's sake.

Two important additions to the Tavistock approach are suggested by Likert: (*a*) that organisations can be regarded as systems of interlocking groups; and (*b*) that these interlocking groups are connected by individuals who occupy through dual membership key positions and thus act as link pins between groups. Shop stewards representing workers in a company as leaders of work groups occupy this position as link pins. This explains why managers often find it difficult to ensure that supervisors are adequately briefed and can in turn inform their sections. The steward as a *link pin* communicates more quickly and effectively with his members. Kahn and his co-workers have however cautioned against ignoring the difference between formal and informal groups. Instead he suggests that the organisation can be viewed as a set of overlapping and interlocking role sets. A person occupies an office within the organisation and this describes his role. The role set is the series of role relationships which the occupant of an office has with other persons in the organisation. The behaviour of people in organisations can be studied in terms of either role conflict or role ambiguity. The personnel function in many companies provides an excellent example of both role conflict and role ambiguity.

The relationship between the organisation and its environment is complex and this must be taken into account in any systems explanation. The definition of the boundaries is however difficult. The organisation is not cut off from its environment in any clear-cut way because its employees are not only members of the organisations which employ them, they are also members of society at large and of other groups and organisations in particular. A British writer, Tom Burns, has attempted to cope with the danger of an over-simplified unitary view of the organisation. He suggests that for a proper understanding of organisational functioning it is necessary to conceive of the existence of at least three social systems which are parallel and continually interacting. These are the work/task system, the political system and the career system. Changes in the work/task system must be acceptable in terms of both the political and career systems particularly in organisations operating in technologically advanced industries. Negotiations between managers and shop stewards often reach an impasse because the existence of one system, the career system, is so often overlooked. This may in part be the result of the socio-economic factors influencing perception which were mentioned previously. The difficulty encountered by managements in dealing with white-collar trade unions for the first time may be traced back to the value placed by the unions on the nature of the career system which is not recognised by the management.

The boldest attempt to bridge the gap between the behavioural scientist's knowledge about organisational behaviour and the conduct of industrial relations has been made by Alan Fox.[4] In an important pamphlet he has been concerned to examine the *frame of reference* through which management view the organisation. Either they regard it as a *unitary* system, analogous to a team, or as a *pluralistic* system, a coalition of interests that may in many areas be divergent. He argues that this framework of reference is important because it determines three factors, (a) how we expect people to behave and how we think they ought to behave, (b) how we react to people's actual behaviour, and (c) the methods chosen in changing behaviour. Fox's work incorporates many of the findings of the behavioural scientist which have been previously mentioned in this chapter. He brings together the research on perception and motivation, on group behaviour and the systems approach to organisations. This integrative task is of great value but it must also be treated with caution. The terms *unitary* and *pluralistic* are in danger of ceasing to be descriptive and of becoming normative.

The unitary system has one source of authority and one focus of loyalty. Three other points can also be said to follow, (a) that organisations have but a single objective, (b) that there exists agreement about the structure of the organisation and the task of individuals within it, and (c) that conflict is invalid and disfunctional. This view of the organisation is outdated in the light of contemporary behavioural science research. The structuralist view of the organisation has been replaced by an open-systems concept. Research on group behaviour has moved beyond the simple human relations findings and our concept of motivations has moved from social man through to complex man. The pluralist frame of reference fully accepts the notion that an industrial organisation is made up of sectional groups with divergent interests with the result that agreement on objectives can only be very limited. If it is recognised that groups are mutually dependent they can be regarded as having a common interest in the survival of the organisation of which they are constituents. This view of the organisation successfully integrates the open systems concept and incorporates the ideas of both Likert and Kahn which were described earlier in this section. The influence of what Fox calls 'structural determinants,' technology and social structure, are the variables described in the Tavistock socio-technical system and the work of Burns and Woodward.

The unitary frame of reference which Fox rejects is the result of a communication gap which exists between the behavioural scientist and the manager. For many managers it still remains a meaningful framework and appears to be functional. This is likely to be the case in those situations where the organisation has not experienced significant change. The pluralistic approach will have been adopted only where for example through productivity bargaining attempts have been made to cope with change. The manager who accepts Fox's strictures about his existing frame of reference may however be excused if he then poses the question: 'How can I make this shift towards pluralism?' The answer in part lies in the application of T-group techniques, the legitimate goals of which are completely reconcilable with the wish to adopt a pluralistic frame of reference. The only practical note of caution which must however be sounded relates to the need to ensure the commitment of the most senior levels of management within the organisation to such a programme.

This chapter has been concerned to identify the contribution which the behavioural scientist can make to the analysis of industrial relations problems. His role in the development of appropriate strategies to resolve the problems identified depends upon two factors. His ability to communicate with a management audience and the manager's recognition that the introduction of change in industrial relations, within the organisational context, is a long process. The desire for quick results is a pressure which has to be resisted by both parties in the interests of effective management and the future development of the behavioural sciences.

References

1 *British Management Thought* by J Child, Allen and Unwin, 1969
2 *Behaviour of Industrial Work Groups—Production and Control* by L R SAYLES, John Wiley, New York, 1963
3 'The Union—Management Intergroup Laboratory: Strategy for Reducing Intergroup conflict', *Journal of Applied Behavioural Science*, Vol. 1 No. 1, 1965
4 'Industrial Sociology and Industrial Relations', *Royal Commission on Trade Unions and Employers' Associations*, Research Paper 3, HMSO, 1966

L

20

The Social Implications of Industrial Relations

The Rt Revd E R Wickham
Bishop of Middleton

This concluding chapter is not about the minutiae of the Code of Industrial Relations Practice. Even less is it about the legal minutiae of the Industrial Relations Act. In a more philosophic vein it is concerned with the intractable industrial and social ground out of which the search for some agreed basis for improved industrial relations has sprung.

The search for reform

It is important to note that this search is not a sectional one. Whatever disagreements may exist about the new Act—and they are strong indeed, and could prove destructive—there has been, however reluctantly, a widespread concession that reforms in the industrial relations field are required, that unwritten rules and traditions are not enough, and that legislation of some kind is inevitable. In the dust of the Act's procession through Parliament it should not be forgotten that before Mr Carr's Bill saw the light of day there was the Donovan Commission; there was Barbara Castle's In Place of Strife; and there was the Labour Government's own Industrial Relations Bill. Leaders, both of the CBI and the Trades Union movement, have expressed the belief that reform is necessary and that the idea of a code of practice is a good one.

The argument is not about reform as such, but about the details, the strengthening of the legal procedures, and the sense of bridling of which the Unions are apprehensive. Only time will show whether the hopes of the legislators, of any legislators, or the fears of their critics are realised. It may be that legislation will simply prove a non-event, with employers wary of resorting to litigation in a field where the parties have to go on living together; and with the larger Unions refusing to register, and withdrawing from the Commission on Industrial Relations, as we are now witnessing. Already this has led to the resignation of Mr Woodcock as Chairman of the CIR, and the TUC in September 1971 adopted a tougher line in instructing their member Unions to deregister. The sabre-rattling continues.

The Code

To the extent that the Act looks less promising, and at best likely to provide a long-stop sanction, the Code could take on more promising significance: because the Code is not a law. It is an attempt—and it sought to be a broad co-operative attempt—of all the parties on the industrial scene—to lay down the conditions most conducive to good industrial relations. It has already been criticised for vagueness, for wickedness, for idealism: but it is important to understand what it claims to be. It is not a body of exact and minute legislation, but a code, a statement of general principles—something like a Ten Commandments for industrial behaviour; and as a wit has said of the Decalogue, 'It doesn't tell you what you have to do, but it does put ideas into your head!' So does the Code. And it puts some very exciting ideas into your head, to an extent that industry has yet to discover. It is not a rule book, but it gives general principles on which rules can be made, and criteria by which practices can be appraised. It provides bench-marks, and it sets a direction. To use theological terms, the Code is about the spirit of the law, and like the marriage vows, there is something radically wrong if you need to look them up every day! They should become axiomatic, natural assumptions about what constitutes civilised industrial relationships. And where such exist, the periodic blow-up is easily containable.

The *idea* of a code of industrial relations practice is good then. It is a sign—whatever industrial tensions exist—of a maturing and civilising of industrial relations. It shows a coming of age of industrial organisation, a seal on the ending of that barbaric era which R H Tawney described as 'autocracy tempered with insurgence'. It can register a high-water mark of current expectation and set a base for further advance. If there is a question mark, it is over the procedures for determining the details of the Code. It was originally published by the Government as a 'consultative document'; discussion and consultation were invited, and in the Foreword the Secretary of State wrote, 'I shall be preparing a further version of the Code which I hope to submit to Parliament for approval before the end of this year'. One may wonder whether this is an adequate procedure for securing the kind of authority that the Code needs. Of course Government has the proper responsibility to take initiative and advance proposals. But if the Code is to command *authority* in the true meaning of that word, as something authoritative, self-authenticating, axiomatic—rather than as something imposed from on high, it must have the general agreement of all the parties most concerned: not only of Government with the broad support of Parliament, but also of the CBI and the TUC and after wide consultation within their respective memberships and constituencies. Should not the Code, though initially proffered by Government, and finally amended and ratified by Parliament, come out of much closer argumentation within the industrial world itself about the areas and details to be comprehended? It would have been in keeping with the spirit of the Foreword in the draft Code which asserted that 'industrial relations in a free society . . . are best conducted by collective bargaining between employers and strong representative trade unions . . .' Not least might that apply to the drawing up of the Code itself. In a free society any workable code must have the broad support of the parties concerned and it has to be won at the grass-roots of industrial life. It will be tragic if the idea of the code, so good in itself, should become an irrelevance through a failure of procedure for establishing it. Parliament may approve it, and it is within the competence of Government to ensure that it does. But that cannot ensure that the industrial community takes it seriously. But these are caveats about procedures, and it is much to be hoped that the Code will precipitate lively debate on fundamental questions about industrial organisation, for the issue of industrial relations is larger than the destiny of the Code and larger than any specific framework of legislation in which they are placed. Industrial relations are about life and how we organise it.

Requirements for good industrial relations

What are the essential conditions of good industrial relations and of improving them? And, more importantly, what are the conditions of good industrial relations not simply measured in terms of industrial harmony, but in terms of the positive and dynamic relationship of all the parties conjoined in the industrial process? After all, there is peace and harmony in the grave-yard.

It is of basic importance to recognise that industrial relations do not exist in a vacuum. No man is an island unto himself, and it is equally true of social groupings, whether it is the family, a social class, an industry, an industrial company or the workshop within it. There is always a larger social context to industrial relations. It is evidence of both the biological fact and the splendid theological affirmation of the unity of the human family, however hard it may be to realise, and notwithstanding the legitimate self-interests of distinctive groups within society. The implications of this social truism are enormous and we ignore them at our peril. It follows that overall confidence in the social organisation of the country is essential as a background for good industrial relations, and this in turn reposes on Government the task of determining social goals that find broad acceptance and securing legislation that manifestly serves them. Even tough measures that may be necessary, if visibly tied to goals that are broadly acceptable can be tolerated without damage to the fabric of society. A general climate of confidence is a *sine qua non* of good industrial relations. It is not easy to secure. There is the long history of distrust stemming from the pre-war period of 'two nations'. There is at present a widespread loss of confidence in any of the political options before us. The current legislations on industrial relations takes place at a time of high unemployment, rising costs of living and industrial re-organisation in basic industries and large companies with much attendant insecurity. The European Economic Community looms ahead casting apprehension in many areas of the country, and not least, we have a Conservative Government. That is fair enough, but it would be naïve indeed to suppose that it can command an enthusiasm amongst workers for legislation in the industrial relations field that even a Labour Government failed to secure.

The problem of confidence and the task of creating a justified confidence are real indeed. They are constituted by the intractable givenness of the social and industrial situation that any consideration of the social implications of industrial relations must reckon with. It is important to see that the problem, and therefore the task, has both *extrinsic* and *intrinsic* aspects. That is to say, there are external, pervasive, determinant factors and forces at work in society that are outside the direct influence of the industrial organisation, though indirectly they are influenced by what happens within industry. And there are intrinsic factors, within industrial organisation, influenced of course by what happens in society at large, but falling within the competence of industry to tackle directly if it has the perceptivity and will to do so. The intrinsic and the extrinsic are subtly related. There is a continuing symbiotic interaction between them, which is one of the reasons why industrial relationships are outside the total determination of either political decisions or of industry itself. Both have their part to play in creating the conditions favourable to good industrial relations.

Extrinsic factors in industrial relations

Responsibility for the *extrinsic* factors falls more directly on Government, though that, of course, does not relieve society as a whole or the industrial community of active concern. But the extrinsic factors fall squarely within Government responsibility, either to tackle directly or to ensure that they are tackled. They are diverse. There is the crucial questions of economic growth and of ensuring the conditions that allow it. There is the need for increased capital investment, in keeping with our investment in research and development. There is the need, one would think, now we have come to visualise their possibilities, and whatever the difficulties, of securing an acceptable incomes policy, and some kind of instrument to replace the National Board for Prices and Incomes, both of which would seem to be eminently desirable in an orderly and civilised society. There is the task of devising new distributive mechanisms and the question of guaranteed income, both of which would be more urgent if technological development was more rapid. There is the matter of the location of industry, of development areas, of areas of high unemployment, and the need for strategic Governmental intervention to advance industrial re-organisation and efficiency. These are all extrinsic factors contributing to a climate of confidence and that in turn is auspicious for positive industrial relations. Certainly without that climate of confidence they are hardly conceivable.

It should be added, that necessary though the right extrinsic *conditions* are, we should beware of thinking that the industrial community is simply to be *conditioned* into positive industrial relations. We should beware of a manipulated and satiated milch-cow society. Among the extrinsic factors, a responsible society ought to be able to count on a wide recognition and endorsement of explicit social goals to which the economic-industrial process is related. We are in fact dominated by the process and there is a severe bankruptcy of vision about the ends it serves. Alongside any acts and codes of industrial relations, we need a great debate on the goals of a responsible society, which is to speak of a true politics, a vision of society without which people perish and fall victim to purely sectional and personal ends.

Assuredly, there are goals of economic life capable of investing the process with meaningfulness and greater sense of purpose, and both process and goals would be better served by their recognition. There is personal livelihood and standards of living of course: but also the fabric of society; the capital to refurbish industry and for research and development; the social capital to build cities and redevelop them; homes and houses, roads and transport, health and social services and social benefits, expanding education, the arts and facilities for leisure. And not least, for a responsible nation, for vulnerable groups and areas of under-privilege at home; and for investment, aid and development in the Third World. Pope Paul's good word that 'development is the new name for peace' is relevant everywhere. At the end of the day the very quality of life we enjoy, or should enjoy, and in its most intangible aspects, has its foundations in the hard realities of economic and industrial life. For good or ill, the industrial-economic process 'maintains the state of the world'. The very excrescences it produces against which the anti-pollutionists fulminate are only eradicable by even more sophisticated technological means.

Social goals—attainment

The attainment of these rational social goals is wholly dependent on the economic-industrial process and its efficient operation, and in turn they are capable of investing the process with high meaningfulness that should make a profound contribution to positive industrial relations. There is a blind-spot about this in our society that desperately requires study. Perhaps our liberal education is too ivory-towered and isolated from social realities, too classical and academic in its background, despising the manual arts and technology. But until there is a clearer understanding of the social ends that are served, and that *can* be served by the economic-industrial process, we shall see an increasing alienation from the process itself. Already it is happening. For some it means protest and a counter-society. For many more it simply means passivity and a kind of general malaise, all protest bought off by a modicum of increased affluence and the soporifics that modern society can provide. However it may show itself, the backlash against economic growth and technology through our failure to relate them, and relate them visibly to humane social goals is a serious danger. The extrinsic factors that ultimately bear upon industrial relations are many indeed. We desperately need to understand them better and how they operate, and to learn how adverse ones can be countered and positive ones engendered. It is the task of a true politics.

Intrinsic factors in industrial relations

The *intrinsic* factors that bear upon industrial relations, subtly related though they are to the extrinsic, are clearly more directly within the capacity of industry itself to tackle. Every company knows that notwithstanding its wider relationships, to other companies and employers' organisations, to the larger Trades Union structure, and notwithstanding its vulnerability in the face of extrinsic factors that may operate, it nonetheless has a certain freedom for controlling its own internal way of life. It is no doubt limited, but within limits it has a real freedom to seek conditions that are conducive to vitality and good industrial relations.

The handbooks on the subject are legion and it is hard to believe that anything new could be said. Rather perhaps, we now need discriminate selection within the industrial relations literature to sift the wheat from the chaff. We need more case-studies of 'causes of industrial peace', and bold experimentation in new models of industrial relations. For certainly models have their day and pass. The pyramids were built with a particular model of industrial relations. Tribal societies have their models. The feudal system provided one. The 'palaeotechnic' phase of industrialisation, to use Lewis Mumford's term, had another, the legacy of which dies hard. There is ample historical evidence that the technological mode of production, as well as the social pressures induced by new means of production have profound effect upon the social organisation of industry, and one does not have to be Marxist to subscribe to this elementary observation. It is inconceivable that the 'biotechnic' phase of technological development, as Mumford called it, which we associate with cybernetics and automation, new forms of power and new synthetic materials, should not require radical changes in the human organisation of work. It would be rash indeed to suppose that the evolution of the industrial organisation is now over.

We have to admit that as yet we do not know what changes in the social organisation of men at work time will bring. What we do know is that the old models derive from a labour-intensive, authoritarian, and at best, paternalistic period of industrial history, and appear increasingly anachronistic. Even the human relations emphasis itself is coming to be regarded as no more than a 'hygiene factor', to use Herzberg's term, that needs to be subsumed in the more important positive satisfactions that come from achievement, recognition, responsibility and the challenge of work itself. We know too that management has to be construed in terms of an integrative planning operation in which everyone involved can be imbued with a managerial attitude and through which untapped energies can be released. So the theories run, and should they simply appear suggestive of more sophisticated management techniques, we can add to them the concepts of industrial democracy, self-determination and workers' control—heady ideas, with a long history, but abroad again, and also indicative of the feeling after new models of industrial organisation. They are all in keeping with the contemporary instinct for a more participative, organic and personalist expression of society.

Model of industrial organisation

Industry cannot and should not be immune from this search, impeded though it may be by rigidities that often seem of a crustacean kind. Transformation cannot happen overnight. Changes are and will be piecemeal. But industry should be open to them. All these factors augur an intensifying search after changing models of industrial organisation, and confusing though they may be, industry should not be fearful of them, simply because work, and the organisation of men in work— which is what industry is about—is elemental, necessary and good. To use a theological term, work is an 'ordinance of creation', that is to say, a given condition without which life cannot exist. It may change, but it has to exist, and fundamentally it is good for man. And many of the essential deepest human needs, the 'human universals' as they are called, are derived from it, such as status in society, the sense of accomplishment and usefulness to the world, the integration into a network of purposeful relationships, into 'organised organisms', participation, security, the exercise of responsibility according to one's capacity, and of course, reward, that should be made in ways that are conducive to enterprise, fairness and human dignity.

Even the malfunctioning of industry cannot wholly preclude the operation of the 'human universals'. It is because they are psychologically necessary for men that at its best, work is fulfilling. It is why unemployment is so destructive. It is why a basic industry can induce at once both intense pride and bloody-mindedness, and why men even become 'fashioned in the image of their craft'. And it is why men may curse work, but go to pieces without it.

The existential character of work makes industrial relations of some kind inevitable. It also makes the unending struggle to improve them imperative.

Bibliography

ALEXANDER K J W and JENKINS C I, *Fairfields: A Study of Industrial Change*, 1970, Allen Lane, The Penguin Press

ALLEN A J, *Management and Men: A Study in Industrial Relations*, 1967, Hallam Press

ANTHONY P and CRICHTON Anne, *Industrial Relations and the Personnel Specialists*, 1969, Batsford

ARMSTRONG E G A, *Industrial Relations—An Introduction*, 1969, Harrap

ARNISON J, *Million-Pound Strike*, 1970, Lawrence and Wishart

BADGER Dr Alfred (Ed.), *Investing in People: the Marlow Idea*, 1966, Geoffrey Bles

BADGER A B, *Man in Employment*, second edition 1966, Macmillan

BAITSELL J M, *Airline Industrial Relations: Pilots and Flight Engineers*, 1966, Harvard University

BARKIN S and others (Eds.) *International Labor*, 1967, Harper and Row

BRITISH INSTITUTE OF MANAGEMENT Information Summary 137, *Company Redundancy Policies*, BIM

BRITISH INSTITUTE OF MANAGEMENT, *Industrial Relations: In Place of Strife*, 1969, BIM

BROWN E H Phelps, *The Growth of British Industrial Relations: A Study from the Standpoint of 1906 to 1914*, 1959, Macmillan

BROWN J A C, *The Social Psychology of Industry*, 1954, Penguin

BROWN W G, *Exploration in Management*, 1960, Heinemann

BYRD S F, *Stategy in Labor Relations?* 1963, Bureau of Business Practice, Waterford, Conn., USA

CENTRAL OFFICE OF INFORMATION, *Labour Relations and Conditions of Work in Britain*, 1967, HMSO

CHANDLER M K, *Management Rights and Union Interests*, 1964, McGraw-Hill

CHILD J, *Industrial Relations in the British Printing Industry: The Quest for Security*, 1967, George Allen and Unwin

CLACK G, *Industrial Relations in a British Car Factory*, 1967, Cambridge University Press

CLARKE M, *Industrial Relations* Notes for Managers, number 11, Industrial Society, 1966

CLEGG H, *The System of Industrial Relations in Great Britain*, 1970, Blackwell

CLEGG H, *How to Run an Incomes Policy—and Why We Made Such a Mess of the Last One*, 1971, Heinemann

CONROY R T W L and MILLS J N, *Human Circadian Rhythms*, 1970, J and A Churchill

DALY G F, *Industrial Relations: Comparative Aspects, with Particular Reference to Ireland*, 1968, Mercier Press

DEPARTMENT OF EMPLOYMENT AND PRODUCTIVITY, *In Place of Strife: a Policy for Industrial Relations*, 1969, HMSO

DEPARTMENT OF EMPLOYMENT AND PRODUCTIVITY, *Gazette*, chapter 15, 'Cost of Equal Pay,' 1970

DEPARTMENT OF EMPLOYMENT AND PRODUCTIVITY, *A Guide to the Equal Pay Act*, 1970

DEPARTMENT OF EMPLOYMENT and CENTRAL OFFICE OF INFORMATION, *Industrial Relations Act 1971: Registration*

DEPARTMENT OF EMPLOYMENT and CENTRAL OFFICE OF INFORMATION, *Industrial Relations Act 1971: The Act Outlined*

DEPARTMENT OF EMPLOYMENT and CENTRAL OFFICE OF INFORMATION, *Industrial Relations: A Guide to the Industrial Relations Act 1971*

DERBER M and others, *Plant Union-Management Relations: From Practice to Theory*, 1965, University of Illinois, USA

DICKINSON A W, *Industrial Relations in Supervisory Management*, 1967, Thomas Nelson and Sons

DUBIN R, *Constructive Aspects of Conflict*, 1969, from *Collective Bargaining* edited by A FLANDERS, Penguin

FLANDERS A, *Can Managers be Taught Industrial Relations?*, 1968, British Institute of Management

FLANDERS A, 'Collective Bargaining: A Theoretical Analysis,' 1968 March, *British Journal of Industrial Relations*, Chapter 4

FLANDERS A, *The Fawley Productivity Agreements*, 1964, Faber and Faber

FORM W H and MILLER D C, *Industry, Labor and Community*, 1960, Harper and Brothers

FOX A, *Industrial Sociology and Industrial Relations: An Assessment of the Contributions which Industrial Sociology Can Make towards Understanding and Resolving Some of the Problems now Being Considered by the Royal Commission*, 1966, HMSO

GOVERNMENT SOCIAL SURVEY, *Workplace Industrial Relations: An Inquiry Undertaken for the Royal Commission on Trade Unions and Employers' Associations in 1966*, 1968, HMSO

HARE A E C, *The First Principles of Industrial Relations*, 1965, Macmillan

HEATH C G, *A Guide to the Industrial Relations Act 1971*, 1971, Sweet and Maxwell

HENDERSON J, *The Industrial Relations Act at Work*, 1971, The Industrial Society

HILTON W S, *Industrial Relations in Construction*, 1968, Pergamon Press

HER MAJESTY'S STATIONERY OFFICE, *National Board for Prices and Incomes: Hours of Work, Overtime and Shiftworking, 1970*, Report number 161, 1970

INDUSTRIAL SOCIETY, *The Industrial Society's Guide to the Report of the Royal Commission on Trade Unions and Employers' Associations: Indicators for Action*, 1968, Industrial Society

INSTITUTE OF PERSONNEL MANAGEMENT, *Industrial Relations: What is Wrong with the System?*, 1965, IPM

INSTITUTE OF PERSONNEL MANAGEMENT, *Report of the Royal Commission on Trade Unions and Employers' Associations: Comment on Some of the Report's Main Conclusions and Recommendations*, 1968, IPM

INTERNATIONAL LABOUR ORGANISATION, *International Standards and Guiding Principles, 1958 to 1961*, 1961, ILO

ISAAC J E and FORD G W (editors), *Australian Labour Relations*, 1966, Sun Books, Melbourne

KAHN-FREUND O (editor), *Labour Relations and the Law: A Comparative Study*, 1965, Stevens and Sons

LAPORTE L, *Labor Relations, Unions and Strikes*, 1968, National Industrial Conference Board, New York, USA

LEAVITT H R, *Managerial Psychology*, 1964, Chicago University Press, USA

LIPTON T, *Management and the Social Sciences*, second edition, 1970, Lyon, Grant and Green

MARRIS R L, *Multiple Shiftwork: A Problem for Decision by Management and Labour*, 1970, NEDO Monograph 1, HMSO

MARSH A, *After Donovan? An Assessment of the Royal Commission and Employers' Associations, 1965 to 1968*, 1968, Pergamon Press

MARSH A, *Industrial Relations in Engineering*, 1965, Pergamon Press

MEPHAM G J, *Problems of Equal Pay*, 1969, Institute of Personnel Management

MINER J B, *Personnel and Industrial Relations: A Managerial Approach*, 1969, Collier-Macmillan

MINISTRY OF LABOUR, *Industrial Relations Handbook*, third edition 1961, HMSO

MORTIMER J E, *Industrial Relations*, 1968, Heinemann

NATIONAL BOARD FOR PRICES AND INCOMES, *Hours of Work, Overtime and Shiftworking 1970*, Report Number 16), 1970, HMSO

NEAL L F and ROBERTSON A, *The Manager's Guide to Industrial Relations*, 1968, George Allen and Unwin

NEWPORT M G, *Labor Relations and the Supervisor*, 1968, Addison-Wesley Publishing Company

NORTH D T B and BUCKINGHAM G L, *Productivity Agreements and Wages Systems*, 1969, Gower Press

O'MAHONY D, *Economic Aspects of Industrial Relations*, 1965, Economic Research Institute, Dublin, Eire

PA MANAGEMENT CONSULTANTS LTD, *Industrial Relations Act: Its Implications for Management*, PAMC

PATERSON P, *An Employer's Guide to the Industrial Relations Act*, second edition 1971, Kogan Page

PATERSON T T, *Glasgow Ltd*, 1960, Cambridge University Press

PATTERSON S, *Immigrants in Industry*, 1968, Oxford University Press

PUGH D S, HICKSON O J and HININGS C R, *Writers on Organisations*, 1971, Penguin

REYNOLDS L G, *Labor Economics and Labor Relations*, fourth edition 1964, Prentice-Hall

RICHARDSON J H, *An Introduction to the Study of Industrial Relations*, 1954, Allen and Unwin

ROBERTS B C, *Trade Union Government and Administration*, 1965, G. Bell

ROBERTS B (Ed.), *Industrial Relations: Contemporary Issues; Selected Papers Given at the First World Congress of the International Industrial Relations Association, Geneva, September 1967*, 1968, Macmillan

ROBERTS B (Ed.), *Industrial Relations: Contemporary Problems and Perspectives*, revised edition 1968, Methuen

ROBERTS P, *Industry: Conflict or Cooperation?*, 1969, Marlow Association

ROSS A M (Ed.), *Industrial Relations and Economic Development*, 1966, Macmillan

ROWAN R L and NORTHRUP H R (Eds.), *Readings in Labor Economics and Labour Relations*, 1968, Richard D Irwin, USA

SAYLES L R, *The Behaviour of Industrial Work Groups*, 1958, Wiley

SEEAR B N, 'The Position of Women in Industry,' *Royal Commission on Trade Unions and Employers*, research paper number 11, 1968

SELEKMAN B M and others, *Problems in Labor Relations*, third edition 1964, McGraw-Hill

SELWYN N M, *Guide to the Industrial Relations Act, 1971*, 1971, Butterworths

SERGEAN R, *Managing Shiftwork*, 1971, Gower Press

SHEIN E H, *Organisational Psychology*, Prentice-Hall, 1965

SLOANE A A and WITNEY F, *Labor Relations*, 1967, Prentice-Hall, USA

SMITH P B, *Improving Skills in Working with People: the T-Group*, DEP training information paper 4, HMSO, 1970

STAGNER R and ROSEN H, *The Psychology of Union-Management Relations*, Tavistock, 1965

TRADES UNION CONGRESS, *Good Industrial Relations: A Guide for Negotiators*, 1971, TUC

TURNER H A and others, *Labour Relations in the Motor Industry*, 1967, Allen and Unwin

WALTON R E and MCKERSIE R, *A Behavioral Theory of Labor Negotiations*, 1965, McGraw-Hill

WEDDERBURN K W, *Cases and Materials on Labour Law*, 1967, Cambridge University Press

WILSON A W and HILL S R, *Industrial Relations: Law and Economics*, 1968, National Extension College course, Longman

Wood J C, *The Industrial Relations Act—An Introduction for Personnel Managers*, 1971, IPM

Wortman M S (Ed.), *Creative Personnel Management: Readings in Industrial Management*, 1967, Allyn and Bacon, Boston

Wright P L, *The Coloured Worker in British Industry*, 1968, Institute of Race Relations and Oxford University Press

Wylie T, *A Concise Guide to Industrial Relations*, fifth edition 1966, Institute of Supervisory Management, Birmingham

Young F J L, *The Contracting Out of Work: Canadian and USA Industrial Relations Experience*, 1964, Queen's University, Kingston, Ontario, Canada

Periodical articles

British Journal of Industrial Relations, volume 10 number 1, summer 1968, pages 39 to 58. 'The Work of Industrial Courts of Inquiry' by W E J McCarthy and B A Clifford

British Journal of Industrial Relations, November 1966, pages 366 to 378, 'Managerial Ideology and Labour Relations' by Alan Fox

Industrial Society, June 1967, pages 26 to 29, 'Industrial Relations and Efficiency' by George Cattell

Management, volume 16 number 1, January 1969, pages 17 to 22, 'Industrial Relations—A Final Comment' by Michael Fogarty

Manpower and Applied Psychology, volume 2 number 1, summer 1968, pages 49 to 53, 'Some Human Factors in Industrial Conflict' by P J R Dempsey

Acts of Parliament etc. Code of Industrial Relations Practice 1972
Industrial Relations Act 1971
Royal Commission on Trade Unions and Employers' Associations, 1965 to 1968. *Report* (1968: the Donovan Report)

Further information: British Institute of Management, Management House, Parker Street, London WC2B 5PT, telephone 01-405 3456

Index

Absenteeism   54, 143, 187, 219, 222, 231
*Absenteeism amongst women manual
   workers* (Ayoub)   219, 220n4
Agency shop agreements   31, 32, 42, 45
Agency shops   31–3 *passim* 35, 46, 55
   challenges to   32
Agricultural industry   14
Amalgamated Engineering Union   271,
   277
Amalgamated Union of Engineering
   Workers   19
Amalgamated Union of Engineering and
   Foundry Workers   89
Arbitration   26, 30, 34, 43, 46, 67, 72, 74,
   155 226
   state   67, 72, 74, 135
Association of Scientific, Technical and
   Managerial staff   89, 261
Atkinson Committee on Equal Pay   208
Autonomy, degree of   23, 24, 88

Ballots   32, 33, 38, 43, 46, 47, 60, 73, 272
Bargaining—*see* collective bargaining
Bargaining units (*see also* sole bargaining
   agents)   38, 63, 74, 131–3 *passim*
   structure of   59
Batch assembly, payment for workers on
   162, 164, 165
Behavioural sciences   285ff
   definition of   286
   group behaviour   291ff
   research   285, 286, 290, 291ff
Behavioural Theory of Industrial Relations
   (Walton and McKersie)   240, 252n5

Behaviour of Industrial Work Groups, The
   (Sayles)   240, 252n6, 294, 301n2
Benefits, distribution of   222
Bonuses—*see* wages/salaries, incentive
   earnings
British Institute of Management   55, 57,
   68, 100, 101, 105
   information from   100, 105
   training schemes   232, 235
British Journal of Industrial Relations   27n6
British Management Thought (Child)   286,
   301n1
British Rail industry   14, 251
*British Workers' View of Industrial
   Relations* (Choudhri)   95n7, 252n8
Building and contracting industry   14

Catering industry   14, 67, 181
   trade union membership in   14
   women in   210, 217
Charity, contributions to   31–3 *passim,*
   55, 74
Check-offs   22, 73, 139
Civil courts   44
Civil servants   14, 208
   new laws for   5
   wages of   15
Closed shop agreements   5, 32, 42
   approved   32, 33, 46
Closed shops   12, 31–3 *passim,* 35, 54, 69
   pre-entry   31
   pre-entry, illegality of   31, 35
Clothing industry   14, 16
   women in   210, 211, 219

Coal-mining industry 14
Code of Industrial Relations Practice 5,
6, 16,
19–22 *passim*, 36, 39, 47, 49, 50, 53–63
passim, 74, 85, 91, 93, 95, 111–13
passim, 117, 120, 123, 127, 131, 134,
161, 167, 303–5 *passim*
Consultative Document 65
Collective agreements (*see also* trade
union/management agreements *and*
work-place agreements/bargaining)
13, 23ff, 36, 37, 39, 40, 117
discriminatory clauses in 212
duration of 94, 133, 134
enforceability of 39, 40, 44, 91, 128
flexibility of 24, 25
procedural 34, 36, 37, 46, 258–60
passim, 262
procedural content of 131ff
substantive 36, 37
substantive content of 137, 138
Collective bargaining (*see also*—
negotiation) 11ff, 30, 32, 36ff, 46,
52, 59, 60, 74, 75, 94, 98, 109–11
passim, 129, 131ff, 222, 227, 231, 258,
305
changes in rules of 20
decentralisation of 18, 19
law's intervention in 20
piecemeal 94
statutory 15, 17
voluntary 15, 17
Collective Bargaining (ed. Flanders) 27n5
Coloured Worker in British Industry, The
(Wright) 196
Commission on Industrial Relations 16,
19, 30, 32, 33, 37, 38, 46, 61, 74, 75,
100, 131, 224, 304
reports of 100, 240
structure and responsibilities of 46
Committees of investigation 75
Communication—*see* information
Community, the, rights/interests of 20,
30, 44, 263, 264, 297
Companies, multi-plant 90, 122
Company Manpower Planning (Department
of Employment) 54
Company Redundancy Policies (British
Institute of Management) 57
Company secretaries, involvement of 129,
130
*Complete Guide to Pensions and Super-
annuation* (Gilling-Smith) 56
Computers 262
Conciliation 30, 43, 47, 66, 71, 72, 74, 94,
135, 226

Conciliation Act 1896 66, 72, 227
Conciliation officers 72, 73, 99
Concise Guide to Industrial Relations
(Wylie) 81, 95n3
Conduct of Collective Bargaining (Anthony
and Crichton) 240
Confederation of British Industry,
publications of 102
structure of 85, 201, 226, 304, 305
Conscientious objectors 31, 33, 74
Conspiracy and Protection of Property
Act 1871 86
Conspectus of Management Courses
(British Institute of Management) 235
Consultative Committees 58, 59, 136, 137,
149, 151, 289
Contracting in/out 86, 87
Contracts, commercial 44
Contracts of Employment Act 1963 33,
35, 45, 66
Contracts of employment, breaches of 44
Cooling-off periods 73
Cost-of-living increases 127
Cotton-spinning industry 14
cotton-weaving 14
women in 210
Courts of Inquiry 13, 75, 240
Craftsmen, employment of 9

DATA 89, 245
De La Rue Index 235
Demarcation 24, 25, 69, 154
Department of Employment 11, 14–16
passim, 47, 49, 50, 54, 68, 73, 74, 75,
99, 135, 197, 201, 209, 212, 227, 240,
305
arbitrators of 72, 226
Conciliation and Advisory Services of
65, 68, 71, 72, 73–9 *passim*, 226
Gazette of 78, 87, 105, 208, 210, 216,
217, 220n3, 236, 243
Manpower and Productivity Services of
99
Manpower Papers 99
publications of 99
training schemes of 231, 232
Department of Health and Social Security
139
Design of Personnel Systems and Records
54
Devlin Committee 75, 122
Director, The 105
Directors, Boards of 6, 19, 117, 118, 120,
123
industrial relations training for 223

Directory of Employers' Associations etc 105

Disciplinary procedures 22, 25, 40, 47, 62, 63, 93, 112, 122, 136

Dismissal—*see* workers, dismissal of

Donovan Commission 4–7 *passim*, 39, 51, 111, 240, 304

Report 4, 10, 14–19 *passim*, 21, 51, 55, 71, 73, 111, 115, 116, 122, 222, 236, 277

Earnings-related benefit 66, 139

Education 14, 110, 194, 198

Efficiency
importance of 18, 52, 57, 110, 132, 164, 296
role of information in 143

Efficiency bargaining—*see* productivity agreements/bargaining

Emergency procedures 42, 43, 46

Employees—*see* workers

Employers' associations/organisations 12, 14, 15, 18, 21, 30, 40, 41, 51, 68, 74, 81ff, 111, 116, 215, 226, 309
advantage of firms' joining 84, 85
attitude towards trade unions 82–4 *passim*
historical background of 82, 83, 114
information services of 101, 102
registration of 40
rights of 40–2 *passim*
role/responsibilities of 42, 85, 127, 135, 227

Employers
court/panel of 274
representatives of (*see also* negotiation) 46, 273
responsibilities of 16, 17, 33, 34, 37, 39
rights of 20

Employment
compensation for loss of 34, 46
conditions/terms of 12, 13, 31–3 *passim*, 35, 38, 50, 55, 56, 90, 113, 127, 132, 134 152, 153, 200, 227, 260, 278
man/woman equality 213, 214
contracts of 33, 34
policies of 53ff
refusal of 31
rules of 11, 12, 22ff
short-term 32
termination of 33, 66
written particulars of 33, 35

Employment rules
procedural 22, 23, 26
substantive 22, 26

Employment Gazette 78, 87, 105, 208, 210, 216, 217, 220n3, 236, 243

Employment of Women and Young Persons Act 1922 66

Engineering Employers' Federation 83, 85, 102
news pamphlet of 102

Engineering industry 14, 16, 26, 91, 236
women in 210

Engineering Industry and the Crisis of 1922, The (Shadwell) 83

Equal Pay Act 1970 66, 207–9 *passim*, 211, 212ff
guide to 212
implementation cost of 216–18 *passim*

Equal Pay Guide (Department of Employment) 214, 215

Escape clauses 128

European Economic Commission 207
Economic Community 207, 306

Exclusion orders 34

Explorations in Management (Brown) 240, 242, 252n1

Factories Acts 11, 66, 109
women's aspects of 219, 220

Factory agreements—*see* work-place agreements/bargaining

Fairfields, a Study of Industrial Change (Alexander and Jenkins) 252n2

Fair Wages Resolution 1946 67

Fawley Productivity Agreements (Flanders) 98, 118, 119, 120n2, 233, 240, 248, 252n9

Feather, Vic 87

Fines 37, 42

Food manufacture industry 14

Foremen—*see* supervisors

Fringe benefits 139, 291

General Post Office 14

Glasgow Ltd (Paterson) 240, 250

Grievance procedures 22, 25, 26, 33, 35, 52, 62, 91, 93, 112, 122, 134, 135, 142, 147, 154–6 *passim*, 231, 259

Groups, rights of 20

Her Majesty's Stationery Office 236

Holidays/holiday pay 33, 56, 57, 67, 83, 90, 94, 116, 127, 128, 130, 137, 138, 154, 243

Hours of work 9, 22, 57, 66, 67, 69, 83, 94, 116, 137, 138, 152, 179, 182, 188, 191, 226, 227
changes in 181, 183–5 *passim*, 188

How to run an Incomes Policy (Clegg)
  27n4
Human relations school   293, 294, 297,
  300
Human Resources Administration
  (Wasmuth et al)   95n6

Immigrants   193ff
  discrimination against   194–6 *passim*,
    199, 200ff
  education for   198, 199
  needs of   199, 200
  problems of   196–9 *passim*, 204
  promotion for   198–200
  resistance to   199
  segregation of   197–9 *passim*
  status of   193, 194, 195, 199
Immigrants in Industry (Patterson)   193,
  199
Income distribution   20
Incomes Data   105, 236, 243
Incomes policies   72, 121, 226, 307
Inducements/threats   32, 34, 38, 41, 42,
  44, 200
Industrial action   73, 77, 135, 278
Industrial Arbitration Board   46, 47, 67,
  73, 74, 212, 215
Industrial conflict—*see* industrial disputes
Industrial Court—*see* National Arbitration
  Board
Industrial Court Awards   105
Industrial Courts Act 1919   67, 72, 227
Industrial disputes   16, 20, 21, 23, 42–4
  passim, 47, 50, 68, 71–3 *passim*, 100,
  134, 135, 142, 155, 222, 231, 239ff,
  273, 274
  avoidance of   25, 60, 71ff, 142, 259, 266
  conference, central   273–7 *passim*
  conferences, local   273, 274
  disputes of interest   134, 250
  disputes of right   134
  handling procedures   25, 30, 37, 43ff,
    71, 72, 90–4 *passim*, 101, 127, 134,
    135, 152–5 *passim*, 239ff, 255ff, 273,
    274, 296
Industrial relations
  changing attitudes in   8, 9, 55, 62, 82,
    84, 110, 111, 285, 286, 289ff, 300,
    303, 310
  economists' view   4
  government supporting services   65,
    66ff, 231
  growth of   6, 7
  influences on   285ff, 307–9 *passim*

legislation for (*see also* Industrial
  Relations Act 1971)   65ff, 128, 129,
  231, 303–6 *passim*
  policies systems of   17ff, 43ff, 112, 113,
    116–18 *passim*, 122, 296–8 *passim*
  politicians' view   4, 5, 9, 19, 29, 39, 49,
    65, 305
  practice of   5, 11, 49, 50, 51, 59, 62, 75,
    97, 98, 257, 264–6 *passim*, 304
  practice of, information on   98, 99
  principles of   29, 30, 43ff, 49ff
  requirements for good   305ff
  research (*see also* behavioural sciences)
    99
  responsibility for   116–20 *passim*
  state intervention in   5, 7, 15–17
    passim, 19, 20, 60, 65ff, 194, 226, 227,
    305, 307
  voluntarism in   226
Industrial Relations Act 1971   4, 5, 10,
  13, 16, 17, 19–22 *passim*, 29ff, 46, 47,
  49, 50, 54, 59, 62, 65, 67, 73–5 *passim*,
  85, 88, 89, 91, 93, 95, 99, 111, 117,
  120, 122, 128, 131, 139, 211, 224, 236,
  266, 267, 285, 287, 303, 304
  legal framework of   5, 11, 29, 47, 65
*Industrial Relations and the Personnel
  Specialist* (Anthony and Crichton)
  241, 248, 252n3
Industrial Relations Handbook (the then
  Ministry of Labour)   11, 12, 15, 27n1,
  81, 86, 95n1
Industrial Relations in Great Britain
  (Clegg)   68
Industrial Relations Journal   236
Industrial Relations Review and Report
  105, 236
Industrial relations training   46, 51, 55,
  91, 100, 113, 221ff, 264
  barriers to   223, 224
  categories of   225ff
  external courses   234, 235
  in-company courses   233, 234
  specialists in   97–9 *passim*, 225, 227,
    229, 230, 245
Industrial Society   54, 56, 58, 59, 101, 230
  services of   101, 232
Industrial Training Act 1964   66, 74, 218
Industrial training   45, 55, 66, 77, 112,
  200, 264
Industrial training boards   55, 198
Industrial Tribunal Reports   105
Industrial tribunals   30, 32, 34–6 *passim*,
  41, 43, 44, 45, 62, 67, 74, 77, 207,
  211, 212, 215, 227
  structure and responsibilities of   45, 46

Industry, influences on output 9, 10
  mechanisation of 9
  social role of 7, 8
Inflation 19, 94
Information, command system 142,
  147–9 *passim*, 151, 156
  consultative system 142, 147, 149, 151,
  152, 156
  disclosure of 39, 45, 46, 74, 75, 103,
  139
  employer to employee 52, 53, 57, 58,
  61, 89, 112, 113, 124, 126, 142ff, 185,
  249, 250, 289, 290, 293
  feedback of 130, 131, 155, 223
  grievance procedure 142, 147, 155, 156
  needs of the individual 142–4 *passim*,
  156
  needs of the organisation 142, 143,
  144ff, 156
  negotiating system 142, 147, 152, 155,
  156
  networks of 146, 147, 223
  problems of 141, 142, 157, 223, 224
  sources of 97ff, 104, 105
  structures of 141ff
In Place of Strife 5, 304
Institute of Directors 105
  women 211
Institute of Personnel Management 8,
  55, 68, 100, 101
  industrial relations training syllabus
  225ff, 232, 233
  information services of 100, 101, 236,
  243
Insurance 85
Internal Adjustment (Anthony and
  Crichton) 240
Is Britain really strike-prone? (Turner)
  251

Job analysis 55
Job descriptions 161, 174, 287
Job evaluation 22, 25, 126, 128, 138,
  161, 164–7 *passim*, 169, 173, 174, 177,
  213
  methods of 174, 212, 216, 217, 220
Job Evaluation (NBPI) 213
Job satisfaction 52, 110, 132, 144, 152
Joint Industrial Councils 15–17 *passim*,
  19, 23, 26, 67, 72, 94
Joint negotiating bodies/panels 37, 38,
  132ff
Joint production and consultative
  committee 136, 137

Joint regulation, principle of 113, 114
Journal of Applied Behavioural Science
  301n3
Journal of Management Studies 236

Labour, efficient deployment of 18, 23–5
  passim, 53, 54, 220, 231
  turnover of 54, 218, 222, 231, 288
Labour Party, creation of 86
Labour Party Bill 10
Labour Relations in the Motor Industry
  (Turner) 95n9
Legal aid 45
Leisure, hours of 179, 180, 183, 184, 188,
  189
Lock-out 34, 43, 47, 250

Magnificent Journey (Williams) 81
Management Abstracts 105
Management, attitude to trade unions 9,
  15, 52, 60, 61, 65, 95, 112, 221, 226,
  230, 232, 239ff, 269ff
  conduct of affairs 5, 22
  definition of 286
  industrial relations training for 223–5
  passim, 227–9 *passim*
  influence of behavioural sciences on
  285ff
  intermediary role of 4, 12, 15, 21, 32,
  39, 40, 52, 60, 88–90 *passim*
  line 116–19 *passim*, 128, 129, 259
  objectives of 8, 9, 111ff, 222, 227, 241,
  242, 250, 280
  research on 105
  responsibilities of 10, 19, 39, 50ff, 61,
  62, 65, 68, 86, 95, 111ff, 123, 130, 131,
  135, 137, 138, 160, 179ff, 194ff, 204,
  206, 230, 236, 237, 242, 246, 296
  salaries of 13, 98, 177, 178
Management Today 105
Managerial Psychology (Leavitt) 240, 248,
  252n7
Manning ratios 21, 138, 161, 162
Manpower *see* labour
Manpower Economics, Office of 76, 100
Million-Dollar Strike (Arnison) 240
Minimum Weekly Wages 24
Ministry of Labour—*see* Department of
  Employment
Motivation to Work (Herzberg et al) 248,
  310
Motor garages industry 14
Multi-unionism 87–9 *passim*

National Board for Prices and Incomes
    7, 19, 100, 116, 121, 122, 213, 307
National Health Service   13–15 *passim*
National Industrial Relations Court   30,
    32, 37, 38, 41, 43–5 *passim*, 59, 67,
    73, 74, 77, 207
    structure and responsibilities   44, 45
National Institute of Psychology   55
National Insurance Acts, various   66
National Joint Industrial Councils   23,
    152
Nationalised industries   15, 116, 241
Negotiating teams/bodies   128, 129, 132,
    135, 153, 154, 242, 243, 245
Negotiation (*see also* collective bargaining)
    30, 31, 36, 38, 39, 40, 42, 43, 52, 60,
    112, 121ff, 152–5 *passim*, 239ff, 259,
    260
    applications for 37, 38
    conduct of   239ff
    distinct from consultation   149
    establishment of parameters   244
    grouping of   94, 95, 248
    information on   239, 240, 243, 244
    lay representation at   261, 262, 264
    machinery of   153–5 *passim*
    meetings for   246, 247, 261
    preparation for   241–5 *passim*
    rights of   38, 75
    training for   239–41 passim
Newspaper printing industry   14, 15
'No-strike' agreements   44
Notice, minimum periods of   33, 35

Occupational Psychology Quarterly   236,
    252n4
Office of Manpower Economics   76, 100
Offices, Shops and Railway Premises Act
    1963   66
Organisations, administrative requirements
    for   42, 48
    definition of   297
    'guiding principles' for   41, 45, 47
    management's view of   299, 300
    qualifications for joining   47, 48
    research on   297–9 *passim*
    relations with environment   298, 299
    social systems within   299, 300
Output, control of   164, 165
Overtime   9, 18, 22, 90, 127, 137, 153,
    162, 182–4 *passim*, 188, 191, 213, 217,
    278

Pattern of the Future, The   209

Pay—*see* wages/salaries, rates of
Pension schemes   56, 139, 149, 152, 217,
    280
Permanent Register of organisations   41
Personnel, records of   54, 204, 209
Personnel Management   105
Personnel managers   4, 5, 50ff, 91, 114ff,
    123, 124, 245, 287
    function/responsibilities of   7, 8, 50ff,
    91, 114, 115, 117–20 *passim*, 128, 130,
    131, 135, 227, 228
    industrial relations training for   223, 224
Personnel Review   105, 236
Picketing   44, 87
Plant agreements—*see* work-place
    agreements
Position of Women in Industry, The
    (Seears)   208, 210, 211, 218, 220n1
Power, use and operation of   20, 21, 204
Printing, general industry   14, 165
Problems of Equal Pay (Mepham)   208,
    211, 220n2
Producing an Employee Handbook
    (McLeod)   58
Productivity   16, 18, 19, 21, 122, 143, 222
    relation of pay to   24, 121, 122, 172
Productivity agreements/bargaining   24,
    25, 56, 85, 94, 99, 116, 121ff, 154, 240,
    285, 291, 296, 300
*Productivity Agreements and Wage
    Systems* (North and Buckingham)   57
Professions, unionisation of   7
Profitability   8, 123, 132, 280
Promotion   21, 112
    immigrants'   198, 200
    opportunities for   55, 56
    training for   58
Provisional Register of organisations   41
*Psychological Research and Industrial
    Relations* (Williams and Guest)   240

Qualifications, misrepresentation of   34
Qualifying periods   25

Race relations (*see also* immigrants)   68,
    193ff
    advisers in   197
    integration as opposed to assimilation
    193
Race Relations Act 1968   45, 66, 193, 194,
    200ff
    complaints under, handling of   201ff
    exemptions from   200, 201
    penalties under   202, 203

Race Relations Board   201–3 *passim*
Racial integration   193ff
    problems of   196ff
Redundancy   21, 34, 45, 53, 56, 66, 68,
    73, 112, 122, 136, 231, 242, 262, 263
Redundancy Payments Act 1965   66, 74
Registration, advantages of   42
    cancellation of   41, 45
    certificates of   41
    eligibility of organisations for   41
    refusal of   45
Remuneration—*see* management, salaries
    of *and* wages/salaries
Restraining orders   43
Restrictive practices   94, 134, 138, 169,
    289
Retail distributors   14, 16, 17, 205, 206
    women in   210, 217
Retail Food Wages Council   17
Retirement   34, 152
    income in   66
Road haulage industry   14
Road passenger transport industry   14
Rota work   162
Royal Commission on Equal Pay   208,
    210, 211
Royal Commission on Trade Unions and
    Employers' Associations 1968   27n2,
    27n3, 69, 82, 85, 90, 95n4, 120n1, 122,
    240, 277, 301n4
Rubber manufacturing industry   23, 91,
    93

Safety committees   57
Safety, health and welfare, requirements
    of   11
Salaries—*see* wages/salaries
Secretary of State for Employment   16,
    17, 37, 38, 40, 43, 45, 65, 71, 73–5
    passim, 100, 111, 201, 212, 215, 224,
    305
Section supervisors (*see also* supervisors)
    53
Sex Discrimination Act 1919   208
Shift premiums   22, 90, 137, 153, 183,
    213, 217
Shift systems (*see also* shiftwork)   21,
    127, 138, 162, 179ff, 213
Shiftwork, administration of   185ff
    continuous working   184
    definition of (*see also* shift systems)   180
    effects of 187–9 *passim*
    health factors/safeguards   187–91
        passim
    management problems of   179–83

    passim, 185, 188ff
    multiple   179–81 *passim*
    need for flexibility   191, 192
    nightwork   180, 182, 183, 185–7
        passim, 189, 220
    recruitment for   186
    three-shift   183, 188
    two-shift   182–4 *passim*, 188
    types of   181–3 *passim*, 262
    white collar workers   180
Shipbuilding industry   14, 16, 143, 164
    women in   210
Shop stewards, facilities for   22, 61, 73,
    100, 113, 132, 274
    historical background   269–71 *passim*
    letters of credential for   132
    new laws for   5, 60, 61
    politics of   281, 282
    qualifications for   61
    recognition for   113, 271, 274
    relations with management   279, 280,
        299
    relations with union   279
    relations with work group   278, 279,
        298
    representative role of   12, 18, 21, 53, 89,
        91, 95, 115, 124, 129, 156, 228, 244,
        247, 269ff
    rights/obligations of   61, 88, 122, 135,
        227, 230, 274, 277, 278
    status of   61, 131, 269ff
    training for   53, 61, 62, 223, 280, 234
Shop Stewards and Works Committee,
    agreement of   271–3 *passim*
    functions of   272, 273
Shop Stewards and Workshop Relations
    (McCarthy and Parker)   95
Sick Pay (Rutter and Otway)   56
Sick pay, schemes of   56, 139, 152, 217,
    243, 248, 280
Social Psychology of Industry (Brown) 159
Social security   68, 111
Sole bargaining agents (*see also* bargaining
    units)   35, 38, 39, 59, 123, 124, 127
    recognition of   38, 39
*Some Examples of Effective Consultative
    Committees* (Henderson)   59
Strikes   18, 26, 34, 40, 43, 47, 69, 73,
    198, 222, 231, 250, 251, 278
    hours lost in   68
    information on   102, 240
    'lightning'   40, 44
    sympathetic   44, 69
    unofficial   20, 44, 69, 73, 251
Supervisors/foremen, consultation with
    91, 118, 129, 155, 156

Supervisors/foremen
  industrial relations training for   223,
    224, 229, 230
  responsibilities of   52, 53, 62, 63, 91,
    113, 135, 172, 185, 293, 294
  *System of Industrial Relations in Great
    Britain, The* (Clegg)   81, 82, 95n2

Tavistock Institute   293, 298, 300
Terms and Conditions of Employment
    Act 1959   67, 72
Textile industry, workers in   84, 95, 211,
    212, 298
Time clocks   138
Trade Boards Act 1909   67
Trade Disputes Acts 1906, 1965   30, 86
Trade Union Acts 1871–1964   41, 86, 227
Trade union committees   90
Trade Union Government and Administration
    (Roberts)   95n5
Trade union/management negotiation
    90, 91, 93, 114, 115, 119, 123, 124,
    131ff, 149ff, 239ff, 255ff
  enforceability problem   91
Trade union officials   4, 50, 88, 93, 256ff
  briefing for negotiations   247, 248
  facilities for   260, 264
  representative role of   5, 12, 18, 21, 59,
    93, 135, 151, 153, 154, 215, 227, 246,
    255ff
  training for   90, 223, 224, 230, 231
  women   219
Trade unions, administration of   88, 89
  appeals against   74
  changes in   256, 261
  compulsion to join   31
  contributions to   31, 32, 54, 74
  craft   154, 155, 256
  creation of   12
  deduction of contributions from wages
    139
  diversity of   255–7 *passim*
  historical background of   7, 36, 86, 87
  independent   30, 34, 38
  information services of   101, 102
  joining   35, 36, 52
  lay representatives   261, 262, 264
  meetings with (*see also* negotiations)
    247, 257ff
  membership of   6, 7, 13, 14, 30–3
    passim, 45, 55, 69, 87, 110,
    women's 219
  non-payment of contributions to   47, 74
  objectives of   227
  place in society   9

  power, increase of   110
  recognition of   13, 36, 38, 40, 52, 60,
    69, 75, 131, 132, 257
  recognition, claims for   60, 258
  recruitment for   12
  refusal to join   31–3 *passim*
  registered   30–2 *passim*, 35, 37–40
    passim, 42, 44, 46
  registration of   20, 30, 40, 304
  resistance to change   241, 242, 245, 291
  responsibilities of   16, 17, 42, 61, 135
  rights of   10, 20, 40, 42, 226, 257
  statistics of   87
  termination of membership of   47
  unregistered   35
  white collar   57, 60, 88, 89, 231, 256,
    261, 299
Trade Unions and Employers'
    Associations, Chief Registrar of   30,
    41, 42, 45
  responsibilities of   41
Trades Union Congress   7, 62, 87, 88, 90,
    201, 211, 304, 305
  Centenary Institute of Occupational
    Health   190
  education service of   62, 230, 232, 264
  information services of   102, 281
  links with unions   88
  resolutions on equal pay for women
    207–9 *passim*
  structure of   88
Transport and General Workers' Union
    19, 24, 90, 248
  information services of   102
  white collar section   89, 261
Treaty of Rome   207

Unemployment   9, 111, 194, 262, 306, 307
  information on   102
Unfair dismissal   5, 31, 34ff, 45, 46, 62,
    63, 74, 136
Unfair industrial practices   20, 21, 30, 32,
    34–8 *passim*, 41, 44, 45, 47, 67, 74
  safeguards against   30, 36, 67

Victimisation   63, 69, 204

Wage claims   17, 72, 102, 245, 259, 274,
    278
Wage drift   85
Wage-fixing bodies   14
Wage restraints   17

Wages councils 14–17 *passim*, 19, 67, 226
  structure of 16, 17
Wages Councils Act 1959   46, 67
Wages inspectors 17
Wages Regulation Orders 17
Wages/salaries (*see also* incentive earnings
    schemes—below)
  additions to basic 18, 169
  age-related payments 213
  comparisons of 172, 215
  information on 97, 98, 101–3 *passim*
  learner rates 213
  rates of 12, 13, 19, 22, 24, 25,45, 55,
    67, 69, 94, 112, 116, 128, 132, 137,
    152, 153, 159ff, 260
  reviews of 245
  salesmens' 173, 177
  sex discrimination in 66, 207ff
  systems of 55, 112, 116, 159ff, 215,
    231, 291
  womens' 207ff
Wages/salaries, manual workers' 160ff
  continuous operation, workers on 165
  guaranteed time rate 169
  incentive earnings schemes 18, 22, 83,
    128, 137, 138, 154, 159–62 *passim*,
    164, 165, 166, 169–72 *passim*, 217
  maintenance workers 172
  measured day work 164–7 *passim*, 169,
    170, 172
  output-based 167, 169–71 *passim*, 215
  payment by results 172, 287
  profit sharing 149, 172
  Rucker plan 171
  Scanlon plan 171
  standard time based 169–71 *passim*
Wages/salaries, staff 173ff
  executive managers 177, 178
  grading of staff 173, 174
  incentives for 173, 177
  job specification/evaluation 153, 173,
    174
  market survey of 174
  personal performance appraisal 173,
    174, 177
  staff report 175
Warnings, disciplinary 63
Whitley Committee 15
  Report 1917 15
Woollen industry 14
  women in 210
Worker/employer relationships 30, 60,
    88, 91ff, 111–13 *passim*, 121ff, 159,
    221ff, 244ff, 255ff, 269ff, 286, 289, 290,
    293, 305

Workers, coercion of 35, 47
  coloured 193ff
  differentials between grades 167, 280
  disabled 186, 187
  discrimination against (*see also* workers,
    women) 31, 35, 74, 194–6 *passim*,
    199, 200, 202ff
  dismissal of (*see also* unfair dismissal)
    32–5 *passim*, 58, 62, 63, 67, 69, 72,
    113, 136, 200
  freedom to vote of 47
  future role in industry of 10
  in basic industries 9
  interchangeability of 24, 25
  lay-off of 136
  legal aid for complaints 36, 45
  local government 14
  loss of earnings 36, 66, 136, 183, 184,
    224
  management participation of 10, 191,
    192, 231
  negotations for 14, 91, 138, 139
  mass production assembly 165, 166
  mobility of 25
  motivation of 144, 287–91 *passim*, 299,
    300
  needs of 8, 290, 294
  new laws for 5, 43ff
  nursing profession 218
  organisations of 12, 40, 41, 44, 52
  part-time 36, 209, 213
  public service 7, 9, 44
  recruitment/selection of 54, 55, 112,
    205
  re-engagement of 46, 202
  representatives of 4, 8, 9, 46, 57, 59,
    60, 93, 110, 115, 124, 134, 136, 137,
    151
  rights of 5, 20, 22, 30ff, 45, 47, 54, 62,
    74
  security of 55–7 *passim*
  suspension of 22, 58, 63, 69
  transfers of 25, 54, 55
  white collar 9, 14, 60, 88, 89, 98, 139
  white collar, union representatives of
    98
  white collar/manual differentials 56, 57,
    139
Workers, women 9, 16, 186, 187, 207ff
  increased opportunities for 218, 219
  maternity leave for 215
  statistics of 209–11 *passim*
  training for 211, 212, 219
  skilled 210, 211, 218

HALLWARD

12

Workers, women, equal pay for 207ff
  arguments against 208, 211, 212
  calendar of 208
  Civil Service moves towards 216
  phasing of 216–18 *passim*
  problems of 211, 212, 214, 218
Work groups, psychological aspects of
  297, 299
  relationships within 295, 296
  relations with shop stewards 278, 279
Working conditions 57, 66, 68, 132
Working practices 24, 86, 128, 134, 137,
  138, 151
Working week 90, 94, 132, 154

Work Place Industrial Relations 84
Work-place agreements/bargaining 16–21
  passim, 26, 56, 59, 60, 94, 110, 121ff,
  131ff, 273, 296
  information on 98, 99
  relation to national agreements of 127,
  133, 137, 153, 154
  strategy of 122ff, 131ff
Work places, multi-union 89
Works committees/councils 26, 126, 132,
  133, 136, 137, 271–4 *passim*, 278, 279
  optimum size of 133
Work study 22, 90, 126, 152, 172, 245